THE FIVE RULES .....

A PATH TO BECOMING A MASTER

3-25-11

{ A NEW VISION }

1:5:1

" BECOMING A MASTER IS A LIFE TIME OF ACHIEVEMENTS! YOUR MIND & BODY ARE NOW FUSED TOGETHER AND ACT AS ONE. M.P.F. "

To: Sally & The A.Y.F.S. program;
Your efforts & dedication to the people of
Auburn is amazing! all my best...
M. Faraday

THE JOURNAL CHRONICLES
OF
MASTER MICHAEL P. FARADAY

COPYRIGHT 2009 U.S.A. INTERNATIONAL MARTIAL ARTS

ISBN # 978-0-557-99171-6

AUTHOR: MICHAEL P. FARADAY / KYOSHI : PROFESSOR {QS} FARADAY

1ST EDITION 2009 { PRIVATE JOURNAL }

* REVISED EDITION 2011

ΤΗΙΣ ΙΣ ΤΗΕ ΦΟΡѠΑΡΔΙΝΓ ΕΣΣΑΓΕ

MY FORWARD MESSAGE TO THE READER :

DURING ALL MY YEARS OF TRAINING & TRAVELING IN THE PERSUIT OF MARTIAL KNOWLEDGE, MY FIRST IN DEPTH PROJECT WAS THE STORY OUTLINED WITHIN THESE PAGES.

IT DIDN'T MATTER HOW MUCH I ALREADY KNEW. IT WASN'T ALL ABOUT THE TECHNIQUES OF SELFDEFENSE, OR THE COUNTLESS PRATICE OF KATAS AND BUNKI'S...

ALSO IT WASN'T ABOUT THE ART OF FIGHTING OR ALL ITS GLORY. IT DIDN'T MATTER HOW MANY TITLES I HAD WON ON MY OWN, NOR ALL THE WORLD TITLES I HAD WON WITH THE UNITED STATES MARTIAL ART TEAM.

A GREAT MASTER ... A GRANDMASTER .. ONCE TOLD ME THIS:

" *AS YOU STAND BEFORE ME FOR JUDGEMENT I DO NOT CARE ABOUT YOUR FIGHTING OR SELFDEFENSE SKILL'S!*

AT THE POINT YOU ARE IN YOUR TRAINING IF YOU DO NOT HAVE THEM AT THIS POINT YOU WOULDN'T BE HERE NOW.

BUT WHAT I EXPECT OF YOU IS NOT STRENGTH OF BODY, BUT STRENGTH IN WISDOM OF SPIRIT!

I WANT TO KNOW WHAT ARE YOUR THOUGHTS ... YOUR IDEAS ... YOUR BELIEFS AND YOUR TRADITIONS. "

THAT MAN WAS SHIDOSHI GRANDMASTER RON " THE BLACK DRAGON " VAN CLIEF.

ONE OF THE MOST RESPECTED LIVING LEGEND ICONS IN THE WORLD OF MARTIAL ARTS TODAY.

HE THEN SAID TO ME THIS:

" *I LIKE YOU MICHAEL. I HAVE A THREE PART PROJECT FOR YOU TO UNDERTAKE. BUT JUST BECAUSE YOU ACCEPT IT AND COMPLETE IT DOESN'T MEAN ANYTHING!*

AFTER YOUR DECISION OF ACCEPTANCE AS WELL AS THE COMPLETION OF THIS SAID PROJECT, I WILL BE THE FINAL VERDICT IN YOUR QUEST, AND RENDER MY THOUGHTS AS TO YOUR SKILL LEVEL AND PROPER TITLE. "

SO HERE IS THE SPIRITUAL JOURNEY THAT LED ME TO WHOM I AM TODAY. EVERTHING WRITTEN IN THIS JOURNAL IS ACCURATE AND TRUE. {M.P.F.}

* MY DISCLAIMER *

ALTHOUGH EVERYTHING WRITTEN WITHIN THESE PAGES OF THE FIVE
RULES, THE PATH TO BECOMING A MASTER IS TRUE AND THE FIRST
AUTOBIOGRAPHY OF MY LIFE IN REGAURDS TO THIS JOURNEY OF SPIRIT,
IT HAS BEEN LABELED BY OTHERS AS CONTROVERSIAL!

EVERTHING PERTAINS TO MY LIFE AND THE PEOPLE IN MY LIFE THAT
CAUSED MISTREATMENT TO ME. EITHER WILLINGLY OR UNWILLINGLY.

BE IT IN A PHYSICAL, OR OF MENTAL BEING.

IN PLAIN ENGLISH I TOLD THE TRUTH OF EVENTS THAT OTHERS DO NOT
LIKE.

HOWEVER I SPEAK MY MIND ON HOW IT REALLY WAS, AND IF YOU DO
NOT LIKE IT THAN YOU SHOULDN'T HAVE DONE IT!

ALL IN ALL IT PLAYED A HUGH PART OF WHO I AM TODAY. SO I THANK
YOU FROM THE BOTTOM OF MY HEART!

BY: KYOSHI "QUICKSILVER" FARADAY

TABLE OF CONTENTS :

INTRODUCTION :

IT WAS DURING THE YEAR OF 2007, THAT I WAS ONCE AGAIN HAVING SERIOUS DOUBTS IN MY TRAINING!

ALTHOUGH I WAS TRAINING VERY HARD NOT ONLY IN MY OWN STYLE OF TAIKYOKUKEN KEN SHO RYU, BUT IN THE ART OF SHOTOKAN WITH SHIHAN WAYNE MELLO, IT SEEMED AS IF I HAD HIT A BRICK WALL!

THERE WERE SO MANY QUESTIONS THAT RAN THREW MY MIND … BUT NOBODY WAS ABLE TO ANSWER THEM FOR ME.

I KNEW THAT I WAS ONCE AGAIN IN NEED OF A CHANGE.

WHY ? BECAUSE I WASN'T PROGRESSING TO MY DESIRED GOAL OF ADVANCEMENT.

I AT THIS POINT HAD NOT TESTED IN QUITE A NUMBER OF YEARS, AND WAS UNDER THE IMPRESSION THAT I NEVER WAS GOING TO AGAIN.

WHEN ALL APPEARED TO BE LOST, AND I THOUGHT I WAS AT MY END …

THEN THREE CIRCUMSTANCES OF LIFE HAPPENED WHICH BROUGHT ME TO THIS FOREVER LIFE CHANGING EXPERIENCE!

FIRST THERE WAS AN OUT OF THE BLUE HEART TO HEART CONVERSATION DURING A TRAINING SESSION WITH MASTER MELLO!

THIS GAVE ME THOUGHT.

NEXT WAS A CONVERSATION WITH SIFU AL DACASCOS!

THIS GAVE ME HOPE.

THEN CAME AN EMAIL FROM RON VAN CLIEF, THAT WAS PURELY A SIGN OF THINGS TO COME?

THIS WAS THE PASSAGE!

THE FOLLOWING OUTLINE OF EVENTS ARE TRUE TO LIFE. THEIR ORGINAL INTENTION WAS IN THE FORMAT OF AN AUTOBIOGRAPHY PRESENTED IN A JOURNAL FORMAT.

THIS WAS ALSO A PRIVATE PROJECT THAT I WAS ASKED TO DO FOR MY SENSEI. SHIDOSHI RON VAN CLIEF.

AFTER THE RELEASE OF MY SECOND WRITTEN BOOK; "LIMELIGHT TO THE DEVIL'S PARADISE" IN 2010, AND THE MENTION OF THIS JOURNAL IN THAT BOOK, I HAD BEEN ASKED SEVERAL TIMES AS TO THE FACT WHERE IT COULD BE PURCHASED.

SO AFTER MUCH THOUGHT I DECIDED TO RELEASE THIS WORK.

HOWEVER; DURING THE PROCESS OF REVISION, AND NOT WANTING IT TO BE EXACTLY THE SAME MATERIAL I HAVE ADDED A FEW MORE THOUGHTS.

THIS WAY THE FIRST COPY WILL STILL BE SORT OF SPECIAL, AND DIFFERENT FROM THIS VERSION.

I REALLY DIDN'T EXPECT THIS TO PAN OUT IN THIS MANNER, BUT AS IT HAS TURNED OUT THIS HAS BECOME MY YING AND YANG!

SO HERE IS MY STORY OF LIFE, THOUGHTS, COMPARISONS, BELIEFS, AND TRADITIONS THAT WERE PERTINENT DURING THIS PERIOD OF MY JOURNEY OF TRAINING.

" THE EVER FLOWING SANDS OF TIME BREAKDOWN AND THEN REBUILD OUR HUMAN SPIRIT! M.P.F. "

PAST & PRESENT:

I WAS BORN ON THE 12TH OF MAY IN THE YEAR 1970. MY FATHER WAS HENERY STELMACK AND MY MOTHER WAS NANCY ANN FARADAY.

I WAS BROUGHT INTO THIS WORLD AT HARRINGTON HOSPITAL LOCATED IN SOUTHBRIDGE MA.

AS AN INFANT DUE TO SEVERAL CIRCUMSTANCES THAT I NEVER FULLY REALIZED UNTIL MUCH LATER ON IN LIFE I WAS LEFT BEHIND BY BOTH OF MY PARENTS!

SO AS FAR BACK AS I CAN REMEMBER WHICH WAS THE AGE OF THREE MY MOTHERS PARENTS CARED FOR MY WELL BEING.

THEY WERE MR. DONALD H. FARADAY AND MRS. MYRTLE G. FARADAY.

AFTER THE SEPERATION OF MY PARENTS AND THEN ME I LIVED A VERY HAPPY LIFE.

THEN AT THE AGE OF SIX MY GRANDPARENTS FULLY ADOPTED ME.

NOT WANTING TO CAUSE TO MANY HEADACHES AT THE TIME MY NAME WAS NEVER CHANGED TO THEIR LAST NAME.

IT WASN'T UNTIL SEPTEMBER OF 1993 THAT I HAD MET MY BELOVED WIFE TAMMY JEAN BARNES THAT I HAD DECIDED TO LEGALLY HAVE MY NAMED CHANGED TO MICHAEL P. FARADAY.

MY OLD LAST NAME DIDN'T SIT WELL WITH ME! SO IN HOPES OF STARTING A FAMILY OF MY OWN I WANTED TO HONOR MY GRANDPARENTS WHO REALLY BECAME MY PARENTS WHEN THEY HAD ADOPTED ME MANY YEARS AGO.

THEN ON THE 23RD OF JULY IN THE YEAR 1995 TAMMY BARNES BECAME TAMMY FARADAY AND WE WERE MARRIED!

NEXT IT WASN'T UNTIL MARCH 2ND 2001 THAT WE WERE BLESSED WITH THE BIRTH OF OUR FIRST AND ONLY CHILD!

MASON DOUGLAS FARADAY WAS NOW THE TRUE BEGINNING OF OUR FAMILY LIFE TOGETHER. MY BEST BUDDY OF ALL IN THE WHOLE WORLD.

TODAY IN LIFE MY FAMILY COMES FIRST! NO MATTER WHAT. THEN MARTIAL ARTS COMES SECOND.

HOWEVER; IT WASN'T ALWAYS LIKE THIS, AND AS TIME WENT ON I CAME TO REALIZE I WAS, AND HAD MADE A HUGH MISTAKE.

AFTER SEEING THE ERROR OF MY WAYS OF THOUGHTS AND ACTIONS, I NEEDED TO CORRECT THIS BEFORE IT WAS TO LATE.

THEN AND ONLY THEN DID I BECOME THE MAN MY WIFE LOVES AND DEPENDS ON, AND WHO MY SON CALLS DAD!

THIS WAS EXTREMELY HARD TO DO. FOR YEARS I NEVER IMAGINED I WAS PUTTING MY MARRIAGE OR MY FAMILY LIFE AT RISK OF FAILURE.

THERE IS NO COMPARISON TO THE LOVE OF A GREAT FAMILY. IT DOESN'T WEATHER THREW TIME IT FLOURISHES!

GROWING UP IN THE SMALL TOWN OF WEBSTER LOCATED IN THE STATE OF MA I ATTENDED THE PUBLIC SCHOOL SYSTEM THERE.

STARTING GRADE K AT THE PARK AVE ELEM IN 1975, THEN GOING TO THE MIDDLE SCHOOL IN 1978 FOR GRADES 4TH THREW 6TH.

I THEN MOVED UP TO THE BARTLETT HIGH SCHOOL AND GRADUATED IN 1989.

NOT ALL OF MY SCHOOL YEARS WERE GREAT, BUT IN THE END I WAS ABLE TO GRADUATE WITH HONORS ALONG WITH SOME ACCREDITED COLLEGE CREDITS IN ADVANCED PLACEMENT ACCOUNTING, AND BUSINESS MANAGEMENT.

THEN IN THE EARLY SUMMER OF 1989 I WAS ACCEPTED INTO NICHOLS COLLEGE LOCATED IN DUDLEY MA 01571.

THIS COLLEGE IS WELL KNOWN FOR ITS COURSES IN THE ARTS OF BUSINESS.

ONCE I STARTED MY STUDIES HERE I REALIZED IT WASN'T FOR ME!

SO DOING THE RIGHT THING I SAT DOWN WITH MY PARENTS AND TOLD THEM HOW UN - HAPPY I WAS.

THIS FOUR YEAR PLAN WAS NOT FOR ME. HOWEVER OUT OF RESPECT FOR THEIR WISHES I DID SEEK A TWO YEAR COLLEGE, AND THIS WAS DUDLEY HALL.

DUDLEY HALL AT THE TIME WAS A SCHOOL STRICTLY RELATED TO THE FIELDS OF BUSINESS, AND WAS LOCATED IN THE CITY OF WORCESTER MA.

I WAS ACCEPTED INTO THIS COLLEGE IN DECEMBER OF 1989.

WANTING TO GET THIS OVER WITH AS SOON AS POSSIABLE, AND MOVE ON WITH MY LIFE I WORKED VERY HARD!

I TOOK EXTRA COURSES DURING THE HOLIDAY BREAKS. THEN I ALSO TOOK MORE CLASSES IN THE EVENING.

NEXT I EVEN TOOK CLASSES DURING THE SUMMER.

AFTER ALL MY HARD WORK AND COUNTLESS EFFORTS TO ACHIEVE THIS GOAL, I OBTAINED MY ASSOCIATES DEGREE THE FOLLOWING FALL IN THE YEAR OF 1990.

MY DEGREE WAS IN ACCOUNTING WITH A MINOR STUDY IN BUSINESS MANAGEMENT.

NOW THAT I WAS OUT OF COLLEGE IT WAS TIME TO FIND WORK. WITH ENTRY LEVEL POSITIONS BEING FAR AND FEW BETWEEN AT THE TIME DUE TO THE STALE ECONOMIC PERIOD IT WAS ROUGH!

BUT THEN MY CHANCE HAD COME. I WAS PICKED UP BY A HUGH CORPRATION WHICH DUE TO UNDERLYING ISSUES I WILL KEEP TO MYSELF.

MY JOB AT THIS COMPANY WAS MAINLY TO GATHER PERSONAL AS WELL AS FINANCIAL INFORMATION IN PREPARING TAXES FOR PEOPLE AND THEIR BUSINESSES.

THAN A SENIOR PLANNER FOR THE COMPANY WOULD TALK TO YOU ABOUT INVESTING YOUR MONEY WITH THEM INTO VARIOUS ACCOUNTS.

IT WAS NOT LONG BEFORE I DISCOVERED WHAT WAS REALLY GOING ON HERE.

THESE SO CALLED PLANNERS WERE ACTUALLY STEALING NOT ONLY MONEY, BUT COMPLETE PROPERTY FROM THE ELDERLY WHO HAD NO FAMILIES TO LEAVE IT TO!

THEY NEVER SAW IT COMING. I MIGHT HAVE BEEN YOUNG BUT I WAS FAR FROM STUPID.

SO NOT BEING ABLE TO CONTROL THIS OR HELP THOSE POOR PEOPLE I RESIGNED IN DECEMBER OF THAT SAME YEAR.

THIS IS NOW THE TIME IN MY LIFE THAT I FELL INTO THE CAREER I CURRENTLY RESIDE IN.

WORKING FOR THE UNITED STATES POSTAL SERVICES AS A LETTER CARRIER.

IT IS HERE I HAVE NOW SPENT THE LAST TWO PLUS DECADES OF MY LIFE DELIVERING THE MAIL IN THE TOWN I GREW UP IN.

PROVIDING A GREAT SERVICE TO THE PEOPLE IN THE TOWN OF WEBSTER.

HOW IT ALL BEGAN :

AS FAR AS MY MARTIAL ARTS INTERESTS I WAS ALWAYS FASCINATED WITH THE CULTURE OF THE ORIENT, AND THE IDEA OF BECOMING A STUDENT OF THE ARTS.

SO AT THE VERY YOUNG AGE OF TWELVE MY UNCLE ON MY MOTHERS SIDE BEGAN MY TRAINING, AND TOOK ME IN UNDER HIS WING SO TO SPEAK.

FOR YEARS HE TAUGHT ME HOW TO PROPERLY TAKE CARE OF MY BODY AND WHAT EXERCISES I NEED TO PERFORM ON A DAILY BASIS.

HE WAS VERY BIG INTO USING WEIGHTS, A JUMP ROPE AND A HEAVY PUNCHING BAG. MY TRAINING STARTED WITH THESE FOUNDATIONS.

NEXT AT THE AGE OF AROUND FIFTEEN HE BEGAN SHOWING ME THE TECHNIQUES OF WESTERN BOXING.

DURING HIS DAYS IN THE MILITARY MY UNCLE HAD LOTS OF EXPERIENCE FROM BOXING AND WAS ON THE MILITARY TEAM.

HE SERVED DURING THE VIETNAM ERA. IT WAS HERE HE BECAME AN ELITE MEMBER OF THE 101ST AIRBORN DIVISION OF THE RANGERS.

WE SPENT A LOT OF TIME TOGETHER WHEN I WAS GROWING UP. HE HAD TAUGHT ME SO MUCH, BUT I HAD NO IDEA HOW MUCH MORE THERE WAS STILL TO LEARN!

THEN THE DAY FINALLY CAME. MY UNCLE STARTED SHOWING ME HIS KNOWLEDGE OF THE MARTIAL ARTS THAT HE HAD LETS SAY ACQUIRED IN HIS TRAVELS OF LIFE.

AFTER A LONG PERIOD OF TIME WENT BY EVERYTHING JUST STARTED TO CLICK!

MY UNCLE HAD TAUGHT ME MUCH ABOUT MYSELF AND HOW TO TAKE CARE OF MYSELF. INSIDE AND OUT.

WHAT AN AMAZING CONCEPT THIS WAS! THEY SAY THAT A PICTURE IS WORTH A THOUSAND WORDS.

BUT THE TIME WE SPENT TOGETHER AND THE THING WE DID WAS PRICELESS!

IT WAS FROM THIS POINT ON IN MY LIFE THAT I KNEW WHAT IT WAS I WANTED.

IT WAS TO PROCEED IN THE STUDY OF MARTIAL ARTS AND LEARN AS MUCH AS I POSSIABLE COULD ABOUT THE MANY CULTURES AND ITS PEOPLE.

THE DIRECTION OF PRINCIPLE THAT THEIR WARRIORS HAD TAKEN TO BECOME WHO THEY WERE, AND HOW THEY CAME TO THIS GREAT ACHIEVEMENT.

THIS WAS NOW MY MAIN OBJECTIVE IN LIFE. FINDING AS MUCH KNOWLEDGE ABOUT THESE PATHS AS I COULD, AND IT STILL IS TO THIS VERY DAY!

THIS PATH THAT I HAVE CHOOSEN IN MY LIFE HAS BEEN LONG AND EXTREMELY DIFFICULT, BUT IT HAS HAD MANY BENEFITS TO ITS PRACTICE AS WELL!

MY LIFE, AND THE LIFE OF MY FAMILY HAS GROWN STRONG BECAUSE OF ITS DIRECTION.

OUR LIFES GO BY SO FAST! IF YOU BLINK YOU JUST MISSED A SECOND.

EVERY SECOND BECOMES A MINUTE. THEN THE MINUTES ADD UP TO HOURS. THIS THEN LEADS UP TO DAYS .. MONTHS … THEN YEARS!

TO HELP STOP THE TIME MAKE EVERY SECOND OF YOUR LIFE MEANINGFUL!

TO YOU, AND TO YOUR FAMILY AS WELL. ALL THE LITTLE THINGS BUILD INTO BIGGER THINGS WHICH MAKES YOU STRONGER!

THE STRONGER YOU ARE THE STRONGER YOUR FAMILY WILL BECOME.

ALL OF THIS LEADS TO WHAT I DESCRIBE AS THE FIVE RULES!

EACH OF THESE RULES ARE THE KEY TO LIVING THE MARTIAL WAY, AND IT IS THIS WHICH SEPERATES YOU FROM THE OTHER PEOPLE WHO CALL THEMSELVES MARTIAL ARTISTS.

RESPECT EACH OF THESE RULES, AND LEARN THE TRUE MEANING OF EACH OF THEM TOO. IT IS ONLY THEN YOU WILL UNDERSTAND MY WAY OF THOUGHT.

THE FIVE RULES :

THROUGHOUT MY MANY YEARS OF STUDIES IN THE MARTIAL ARTS I DO NOT CONCIEVE IT TO BE A TYPE OF TRAINING, BUT RATHER A WAY OF LIFE TO ME!

I LIVE BY WHAT I CALL THE FIVE GOLDEN RULES OF MARTIAL ARTS. THESE RULES ARE:

EFFORT ~ ETIQUETTE ~ CHARACTER ~ SINCERITY ~ SELF CONTROL!

ACTUALLY SOME OF THE BEST LESSONS IN MY TRAINING WERE THE EXPERIENCES I ENCOUNTERED IN LIFE.

IT DID TAKE ME SEVERAL YEARS OF BUILDING MY FOUNDATIONS WITH THE CONDITIONING OF MY MIND AND BODY ALONG WITH EXTREME TRAINING OF MY INNER SPIRIT.

THIS INNER SPIRIT WE CALL CHI. IT IS THE ENERGY FROM WHICH WE DRAW OUR POWER, AND THE MEANS IN WHICH MARTIAL ARTS FLOWS THROUGHOUT OUR BODIES.

LEARNING HOW TO HARVEST THIS AND HOW TO CONTROL THIS FORCE IS NO EASY TASK! YOU COULD WORK ON IT FOR A LIFE TIME AND NEVER FULLY UNDERSTAND ITS MEANING.

BUT BY PRACTICING OUR BASICS AND TECHNIQUES THREW PRACTICAL MEASURES THIS IS WHAT I HAD INDEED LEARNED ON MY OWN AS AN INDIVIDUAL.

THE KNOWLEDGE THAT WAS SHARED WITH ME IN RELATIONSHIP TO MY PERSONAL BELIEFS AND SELF VAULES ALONG MY FELLOW COLLEAGUES WAS A HUGH BENEFIT TO MY TRAINING.

THE MARTIAL ARTS HAS TAKEN ME ALL OVER THE WORLD! FROM THE EAST COAST OF THE UNITED STATES ALL THE WAY TO SYDNEY AUSTRALIA, AND EVERYWHERE IN - BETWEEN!

I HAVE LEARNED SO MUCH ABOUT MY SELF AND HOW TO IMPROVE MY ABILITIES FROM OTHER MARTIAL ARTISTS BY TRAVELING TO THEIR COUNTRIES DURING MY TIME SPENT ON TEAM AMERICA.

TEAM AMERICA IS THE UNITED STATES TEAM OF VERY TALENTED MARTIAL ARTISTS FROM ALL OVER OUR GREAT COUNTRY.

TOGETHER WE STAND AND PROVIDE REPRESENTATION OF GREAT CHARACTER, WHICH IN TURN REFLECTS UPON OUR COUNTRY THAT WE LOVE!

THE UNITED STATES OF AMERICA. OUR CULTURE. OUR SPORTSMANSHIP, AND THE SOCIAL MANNERISM THAT PEOPLE RESPECT IN WORLD PEACE!

IN AUSTRALIA I LEARNED THAT TRADITION IS NOT CONFINED OR PRATICED IN A DOJO. BUT RATHER WHERE EVER I MAY CHOOSE TO BE. THE WORLD IS MY DOJO.

THIS PRINCIPLE OF RULE IS CALLED **ETIQUTTE!**

IN HAWAII I LEARNED THE BEAUTY OF DIVERSITY IS IN OUR SELF BEING. THIS IS WHAT MAKES US UNIQUE AND THE PRINCIPLE OF OUR **SINCERITY!**

WHEN I TRAVELED TO THE COUNTRY OF IRELAND PERHAPS MY MOST VAULABLE LESSON EVER WAS TAUGHT TO ME.

THIS LESSON WAS THAT I AM NOT INVINCIBLE, AND NO MATTER HOW GOOD YOU ARE MAY THINK YOU ARE THERE IS ALWAYS SOMEBODY OUT THERE WHO IS BETTER!

THIS WAS VERY GOOD TO PUT MY LIFE BACK INTO PERSPECTIVE.

HOWEVER; EVERYTHING YOU DESIRE IN LIFE SHOULD BE SOUGHT WITH GREAT RESPECT AND PATIENCE.

THIS PRINCIPLE WE CALL **SELFCONTROL!**

WHILE IN THE COUNTRY OF MEXICO THE SUBJECT WAS THAT THERE IS ALWAYS ROOM FOR IMPROVEMENT.

NO MATTER HOW WELL YOU PRECIEVE YOUR PERFORMANCE TO BE!

THIS PRINCIPLE IS THE **EFFORT** WE PUT FORTH FROM HARDWORK!

LAST BUT NOT LEAST. ALTHOUGH THERE ARE MANY DIFFERENCES FROM THE EAST COAST TO THE WEST COAST ONE CONCEPT REMAINS THE SAME …

THAT CONCEPT IS FRIENDSHIP, AND THOSE FRIENDSHIPS GO A LONG WAY. THEY ARE NEVER FORGOTTEN BY THE PEOPLE WHO ARE YOUR TRUE FRIENDS.

HOW DO WE COME TO THIS YOU MAY ASK? IT IS ALL ABOUT WHAT YOU ARE MADE OF, AND EVERYTHING THAT YOU STAND FOR.

THIS LAST RULE OF PRINCIPLE IS CALLED **CHARACTER!**

YOUR CHARACTER IS WHAT HOLDS TRUE TO AND ABOUT ONES SELF.

THE STRONGER YOUR CHARACTER IS THE MORE RESPECT YOU WILL RECEIVE!

IF YOU REMEMBER NOTHING ELSE IN LIFE PLEASE REMEMBER THIS RESPECT IS NOT SOMETHING YOU ARE GIVEN.

RESPECT IS SOMETHING YOU EARN! IT IS OF THE HIGHEST VALUES.

ONCE YOU FIGURE THIS OUT YOU WILL BECOME NOT ONLY MORE PRODUCTIVE BUT A FAR BETTER PERSON TO ALL AS WELL.

" THE LOVE OF HEART IS WHAT MAKES THE WORLD GO ROUND! M.P.F. "

" THE SEEDS WE PLANT IN LIFE WILL GROW INTO THE FUTURE OF TOMORROW! M.P.F. "

KEEPING THE TRADITION :

IN OUR TRAINING WITHIN THE MARTIAL ARTS TODAY I HAVE BEEN EXTREMELY BOTHERED BY WHAT I HOLD AS HIGH VAULE.

THIS VALUE IS TRADITION! TRADITION IS EVERYTHING TO ME. THIS IS WHERE WE DEVELOP OUR ROOTS.

THIS IS ALSO WERE IN MY OPNION HONOR IS UP HELD!

THESE PAST FEW YEARS WHAT I HAVE BEEN SEEING IN PERSON WHEN TRAVELING, AND BY VISITING DOJOS AROUND THE WORLD …

AND WHAT I HAVE BEEN HEARING FROM THE STUDENTS OF ALL SKILL LEVELS FROM THESE DOJOS IS APPALLING!

THERE ARE SCHOOLS OUT THERE THAT HAVE PEOPLE INSTRUCTING THE ARTS THAT HAVE NEVER TAKEN A CLASS IN THEIR ENTIRE LIFE!

THERE ARE INSTRUCTORS THAT ARE OUT THERE TEACHING THEIR STUDENTS WORTHLESS MATERIAL, AND SWELLING THEIR HEADS WITH FALSE HOPES!

MEANWHILE THESE SO CALLED INSTRUCTORS AND THEIR SCHOOLS ARE BRINGING IN SOME SERIOUS CASH FLOW EVERY MONTH OF EVERY YEAR!

IT ISN'T ABOUT MONEY! IT IS ALL ABOUT THE FIVE RULES. AND IF YOU ARE ONE OF THESE PEOPLE AND BELIEVE ME THEY KNOW WHO THEY ARE.

THAT TRAIN THEIR STUDENTS IN THIS FASION, ONE DAY THEY MIGHT, NO ONE DAY THEY WILL GET THEMSELFE INTO SERIOUS TROUBLE NOT TO MENTION SERIOUSLY HURT!

THIS IS VASTLY DANGEROUS. PLEASE EXCUSE THE FOLLOWING PHRASING BUT IT WILL GET MY POINT ACROSS.

" THE STUDENTS OF THESE SO CALLED MASTERS OF THE MARTIAL ARTS COULDN'T FIGHT THEIR WAY OUT OF A WET PAPER BAG! "

NOT ONLY ARE THESE STUDENTS GETTING EXTREMELY HURT IN THE DOJO, BUT EVEN WORSE IN THE STREETS.

WHEN I COME ACROSS THIS ISSUE WHICH BY THE WAY IS ALL TO FREQUENT I TRY MY BEST TO EDUCATE THE PEOPLE INVOLVED WHO HAVE BEEN WRONGED.

HOWEVER; NOT ALL FEEDBACK IS ACCEPTED. THEIR MINDS HAVE BEEN TO WASHED AWAY BY THIS POINT, AND BEYOND REASONING!

IF THEY REALLY ONLY KNEW WHAT THE MARTIAL ARTS WAS SUPPOSED TO BE ABOUT… BUT THEY NEVER WILL!

I HAVE NO PROBLEM WITH SOMEBODY TRYING TO MAKE A LIVING, BUT DON'T STEAL IT!

AT LEAST TEACH YOUR STUDENTS GOOD SOLID MATERIAL THAT ACTUALLY WORKS, AND DO IT FOR A FAIR PRICE!

WHEN I AM APPROACHED BY AN INDVIDUAL OR EVEN A GROUP ASKING MY ADVICE WHEN SEEKING OUT A SCHOOL MY NUMBER ONE TOPIC IS SELFDEFENSE.

IF YOU VISIT A SCHOOL AND YOU NOTICE THAT NO ONE IS ALOUD TO PHYSICALLY TOUCHONE ANOTHER THEN YOU DO NOT WANT TO BE THERE!

HOW WILL YOU EVER KNOW IF WHAT YOU ARE TAUGHT WILL REALLY WORK WHEN IT COUNTS?

ALSO IF YOU NEVER GET HIT OR RECEIVE SOME BRUISES THEN HOW DO YOU THINK YOU WILL REACT TO THE FIRST TIME YOU GET INTO A REAL FIGHT?

NOT A GOOD THING!

NEXT LOOK AT THE VALUE OF YOUR DOLLAR COMPARED TO THE DURATION AND FREQUENCY OF THE CLASS TIMES.

YOU SHOULD BE RECEIVING AT LEAST THREE DAYS OF CLASS TIME, FOR ABOUT ONE HOUR PER DAY.

THIS IS FAIR AND THE PRICE SHOULDN'T BE MORE THAN $90.00 A MONTH.

I DO NOT KNOW ANYBODY AROUND MY LOCAL AREA AS FAR AWAY AS IN A CIRCUMFRENCE OF ONE HUNDRED MILES THAT IS WORTH MORE THAN THIS!

HOPEFULLY THIS STATEMENT TELLS YOU A LITTLE SOMETHING.

LASTLY BE VERY CONCERNED IF YOU ARE ASKED TO TEST A LOT FOR EXTRA FEES IN EXCESSIVE AMOUNTS!

THERE IS NO NEED TO RUSH YOUR TRAINING. YOU HAVE YOUR WHOLE LIFE TO DO SO. WHEN YOU ARE READY THE TIME WILL COME. LET IT BE NATURAL.

WHAT YOU PUT INTO IT IS WHAT YOU WILL GET OUT OF IT, AND WHAT YOU PAY FOR IS WHAT YOU GET AS WELL!

" REMEMBER THE OLD SAYING ... TIME IS MONEY? AND MONEY IS TIME! "

MY SIDE PROJECT OF LOCAL DOJOS VS TRADITION :

IN REFRENCE TO THE PREVIOUS CHAPTER I DECIDED TO CONDUCT A SECRET TEST.

THIS TEST WAS TO FIND OUT WHAT TRADITION MEANT TO MARTIAL ART TRAINING AT NOT ONLY LOCAL DOJOS IN MY AREA, BUT ABROAD AS WELL.

WHAT I HAD DISCOVERED WAS ALL TOGETHER SHOCKING! IN WHAT I WITNESSED FIRST HAND.

NOT TO MENTIONED WHAT I WAS TOLD BY SENSEI AND STUDENTS IN RELATION TO MY QUESTION OF TRADITION WAS SCARY!

THE BEST OF ALL CAME FROM A SCHOOL THAT PREACHES ABOUT TRADITION AND ITS VAULE.

I DO NOT WANT TO SAY THE NAME OF THIS DOJO HOWEVER LET IT BE KNOWN THAT IT IS IN ANOTHER COUNRTY.

HOWEVER SEVERAL LOCAL SCHOOLS IN MY AREA WERE NOT TO FAR OFF FROM ALMOST THE SAME ANSWERS.

" I DO NOT HAVE A HIGH VAULE TO TRADITION. IN MY MARTIAL ARTS TRAINING! WHAT EXACTLY DOES IT MEAN? I ONLY LEARN HERE. I AM NOT THE OWNER! "

THIS IS A TRUE STATEMENT THAT WAS SPOKEN TO ME FROM A BLACKBELT AFTER A CLASS HAD LET OUT WHEN I ENQUIRED ABOUT.

AS I PREVIOUSLY MENTIONED … THERE IS NO NEED TO DISCLOSE THE LOCATION OR NAME OF THIS DOJO OR ALL THE REST.

BUT KEEP IN MIND IF YOU ACTUALLY KNEW WHO I WAS REFERING TO IT WOULD PUT YOU ASIDE YOURSELF!

BECAUSE THEIR WERE MORE THAN ONE. THERE WERE SEVERAL!

AFTER MUCH REGRET I FINALLY FOUND ONE DOJO THAT HELD TRADITION WHICH WAS TO MY STANDARD.

THEY KNEW WHAT TRADITION WAS, AND HOW TO ABIDE BY IT!

AFTER TALKING TO ITS HEAD INSTRUCTOR AND OWNER I HAVE HIS PERMISSION TO INCLUDE HIS THOUGHTS AS TO TRADITION IN MY FIELD STUDIES.

THANK YOU! BECAUSE YOU WERE THE ONLY ONE AROUND THAT MADE THE CUT. TO A STANDARD THAT I APPROVE OF IN ALL ASPECTS.

IN TODAYS WORLD OF MARTIAL ARTS THIS IS A RARITY!

THE FOLLOWING IS AN EMAIL THAT THIS SENSEI SENT TO ME IN REGAURDS TO OUR CONVERSATION EARLIER THAT DAY.

HIS NAME IS SENSEI MIKE MILLETT. HE HOLDS THE RANK OF SANDAN. WHICH IS THE PROPER RANK TO BE A SENSEI.

A SANDAN IS A THIRD DEGREE BLACKBELT.

HE IS THE HEAD INSTRUCTOR AND OWNER OF THE KENSHO RYU KENPO DOJO LOCATED IN OF ALL PLACES WEBSTER MA.

MR MILLETTS EMAIL:

" IT HAS BEEN MY THOUGHT THAT WITHOUT TRADITION, MARTIAL ART TEACHINGS WOULD BE LOST.

ENTIRE SYSTEMS HAVE BEEN LOST IN THE PAST, AND THE ONES THAT HAVE BEEN AROUND FOR HUNDREDS OF YEARS ARE FULL OF TRADITION.

IN THE KENSHO RYU SYSTEM, TRADITION STARTS AS SOON AS YOU GET TO THE DOJO.

THERE IS A BOW BEFORE YOU ENTER. EVERYONEIS WEARING A GI, AND YOUR OBI IS TIED IN A SPECIFIC WAY. ALL OF WHICH ARE TRADITION.

WHEN TEACHING MARTIA ARTS TRADITION PLAYS A MAJOR ROLL.

EVERYBODY HAS DIFFERENT TEACHING STYLES, BUT IN THE END ITS ALL ABOUT HAVING YOUR STUDENT UNDERSTAND THE CONCEPTS.

THE TRADITION OF PASSING ON THE MOVEMENTS AND CONCEPTS OF KATA IS ESSENTIAL TO KEEPING THE ART ALIVE.

WHEN A MARTIAL ARTIST UNDERSTANDS THE BASICS, IT GIVES THEM THE STRONG FOUNDATION TO BUILD ON.

STRONG BASICS EQUAL STRONG KATA. STRONG KATA EQUALS STRONG SELFDEFENSE.

WITHOUT TRADITIONAL TEACHING OF THEBASICS THE REST OF THE INFORMATION THE STUDENT HAS WILL LACK IN THE SUBTLETIES NEEDED TO BE A PROFICIENT MARTIAL ARTIST.

MY INSTRUCTOR, GRANDMASTER MARK SHEELEY, ALWAS SAYS TO US "" ITS NOT HOW MUCH YOU HAVE, BUT HOW WELL YOU DO IT ""

IN ONE WAY OR ANOTHER, THAT LESSON WAS TAUGHT TO HIM FROM PROFESSOR NICK CERIO, AND I TELL MY STUDENTS THE SAME THING.

I HOPE ONE DAY MY STUDENTS PASS ON THE SAME LESSON.

THIS IS AN EXAMPLE OF HOW TRADITION, AND THE TEACHING OF THE ART IS IMPORTANT TO KEEPING THE ARTS ALIVE.

IN CONCLUSION ... BASICS. BASICS .. BASICS ...!

I COULD GO ON FOREVER, BUT I NEED TO STOP SOMEWHERE. I HOPE THIS CAN HELP IN ANY WAY.

MICHAEL MILLETT, SANDAN, KENSHO RYU KENPO KARATE "

MY EMAIL BACK TO SENSEI MIKE :

" NICE JOB SENSEI MIKE! THANK YOU. YOU WILL SEE THIS IN MY BOOK, WITH YOUR NAME FOR WRITING IT AS PART OF MY SIDE PROJECT OF TRADIION AND DOJOS.

DO YOU WANT YOUR SCHOOL NAME TO BE MENTIONED AS WELL? LET ME KNOW!

AS I EXPRESSED TO YOU YOUR ANSWER IS THE ONLY ONE AROUND FOR A FARE DISTANE THAT I LIKED AND AGREE WITH.

SO AFTER I ASKED YOU TO WRITE THIS PASSAGE I STARTED GOING BY YOUR DOJO TO CHECK UP ON WHAT I WOULD SEE.

THIS IS WHAT I NOTICED: YOU ARE WELL RESPECTED BY YOUR PUPILS.

I HAD ACTUALLY SPOKE TO A COUPLE OF THE PARENTS ANNOUMNASLY. { SORRY SLEEP DEPRIVED }

THEY HAD GREAT THINGS TO SAY ABOUT YOU, AND YOUR INFLUENCE ON THEIR CHILDREN.

DURING YOUR CLASSES I NOTICED GOOD ATTENTION TO DETAIL IN THE BASICS!

ALTHOUGH YOUR AULT CLASS ES WERE SMALL YOU MADE UP IN THE YOUTH.

THE BIGGEST PART WAS THIS ...

I NEVER SAW ANY FOOLISH PLAY OR HAPPY FACES DURING A TRAINING SESSION!

BUT AFTER YOUR CLASSES WERE FINISHED I SAW BIG SMILES!

WHAT THIS TELLS ME IS THAT YOU ARE DEDICATED TO YOUR TEACHING THREW YOUR STUDENTS!

YOU VALUE TRADITION, AND RUN A GOOD SHIP.

ALSO YOUR PEOPLE ARE HAPPY TO BE THERE. AND ABOVE ALL YOUR MATERIAL IS SOLID AND VERY PRACTICAL!

FOR WHAT I NOTICED AFTER SEVERAL VISITS.

HOPE YOU ENJOY THIS MESSAGE.

REMEMBER THIS IN TEACHING TO OTHERS - YOU ARE ALSO TEACHING YOURSELF!

MUCH MORE THAN YOU MIGHT RELIZE.

YOU CAN LEARN MORE FROM A WHITE BELT THAN A MASTER. WHY YOU MAY ASK?

EASY. BECAUSE THE WHITEBELT HAS NOTHING TO LOOSE!

HOWEVER THE MSTER HAS TO MUCH KNOWLEDGE TO DRAW FROM ...

THIS IS WHY SIMPLE BASICS IS AWESOME & BEST!!!

HOW MANY KATAS DO YOU REALLY NEED? HOW MANY TECHNIQUES DO YOU REALLY NEED?

IN MY OPNION YOU NEED AT LEAST 5 KATAS FOR UNDERBELTS & 2 FOR EACH

DAN LEVEL. ONE EMPTY & ONE WEAPON. 10 TECHNIQUES & 3 HAND STRIKES:

{ FRONT PUNCH ~ THRUST PUNCH ~ KNIFEHAND }

LASTLY THREE GOOD KICKS:

{ FRONT ~ SIDE ~ CRESCENT }

BY USING THE ABOVE THE COMBOS YOU CAN CREATE ARE INDEFINATE!

ALSO REMEMBER YOU NEVER KNOW WHO IS WATCHING YOU?

DID YOU KNOW I DID ALL THIS?

ON TOP OF ALL MY WORK LOAD: WITH FAMILY & TRAINING?

MY STUDENTS & MY SELF..

THEN TRYING TO OMPLETE THIS PROJECT ON TOP OF ALL THAT.

PLEASE GET BACK TO ME & HAVE A GREAT WEEKEND. YOUR FRIEND MIKE. "

WITHIN THESE PASSAGES YOU WILL SEE HOW YOU NEED TO BE AWARE OF YOUR SURROUNDINGS!

YOU JUST NEVER KNOW WHO IS OUT THERE? OR WHAT THEY ARE DOING!

HOWEVER; BY GOING UNDER COVER IT WAS REFRESHING TO FIND AT LEAST TWO TRUE TRAINING HALLS OF TRADITION.

ONE IS MELLO'S MARTIAL ARTS CENTER & THE OTHER IS KENSHO RYU KENPO KARATE.

BOTH PLACES DO AN EXCELLENT JOB! EVEN THOUGH I NO LONGER TRAIN WITH SHIHAN MELLO FOR MY OWN REASONS...

HE IS THE BEST AROUND THESE PARTS IN THE EDUCATION OF SHOTOKAN.

BUT HOW SCARY IS IT? TO FIND OUT THAT THE MAJORITY OF THE DOJOS, NOT ONLY THEIR STUDENTS, BUT THEIR INSTRUCTORS AS WELL HAVEN'T A CLUE!

WELL; THIS PROJECT TELLS IT ALL! ABOUT THE QUALITY OF TEACHINGS AND STUDENTS AT ALL THE REST OF THE MARTIAL ARTS SCHOOLS AROUND MY AERA.

VERY. . . NO! EXTREMELY SAD!!

*ALL INFORMATION PROVIDED ON THIS STUDY IS TRUE AND ACCURATE. JUST KEEP IN MIND HOWEVER IT IS ONLY MY OPNION OF MY OWN STANDARDS.

BUT MY STANDARDS ARE EXTREMELY HIGH.

ALL THE REST OF THESE SCHOOLS NEEDAMPLE WORK TO EVEN OME CLOSE TO THESE TWO DOJOS!

AS FOR MY OWN STANDARDS OF TRAINING AND TEACHING; IT WOULD BE IMPOSSIABLE FOR THEM TO CATCH UP.

TO BREAK BAD HABITS AND FIX POOR INTELLECT IS EASIER SAID THAN DONE.

BESIDES PEOPLE DO NOT TAKE WELL TO CHANGE. NOT AT ALL!

I SEE THIS EVERYDAY IN LIFE. IN MY OWN, AT WORK, AND IN TRAVELING ABOUT.

NO ONE IS PERFECT. WE ALL HAVE PLENTY OF ROOM FOR IMPROVEMENT!

ALTHOUGH NO ONE IS BETTER THAN ANYONE ELSE SO IT MAY BE SAID...?

I BELIEVE SOME PEOPLE WORK MUCH HARDER THAN OTHERS. THIS IS WHAT MAKES YOU BETTER! THE STRIVE FOR EXCELLENCE OF ACHIEVEMENTS.

I WISH THE BEST OF LUCK AND SUCCESS TO ALL YOU LEAN TO IMPROVE THEIR LIFES!

NO MATTER IN WHAT DIRECTION THEY NEED TO FOLLOW. BECOME INSPIRED! DO NOT BE A FOLLOWER! BECOME A LEADER.

" DIRECTION. WHICH IS YOUR'S? CHOOSE WISELY. "

BECOMING A BLACKBELT :

JUST WHEN TIME SEEMED TO COME AT A COMPLETE STANDSTILL … IT FINALLY CAME.

MY INVITATION TO TEST FOR MY SHODAN. { 1ST DEGREE BLACKBELT }

IT WAS VERY EXCITING! FINALLY ALL THOSE LONG HOURS, THE DURATION OF PAIN, THE SPAN OF TIME…

ALL MY HARDWORK WAS ABOUT TO HOPEFULLY COME INTO A REALITY AND PAY OFF.

WELL MY TEST DAY FINALLY ARRIVED. THAT NIGHT I COULDN'T SLEEP AT ALL!

THEIR WERESO MANY THOUGHTS AND QUESTIONS RUNNING THREW MY MIND!

MY TEST WAS SCHEDULED TO LAST FOR SIX HOURS. DURING THIS TIME THERE ARE NO BREAKS OR RESTS. THIS IS A TEST!

TO SAY THE LEAST, THIS DAY WAS FULL OF SURPRISES.

EVEN WITH ALL THE YEARS OF PREPARING FOR THIS ONE DAY, IT FELT LIKE I HAD NEVER EVEN STEPPED INTO A DOJO BEFORE AT ALL!

IT WAS TO SAY THE LEAST EXTREMELY INTENSE.

THEN TOWARDS THE END OF THE EXAM A SIGH OF RELIFE FELL OVER ME.

THE TESTING PANNEL HAD ANNOUNCED THAT WE WERE GOING INTO THE FINAL HOUR.

AWESOME! NEXT UP THE SPARRING SESSIONS. WE DID ONE ON ONES, THEN TWO ON ONS, SOME GRAPPLING EXERCISES, AND ETC…

THE NEXT THING I REMEMBER ? I WAS IN THE BACK ROOM WITH THE

MASTER STANDING ABOVE ME AND THE REST OF THE PANNEL SURROUNDING ME.

IT WASN'T WHAT YOU MIGHT THINK. I WAS ACTUALLY BEING WOKEN UP BY MASTER ALAN D ' ALLESSANDRO.

HE HAD KNOCKED ME OUT! THIS WAS MY FIRST TIME EVER BEING KNOCKED OUT. THE FEELING IS VERY BIZARRE!

I STILL TO THIS DAY CAN'T REMEMBER WHAT HAPPENED AT ALL.

THEN I WAS COMPLETELY WITHDRAWN! AFTER ALL THIS HARDWORK AND THE TIME SPEND ON THIS EXAM…

I WAS TOLD TO GO HOME! I DIDN'T MAKE IT. I JUST COULDN'T BELIEVE IT!

I NEVER SAID I QUIT! I WANTED TO FINISH. ALTHOUGH MY CLOCK HAD BEEN CLEANED … I STILL NEVER HEARD THE BELL!

I ONLY HAD LIKE TWENTY MINUTES LEFT BEFORE THE TEST WAS OVER.

BUT I WAS TOLD BELIEVE IT. YOUR TEST IS OVER! BETTER LUCK NEXT TIME.

WOW! FIVE HOURS AND FOURTY MINUTES LATER, AND NOTHING TO SHOW FOR IT.

THEN I WENT HOME. FEELING A BIT OF DESPAIR. WHEN I REACHED MY HOUSE MY WIFE AND FAMILY HAD PLANNED A HUGH CELEBRATION PARTY FOR ME.

TO CELEBRATE MY SUCCESS OF REACHING MY GOAL AND BECOMING A BLACKBELT!

UPON MY ARRIVAL; THEIR WERE LIKE SIXTY PEOPLE AT MY HOME! MY HEART FELT LIKE IT WAS GOING TO SPLIT.

AS I WALKED INTO THE HOUSE … THERE WERE CHEERS OF JOY AND SUCH. ALL KINDS OF FOOD AND DRINKS TOO.

BOTH INSIDE AND OUT OF THE HOUSE. THEN I HAD TO PERHAPS DO THE MOST HARDEST THING IN MY LIFE EVER.

""   THANK YOU ALL VERY MUCH FOR ALL YOUR KIND WORDS AND THOUGHTS. ALL YOUR SUPPORT HAS BEEN AWESOME! BUT ... I DID NOT PASS. ""

NEXT THE SILENCE WAS SPOOKY. IT WAS LIKE YOU COULD HEAR THE WATER BUGS SKIMMING ACROSS THE WATER IN MY NEIGHBORS POND.

REALLY; THIS WAS AN UNCOMFORTABLE FEELING TO PROCESS. YOU SHOULD HAVE SEEN THE LOOKS ON ALL MY FAMILY AND FRIENDS FACES!

THEN MY WIFE TAMMY SAID ... *"" ARE YOU SERIOUS? ""* ... I THAN TOLD HER YES.

SHE THEN SAID ... *"" I KNOW YOU GAVE IT YOUR ALL AND WE ARE ALL VERY PROUD OF YOU! ""*

THIS MADE ME FEEL AWESOME!

THE LOVE THIS WOMAN GIVES TO ME, THE LOVE SHE STILL GIVES TO ME TODAY IN EVERYWAY IS THE BEST PART OF MY LIFE!

LATER ON THAT EVENING MY FELLOW CLASSMATES CAME OVER AS WELL AS THE TESING BOARD.

THEY TOLD ME I DID AN AWESOME JOB UNTIL I GOT KNOCKED OUT.

BUT IN SIX TO NINE MONTHS I WOULD BE ELIGIBLE TO RE - TEST AGAIN.

WELL THE WEEKEND HAD PASSED, BUT THE PAIN OF MY FAILURE WAS STILL HAUNTING ME.

NOT TO MENTION ALL THE SORENESS OF MY MUSCLES FROM THE TEST ITSELF!

ON MONDAY NIGHT TWO DAYS AFTER MY ORDEAL I WALKED INTO THAT DOJO LIKE NOTHING EVER HAPPENED.

I PUT MY BROWN BELT ON, AND STARTED TRAINING WITH MY PEERS. I NEVER SAID A WORD.

SEVEN MONTHS LATER .... I RECEIVED MY BLACKBELT! AFTER FINALLY COMPLETING THE SIX HOUR EXAMINATION.

IF THIS ISN'T CLASSIFIED AS HUMILITY THEN THE TEXT NEEDS TO BE RE - WRITTEN!

BUT NONE THE LESS IT BECAME A CLASSIC LESSON TO ME. NOW WITH THIS OBSTACLE OUT OF THE WAY MY JOURNEY CONTINUES …

"" LOOKING BACK … ALTHOUGH IT WAS A HARD DECISION TO MAKE …

IT WAS PERHAPS THE BEST ONE I EVEN MADE! ""

BEYOND BLACKBELT THE NEXT STEP :

THE NEXT STEP CAME WITH MANY MORE HARD LESSONS TO ENDURE. BOTH IN TRAINING AND LIFE.

WHEN YOU ACHIEVE YOUR FIRST DAN LEVEL YOU ARE NOW SUPPOSED TO TAKE ALL THAT YOU WERE TAUGHT, AND ADOPT IT TO FIT YOUR SKILLS.

THIS MEANS TO MAKE EACH TECHNIQUE YOUR OWN, AND CREATE SOMETHING NEW FOR YOURSELF. LIKE A TAILORED FIT.

SO MY NEW TASK WAS TO START THINKING OUTSIDE THE BOX, AND THINKING FOR MYSELF.

IT WAS DURING THIS PHASE OF MY TRAINING THAT I STARTED ASKING LOTS OF QUESTIONS.

QUESTIONS SUCH AS: *"" WHAT IS THE NEED FOR ALL THESE EXTRA STRIKES? THE ACTUALLY TECHNIQUE WAS FINISHED THREE MOVES AGO. ""*

THEN I STARTED THINKING: *"" WHAT IF I WAS DISABLED OR BECAME HANDICAPPED IN SOME MANNER? ""*

SO I STARTED TAKING ALL THE MATERIAL I HAD LEARNED, AND TRIED TO SIMPLIFY THE TECHNIQUES.

THINKING WHAT EVER THE DISABILITY MAY BE WHY WASTE EXTRA ENERGY. JUST DO WHAT YOU NEED TO, TO FINISH!

THEN GET AWAY. IN OTHER WORDS DO YOUR OWN THING. GET IN, AND THEN OUT AS SOON AS POSSIABLE.

ALSO REMEMBER TO CONSERVE AS MUCH ENERGY AS YOU CAN TOO. BECAUSE YOU NEVER KNOW WHAT ELSE MAY BE COMING.

WELL MY IDEA WAS TAKEN INTO CONSIDERATION. THE NEXT THING I KNOW …

IT WASN'T MY IDEA ANYMORE! IT WAS NOW THE MASTERS PLAN, AND NEW IDEA.

I NEVER RECEIVED ANY CREDIT AT ALL. PLUS I WAS LOOKED STRAIGHT IN THE EYE WITH NO RECOURSE OF GUILT!

SO I THOUGHT OK. HES THE MASTER, AND I AM BUT HIS STUDENT. WHO AM I TO MAKE POLICY.

AFTER SOME MORE TIME HAD PASSED BY I STARTED EXPERIMENTING WITH MORE OF MY OWN THOUGHTS.

THEN IN WHAT WAS CALLED FREE TIME, DURING LINE DRILLS FOR SELFDEFENSE I STARTED TO TRY THEM OUT.

WHEN I WAS ASKED: "" *FARADAY .. WHAT THE HELL ARE YOU DOING? .. THAT ISN'T IN OUR SYSTEM!* ""

MY ANSWER: "" *I CALL IT THINKING OUTSIDE THE BOX.* ""

WELL GUESS WHAT? THIS WAS ALSO NOT ACCEPTED.

HOWEVE; WHEN I NOTICED ANOTHER MORE "" ADVANCED "" BLACKBELT THAN ME FREE STYLE IT WAS LABELED AWESOME!

NICE JOB. GREAT THINKING! THAT LOOKED GREAT IN THERE.

AGAIN I WAS LIKE WHAT IS GOING ON HERE? IN MY MIND!

SO THAT EVENING I WENT HOME. AS I SAT DOWN AT MY COMPUTER I STARTED WRITING WHAT LATER ON BECAME MY OWN MATERIAL.

I WORKED ON THIS MATERIAL FOR ALMOST TWO YEARS. THROUGH TRIALS AND TRIBULATIONS OF FIELD TESTING TO PROVING THE MATERIAL WITHOUT ANY DOUBT.

NEXT WHEN I FINISHED THE KYUS SECTION { WHITE TO 3RD BROWN } I PLACED ALL THE WORK INTO A REAL NICE BINDER.

THEN I WORKED ON PRODUCING MY OWN LOGO, AND BUSINESS CARD. I WANTED TO BE DIFFERENT BUT ALSO UNIQUE TO ME.

HENCE U.S.A. INTERNATIOAL MARTIAL ARTS, AND THE STYLE OF TAIKYOKUKEN KEN SHO RYU WAS BORN!

THIS WAS ALL MY OWN MATERIAL. SO IN EFFECT ALTHOUGH I WAS FAR FROM BEING A MASTER IN THE ARTS I WAS THE SOKE { FOUNDER OF } THIS STYLE OF MARTIAL ARTS.

NOW WITH ALL THIS WORK FINISHED I NEEDED OR SHOULD SAY WANTED THE OPNION OF MY TRAINING PARTNER AT THE TIME.

HIS NAME WAS CHARLES TARR. WE HAD TRAINED AS WELL AS CAME UP THE RANKS TOGETHER FOR MANY YEARS.

HIS THOUGHTS TO MY MATERIAL WAS OF HIGH VAULE TO ME.

CHUCK TOOK MY BINDER HOME. HE EXAMINED IT FOR MONTHS AND ASKED ME SEVERAL QUESTIONS ABOUT IT.

THEN HE ASKED ME TO DEMO THEM TO HIM. BECAUSE HE WATED TO FEEL THE EFFECTS OF THE TECHNIQUES.

AFTER ALL THIS HE THEN TOLD ME: "" *MIKE IT ALL LOOKS GREAT TO ME. ARE YOU NOW READY TO APPROACH ALAN?* ""

CHUCH WAS REFERRING TO MASTER ALAN D ' ALLESSANDRO.

MY REPLY WAS: "" *YES I BELIEVE I AM NOW READY.* ""

NEXT STEP PROPOSING MY PLAN, AND PROJECT TO MY AT THE TIME MASTER. ALAN D ' ALLESSANDRO.

I WAS VERY NERVOUS, BUT ALSO EXTREMELY EXCITED TO GET HIS OPNION OF MY WORK!

I HAD PUT IN A VAST AMOUNT OF TIME, AND EFFORT INTO THIS PROJECT.

SO IT ALL CAME DOWN TO THIS MOMENT …

DOUBLE CHECKING ALL MY THEORIES, AND PROVING THEM IN THE CLASS ROOM { DOJO }, AND SEEKING THE FEEDBACK FROM ANOTHER DAN.

SO I APPROACHED AL AND ASKED HIM IF HE COULD PUT SOME TIME ASIDE FOR ME TO SHARE A PROJECT WITH HIM.

HE SAID YES. *"" HOW ABOUT NEXT WEEK? ""*

I COULDN'T WAIT! THE NEXT WEEK DIDN'T COME FAST ENOUGH!

WHEN IT DID ARRIVE, AND WE MEET WHAT HAPPENED NEXT CHANGED MY LIFE FOREVER!

BEFORE I HAD EVEN ENTERED THE OFFICE DOWN AT THE DOJO, ALAN BEGAN SCREAMING AT ME.

HE JUST TOTALLY BLEW UP AT ME! HETOOK MY BOOK THREW IT ACROSS THE ROOM, AND SLAMMED THE DOOR.

HE STARTED YELLING: *"" WHO THE HELL DO YOU THINK YOU ARE? WHAT THE HELL ARE YOU DOING? ""*

I REPLIED: *"" I THOUGHT YOU WOULD BE PROUD OF ME! HAVING ONE OF YOUR OWN BLACKBELTS TAKE ON SUCH A PROJECT.*

I JUST DON'T WANT TO BE A MAN WEARING A BELT. I WANT TO BE A MAN WEARING A BLACKBELT!

ONE WHO CAN THINK FOR HIMSELF, AND ASK QUESTIONS, AND TRY OUT NEW IDEAS OF MY OWN! ""

LETS JUST SAY THIS… I WAS STRONGLY FROWNED UPON FOR DOING SUCH A PROJECT!!!

I WANTED TO SPREAD MY WINGS, AND I WAS SO FULL OF HOPE.

THEN SHOT DOWN AND DEGRADED LIKE I WAS JUST PLAIN USELESS.

AFTER THE BLOW UP SESSION AND SUCH ALAN DECIDED TO TAKE MY REFRENCE BOOK HOME TO STUDY.

THEN SHORTLY AFTERWARD LIKE THE NEXT WEEK, WHEN I ENTERED THE DOJO NO ONE WOULD BOW RESPECT TO ME!

THEY HAD ALWAYS HAVE BEFORE THIS HAPPENED, AND NOW EVEN A FEW OF THE HIGHER RANKING DANS ALL OF A SUDDEN REFUSED TO WORK WITH ME.

THEY TOLD ME THAT ALAN HAD TOLD THEM I WAS PERFORMING DANGEROUS MOVES AND NOT TO WORK WITH ME, BUT BE DISGRACED BY ME!

I WAS LIKE: "" *WHAT?!* "" THEN I NOTICED LIKE THE NEXT WEEK THAT ONE OF MY TECHNIQUES FROM MY BOOK WAS BEING TAUGHT!

DO YOU THINK I WAS GIVING CREDIT FOR THIS? NO I WAS NOT!

THEN I STARTED OF TIME TO NOTICE THAT STUDENTS BELOW ME WERE RECEIVING MORE CREDIT THAN I, AND IT ALSO SEEMED THEY WERE ADVANCING VERY QUICKLY TO REACH MY CURRENT LEVEL.

SO I ASKED: "" *IS SOMETHING WRONG?* ""

THEN ANOTHER ONE OF MY SO CALLED BUDDIES CAME UP TO ME AND HE SAID: "" *I HEARD THE RUMOR THAT YOU ARE NEVER GOING TO MOVE UP IN RANK ANY TIME SOON. YOU KNOW WHAT I MEAN?* ""

BUT STILL A LITTLE MORE TIME WENT BY… THEN SOME MORE OF MY TECHNIQUES WERE BEING TAUGHT!

THIS WAS PRETTY MUCH THE LAST STRAW FOR ME, AND I STARTED FORMATTING THE PLAN FOR WHAT I CALLED MY DRY RUN.

TO THIS VERY DAY 10 / 16 / 2010 I STILL HAVE NOT RECEIVED MY TEXT BOOK BACK THAT I WROTE ABOUT A DECADE AGO.

MY FEELINGS WERE AND STILL ARE: ONE ~ REMEMBER WHO WROTE IT, AND TWO ~ ENJOY IT!

BECAUSE I HAVE RE - COMPLETED MY MATERIAL SINCE THEN AND IT IS VERY DIFFERENT.

WHEN WE BECOME BLACKBELTS WE ARE HELD TO A MUCH HIGHER STANDARD THAN THAT OF OTHERS.

AND AT THIS LEVEL WE ARE ENCOURAGED TO THINK OUTSIDE THE BOX.

SO I PHRASE OR RE - PHRASED IT TO THIS:

"" WHEN FACED WITH ADVERSITY OVER COME AND ADAPT! "" "" THAT IS THE TRUE NATURE OF A REAL BLACKBELT. ""

ALSO YOU NEED TO BE ENCOURAGED BY THE RIGHT MASTER. DO YOU KNOW WHAT I MEAN? ...

WITH THAT BEING SAID I DID! I OVER CAME AND ADAPTED TO BEING ON MY OWN.

TO TRULY BECOME A BLACKBELT YOU NEED TO INCORPRATE WHAT YOU HAVE LEARNED AND CHANGE IT SO THAT IT WORKS AND FLOWS TO YOUR THOUGHTS!

EVRYONE HAS A DIFFERENT BODY TYPE, AND EACH OF US HAS ARE OWN PERSONALITY. DRAW FROM THESE TRAITS IF YOU WANT TO BECOME SUCCESSFUL.

THE NEED TO CUT BACK OR TO ADD ON TO YOUR TECHNIQUES DEPENDS ON HOW YOU READ INTO YOUR MATERIAL THAT YOU WERE TAUGHT.

WHAT DOES THIS AL MEAN TO YOU?

THIS IS JUST ANOTHER PART OF HOW YOU CAN MAKE YOURSELF STANDOUT AS A GREAT MARTIAL ARTIST!

GOOD LUCK TO YOU AND DO NOT LET ANYONE OR ANYTHING STAND IN FRONT OF YOU AND YOUR GOALS.

NEVER! CHIEN; KYOSHI {QS} FARADAY 10 / 16 / 10.

"" THE N.E.K.A. CLAN ""

<u>MY TEACHING PHILOSOPHY :</u>

"" TO BE ABLE TO SHARE MY LIFES EXPERIENCES IN THE MARTIAL ARTS WITH OTHER PEOPLE.

BY USING MY OWN PERSONAL THEORIES, BELIEFS, AND MY TRADITIONS IN A WAY THAT CAN BENEFIT THE COMMON INDIVIDUAL.

THROUGH { EFFORT ~ ETIQUETTE ~ SINCERITY ~ CHARACTER ~ & SELF - CONTROL } I.E. GOOD OLD FASHION TRADITION! ""

WHEN IT COMES DOWN TO MY TEACHING I ONLY TEACH PRIVATELY. I ALSO DO NOT BELIEVE IN FOUR WALLS.

EVERYTHING THAT I DO EXCEPT WHEN I PROVIDE A SEMINAR IS COMPLETED OUT SIDE!

DURING ONE OF MY SESSIONS IT IS VERY RARE THAT YOU WILL FIND MORE THAN EIGHT AT A TIME.

BECAUSE I LIKE THE NUMBERS TO BE LOW SO THAT THE MATERIAL HAS THE CHANCE TO SET IN DEEP WITHIN THE PUPUIL. IT IS LIKE BEING A PERSONAL TRAINER.

I AM NOT IN IT FOR THE MONEY, BUT I AM IN IT TO HELP OTHERS!

MY FEE TO MY STUDENTS IS THEY DO ONE OF TWO THINGS:

ONE THEY GIVE ME FOURTY DOLLARS A MONTH, OR SECOND THEY GET A GIFT CERTIFICATE IN THAT SAME AMOUNT SO I CAN HAVE FUN WITH MY FAMILY.

BECAUSE OF THE WAY I CHOOSE TO TEACH I BELIEVE MY SKILLS ARE BROADENED AS AN INSTRUCTOR.

EVERYTHING THAT I ASK OF MY STUDENTS I IN TURN DO WITH THEM 100%. I WILL NEVER ASK THEM TO DO ANYTHING THAT I HAVE OR WILL NOT DO ALONG SIDE OF THEM!

EVEN THOUGH I HAVE BEEN IN THE GAME FOR DECADES I STILL LEARN FROM ALL OF MY STUDENTS THEMSELVES.

IF YOU ARE A GOOD INSTRUCTOR, AND YOU CAN NOT ADMIT TO THIS STATEMENT THEN YOU WILL NEVER BECOME A GREAT INSTRUCTOR!

YOU CAN LEARN FROM EVERYONE REGARDLESS OF WHO THEY ARE OR WHAT RANK THEY MIGHT HOLD.

"" THE ONLY RANK TO FEAR IS THE WHITE BELT1 BECAUSE THEY HAVE NOTHING TO LOOSE, BUTEVERYTHING TO GAIN! "" M.P.F.

THE MATERIAL THAT I HAVE SELECTED IS DRAWN FROM ALL MY MANY YEARS OF TRAVELING THROUGH TRIBULATIONS.

IT IS PUT TOGETHER INTO WHAT I CALL TAIKYOKUKEN KEN SHO RYU. THIS IS MY STYLE OF MARTIAL ARTS THAT I HAVE FOUNDED.

THE TRANSLATION OF THIS STYLE WHICH IS A COMBINATION OF BOTH JAPANESE AND CHINESE IS THIS:

THE ULTIMATE FIST STYLE OF KENPO AND SHOTOKAN.

AS I EXPLAINED EARLIER I TEACH OUTSIDE ALL YEAR ROUND. I HAVE NO CONCERN ABOUT WHAT THE WEATHER MAY HAVE IN STORE!

WHAT IT IS, IS WHAT IT IS! NO MATTER WHAT. IF YOU DO NOT LIKE IT THEN YOU ARE NOT INTERESTED IN MY TRAINING OR DO YOU WISH TO BE A STUDENT OF MINE.

THIS MAY SOUND HARSH, BUT I DO HAVE MY REASONS FOR WHICH LEADS ME TO THIS DECISION.

LIFE IS IN NO WAY AN EASY RIDE AND NEITHER IS MY CLASSES! I AM NOT HERE TO BE YOUR FRIEND.

I AM HERE TO BE YOUR TEACHER! THERE IS A HUGH DIFFERENCE BETWEEN THE TWO.

IN TEACHING THIS WAY WITH THIS MIND SET I HAVE GAINED MUCH RESPECT FROM MY STUDENTS, PEERS, AND IN A WAY TO MYSELF.

ONE ISSUE THAT I HAVE BEEN QUESTIONED ON IS MY BELIEF OF NOT USING HEAVY WEIGHTS IN TRAINING.

MY ANSWER IS … I DO NOT BELIEVE IT IS GOOD FOR YOU IN THIS SPORT. YOU DO NOT HAVE TO BE HUGH WITH OUTLANDISH MUSCLES.

HOWEVER YOU DO NEED STRENGTH AND DEFINED MUSCLES! THERE IS ALSO A HUGH DIFFERENCE BETWEEN THE TWO OF THESE THOUGHTS.

IN MARTIAL ARTS YOU NEED TO BE FLEXIABLE, LEAN, AND POWERFULL!

THIS WILL MAKE YOU QUICK. THIS IS WHAT YOU WANT. THE BIGGER YOU ARE THE HARDER IT IS TO GAIN THESE TRAITS.

THERE IS NOTHING WRONG WITH WEIGHT TRAINING OR BEING BIG, BUT IT WILL SLOW YOU DOWN A BIT.

AS FOR ME ALL MY WEIGHT TRAINING IS PERFORMED WITH MY TOTAL BODY WEIGHT, AND THE WEIGHT OF MY TRAINING PARTNERS.

OCCASIONALLY I WILL USE TEN TO TWENTY LBS OF CASTLE BLOCK STONE.

BUT AS A RULE I LIKE TO STICK TO THE BODY WEIGHTS THAT I HAVE TO WORK WITH. OLD FASION TRAINING.

IE. BODY AGAINST BODY PARIED INTO PARTNERS. EVERYONE IS DIFFERENT SO THIS IS WHAT MAKES YOUR WORKOUT!

IS THEIR AN EXCEPTION TO MY RULE? OF COURSE THERE IS. IN MY CROSS TRAINING I LIKE TO DO CIRCUIT TRAINING.

WHEN I EXERCISE IN THIS FASHION I WILL USE UP TO BUT NOT OVER FIFTY LBS.

NOW; WHEN IT COMES TO TESTING { *RANK ADVANCEMENT* } I AM VERY OLD FASHION.

I ONLY AND STRONGLY BELIEVE THAT THERE ARE ONLY TWO COLORS.

WHITE AND BLACK! NO IN BETWEENS. AFTER ALL THE YEARS OF HARD TRAINING YOUR WHITE BELT WILL START TO TURN BLACK.

THIS NATURAL COLOR COMES FROM THE SWEAT OF YOUR BODY COMBINED WITH DIRT. THEN IF YOU ARE LUCKY YOU WILL BLEED FROM YOUR TRAINING TIME TO TIME.

THIS TOO ADDS NOT ONLY TO THE COLOR OF YOUR BELT, BUT THE SPIRIT WITHIN IT TOO!

AS FAR AS ALL THE WHAT I CALL THE IN BETWEEN COLORS…

THESE ARE NOTHING MORE THAN POSITIVE REINFORCEMENTS TO THE STUDENT.
THE SOCIETY FOR WHICH WE LIVE IN TODAY IS ALL ABOUT STATUS AND MONEY. I THINK THIS IS VERY, VERY WRONG!

SO WHAT HAPPENS … ? INSTRUCTORS CHARGE OUTRAGEOUS FEES FOR TESTING THAT IS NOT NEEDED, AND IN TURN THE STUDENTS FEEL FALSE PRETENSES OF STATUS.

PEOPLE ASK ME … DO YOU TEST YOUR STUDENTS? MY ANSWER IS YES.

HOWEVER; FOR ONE I HAVE NO SET TIME IN THEIR TRAINING. WHAT THIS MEANS …

WHEN THEY ARE READY, THEY ARE READY! FINAL.

THEY ALL KNOW MY FEELING TO THE MATTER AT HAND. SO I ASK THEM WHAT THEY WANT, AND I THEN GIVE IT TO THEM.

BUT! I DO NOT CHARGE THEM CRAZY MONEY FOR IT EITHER.

THERE IS ALWAYS TWO STORIES I TELL MY STUDENTS WHEN THEY FIRST START TO TRAIN WITH ME:

IST ~

"" FIRST IF YOU EVER COME INTO THE NEED TO PROTECT YOURSELF OR LOVED ONES I WANT TO HEAR ABOUT IT FROM YOU. I DO NOT WANT TO BE READING ABOUT YOUR MISFORTUNE IN THE LOCAL PAPER. ""

2ND ~

"" NO MATTER HOW GOOD YOU MAY THINK YOU ARE THERE IS ALWAYS SOMEBODY OUT THERE WHO IS MUCH BETTER THAN YOU! AND YOU WILL NEVER KNOW WHO THAT SOMEBODY MAY BE ... OR WHO IS WITH THEM! ""

BY THESE TWO STATEMENTS I LET THE POTENTIAL STUDENT KNOW RIGHT AWAY WHERE I STAND AND WHERE THEY STAND.

IT IS ALSO A GREAT REMINDER TO ALL CURRENT STUDENTS TOO.

THIS IS WHY I TEACH IN THE MANNER FOR WHICH I TEACH, AND I ONLY TEACH SOLID MATERIAL.

NOTHING FLASHY OR TRENDY. JUST TECHNIQUES THAT WORK, AND ARE LEARNABLE BY ALL!

SO MOVING ON ... WHEN IT COMES TO COMPENSATION I CHARGE $40.00 PER MONTH FOR ONE AND A HALF HOURS OF CLASS TIME.

AS FAR AS TESTING GOES THE PRICE IS $ 50.00 FROM 10TH KYU TO 1ST KYU. EACH DAN LEVEL IS $ 250.00.

FOR ALL TESTING FEES THIS COVERS THE CLASS TIME FOR THE TEST, AND COMES WITH YOUR NEW BELT AND CERTIFICATE CREDITS.

"" THE DRY RUN EXPERIMENT ""

THIS EXPERIMENT TOOK PLACE IN EARLY SPRING OF THE YEAR 2003. IN THIS EXPERIMENT THEIR WERE NINE TESTING SUBJECTS.

ALL RANGED FROM DIFFERENT AGES, AND BACKGROUNDS. THE ONE FACTOR THAT ALL OF THEM SHARED WAS THE INTEREST IN THE LEARNING OF MARTIAL ARTS.

THEIR WERE SEVEN MEN:

{ ROBERT KOKOCINSKI 50 YRS OF AGE ~ TODD MARCIN ~ CHRIS CARDELLA MID TWENTIES ~ BRIAN WILLARD ~ TOM WHEELER ~ JOHN JOHNSON ALL TWENTY FOUR YEARS OF AGE. }

THEN THERE WERE TWO WOMAN:

{ NICOLE TRABUCCO SIXTEEN YEARS OF AGE ~ KAITIE FLYNN TWENTY THREE YEARS OF AGE. }

DURING THIS TIME I WANTED TO SEE FIRST HAND HOW BY IMPOSING MY WILL OF THE WAY I TRAIN WOULD IMPACT THESE SELECTED STUDENTS.

MY EXPERIMENT ENDED WITH THESE NINE STUDENTS WHEN I CAME DOWN TO THE LAST ONE.

THIS BY MY SURPRISE WAS MS. FLYNN IN JULY OF 2006. SHE HAD OUTLASTED ALL THE OTHERS!

SHE HAD STUCK WITH ME AND MY TRAINING NO QUESTIONS ASKED. A TRUE SPIRIT OF A WARRIOR.

JUST TO LET YOU KNOW WAY BACK THEN SOAKING WET KAITIE WAS ABOUT 110 LBS, AND THIS IS WHAT HELD THREW THE GUYS WHO THOUGHT THEY WERE BIG AND TOUGH!

SHE HAD SHOWN ME A LOT OF HEART, AND DETERMINATION. I WAS THEN AND STILL TODAY VERY PROUD OF HER!

TO TRAIN IN THESE TYPES OF CONDITIONS AND CIRCUMSTANCES IS BY NO MEANS AN EASY TASK.

AS FAR AS I KNOW, AND LED TO BELIEVE THERE IS NO ONE AROUND ME WITHIN AT LEAST SIX STATES THAT HAS SUCH A PROGRAM LIKE MINE.

I LOVE IT! THIS IS WHAT I DO, AND HOW I LIKE TO DO IT. THIS IS MY WAY OF TRAINING IN THE MARTIAL ARTS.

DUE KEEP IN MIND HOWEVER I ONLY ACCEPT SO MANY INTO MY PRIVATE PROGRAM.

OF THOSE THAT I DO ACCEPT I CHOOSE THEM AFTER AN INTERVIEW ALONG WITH A SPECIAL ONE ON ONE CLASS.

I DO NOT TAKE JUST ANYBODY. BECAUSE IN THE MANNER FOR WHICH I TRAIN I ALSO DO NOT ACCEPT ANY KIDS UNDER THE AGE OF EIGHTEEN.

I HAVE NO PROBLEM PROVIDING SEMINARS OR SPEAKING TO THE YOUTH THAT ARE INTERESTED IN THE ARTS, BUT AFTER MY PRESENTATION I DIRECT THEM TO A PROPER INSTRUCTOR THAT MEETS MY STANDARDS.

AS OF THIS 20TH DAY IN OCTOBER, IN THE YEAR 2010 THE ONLY PERSON I TRULY BELIEVE IN FOR THIS JOB IS SENSEI MIKE MILLETT, AND HIS SCHOOL THE KENSHO RYU KENPO KARATE SCHOOL.

SPEAKING OF SEMINARS I AM AVAILABLE TO PROVIDE THEM ON A LIMITED BASIS. FOR MORE INFORMATION , AND A PRICING GUIDE PLEASE FEEL FREE TO CONTACT ME AT:

FARADAYPOWER@MSN.COM

IN THE SUBJECT MATTER LIST MARTIAL ARTS SEMINARS SO I KNOW I NEED TO GET BACK TO YOU, AND THAT YOU ARE M ARTIAL ARTS ORIENTATED.

OTHERWISE I HAVE KNOW IDEA WHO YOU ARE OR WHAT YOU WANT AND ALL CORRESPONDANCE WILL BE TREATED AS INTERNET SPAM.
THANK YOU FOR YOUR UNDERSTANDING AND INTERESTS.

TODAY I HAVE ONLY TWO PRIVATE STUDENTS KAITIE AND BRIAN, AND WORK WITH THREE OTHER DANS.

THEY ARE SENSEI JOHN GIAQUAINTO ~ SENSEI MIKE MILLETT ~ AND MASTER CHARLES TARR.

THEN I TAKE DIRECTION UNDER MY SENSEI. THE LIVING ICON LEGEND SHODOSHI RON " THE BLACK DRAGON " VAN CLIEF.

IN THE YEAR OF 2005 I HAD LOST BRIAN DUE TO PERSONAL REASONS IN HIS LIFE THAT WERE CONFLICTING TO HIM.

AFTER HE WORKED OUT HIS WORRIES HE CAME BACK TO ME IN THE WINTER OF 2010.

AS FOR KAITIE SHE HAD A LOT ON HER PLATE!

AFTER BEING THE LAST ONE TO SURVIVE MY DRY RUN EXPERIMENT IN 2006 SHE HAD JUST FINISHED UP HER STUDIES AT WHAT IS NOW WORCESTER STATE UNIVERSITY.

LIKE MOST COLLEGE GRADUATES SHE NEEDED TO FIND HER PLACE IN SOCIETY.

UNFORTUNATELY IN THE WORLD WE LIFE IN TODAY THIS IS ALSO NO EASY ADJUSTMENT!

THEN TO ADD TO HER DIFFICULTY HER MOTHER WAS STRICKEN SERIOUSLY ILL, AND SHORTLY AFTER HAD PASSED.

KAITIE NEEDED TO HAVE PERSONAL TIME. DURING THIS TIME SHE WAS GONE FOR THREE YEARS.

AFTER GOING THREW SOME MORE SOUL SEARCHING SHE HAD REALIZED THAT EVERY WHERE SHE WENT AS FAR AS MARTIAL ARTS TRAINING WAS NOT THE SAME.

THE SKILLS THAT SHE DEVELOPED FROM TIME SPENT WITH ME WAS WHAT SHE CALLED WAY BEYOND THE QUALITY OF OTHER STUDENTS THAT SHE HAD ENCOUNTERED.

THIS MADE ME FEEL GREAT! WHY? BECAUSE I KNEW THAT WHAT I HAD TAUGHT HER SHE RETAINED, AND ITS QUALITY OF MATERIAL WAS SOLID.

AFTER HEARING FROM HER SEVERAL YEARS SINCE SHE HAD LEFT WE WERE REUNITED THREW FACEBOOK.

SHE HAD TOLD ME THAT EVERYTHING THAT WAS GOING ON HER LIFE AT THE TIME WAS GETTING EXTREMELY ROUGH, AND THAT SHE WAS UNABLE TO HANDLE IT ANYMORE!

I COULD CERTAINLY UNDERSTAND THIS AND HAD NO HARD FEELINGS ABOUT IT.

THEN SHE ASKED ME IF SHE COULD PICKUP WHERE SHE HAD LEFT OFF …?

I TOLD HER YES. SO AS OF OCTOBER OF 2009 MS. FLYNN WAS BACK AND BETTER THAN EVER.

NOW ONLY HAVING TWO PRIVATE STUDENTS IS PERFECTLY FINE WITH ME. AT LEAST I KNOW THEY ARE WILLING TO PUT IN THE EFFORT.

BECAUSE UNTIL I COME ACROSS SIX MORE PEOPLE WHO WANT TO GIVE ME THIS TYPE OF COMMITMENT, AND TRAIN IN MY FASHION WHAT I HAVE TO WORK WITH WILL DO.

AND I AM VERY PLEASED WITH THIS FACT. THIS IS MY TRADITION. THIS IS THE LEGACY!

AS I HAVE DISCUSSED EARLIER IN GREAT DETAIL TRADITION IS EVERYTHING TO ME.

I BELIEVE I HAVE SUPPORTED MY CAUSE FOR THIS TOPIC. SO I LEAVE THIS SECTION WITH MY LITTLE RIDDLE TO YOU…

"" *WHAT DO YOU CONSIDER TO BE YOUR MOST VAUABLE ASSET IN YOUR MARTIAL ARTS TRAINING AS FAR AS TRADITION?* ""

"" *IS IT KATA … BASICS … OR THE BASICS WITHIN YOUR KATA?* ""

IN TALKING WITH MY FRIEND SIFU ALAN DACASCOS ANOTHER MARTIAL ARTS LEGEND FROM HAWAII HE TOLD ME THAT MY FEELINGS ON THE MATTERS FOR WHICH I EXPRESSED ON TRADITION WERE WELL WARRANTED.

HE ALSO TOLD ME THAT WE ALL FEEL LIKE WE HIT THE BRICKWALL SOMETIMES IN OUR TRAINING!

BUT THE WAY I PERCIEVE AND CORRESPONDE TO IT IS WHAT TRULY MAKES ME STAND OUT AS A GREAT MARTIAL ARTIST!

NOW LETS FINISH MY RIDDLE. TRADITION IS A SEQUENCE OF HISTORY THAT IS PASSED ON FROM ONE TO ANOTHER OVER TIME.

KATA IS AN EMPTY BUNKI. ITS CONSTRUCTION IS DESIGNED TO TEACH YOU TO LEARN HOW TO FIGHT IN MULTIPLE SITUATIONS.

BASICS ARE THE MOST FUNDEMENTAL OF THE BUILDING BLOCKS! THEY ARE THE MAIN FOUNDATION OF ALL TRUE MARTIAL ARTS.

SO … MY RIDDLE EXPLAINS IT SELF.

"" *THE BASICS WITHIN YOUR KATA SHOULD BE YOUR MOST VALUABLE ASSET IN YOUR TRAINING AND YOUR TRADITIONS!* ""

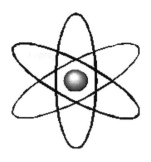

THE CONCEPTION OF MY LOGO :

WHEN I WAS DECIDING ON A LOGO I HAD MANY THOUGHTS IN MIND. IT ACTUALLY TOOK ME QUITE AWHILE TO COME UP WITH ONE.

THEN ONE DAY IT JUST CLICKED!

BEING VERY PATRIOTIC AND A CURRENT MEBER OF THE UNITED STATES TEAM / TEAM AMERICA AT THE TIME, PAIRED WITH THE LOVE OF EAGLES BY MY SON MASON I HAD MY VISION!

MY LOGO HAD COME TO BE. IT IS AN EAGLES HEAD OUTLINE. THE FACE IS JUST LIKE THE BIRD, BUT THE HEAD HAS A WAVE TO IT TO RESEMBLE OUR COUNTRIES FLAG.

IT HAS RED AND BLUE STRIPS WITH STARS. THEN IN A CIRCULAR SHAPE GOING AROUND THE WHOLE EAGLE IS MY SCHOOLS NAME.

U.S.A. INTERNATIONAL MARTIAL ARTS. I PICKED THIS NAME FOR THE SIMPLE REASON THAT I AM PROUD TO BE AN AMERICAN!

AND I HAVE TRAVELED INTERNATIONALLY ALL AROUND THE WORLD REPRESENTING THE UNITED STATES IN THE SPORT OF MARTIAL ARTS.

HENCE THE NAME: U.S.A. INTERNATIONAL MARTIAL ARTS AND THE FOUNDING OF THE STLYE TAIKYOKUKEN KEN SHO RYU WAS BORN!

"" FINAL DESIGN 2000 ""

HOW TO CORRECTLY PRATICE YOUR KATA :

FIRST AND FORMOST WHEN YOU ARE PRATICING YOUR KATAS KEEP IN MIND THAT A MIRROR IS YOUR BEST FRIEND.

CHECK YOUR STANCES REGULARLY! ARE YOUR BLOCKS IN GOOD FORM?

DID YOU REMEMBER TO LOOK BEFORE YOU CHANGED DIRECTION? WAS YOUR BREATHING DONE CORRECTLY?

IF YOUR ANSWER IS NO TO ALL THE ABOVE THEN YOU NEED TO PRATICE MORE!

MUCH ~ MUCH ~ MORE! THESE QUESTIONS ARE ASKED FOR A REASON.

THEY ARE VERY IMPORTANT IF YOU WANT TO PERFORM AND PRATICE YOUR KATAS CORRECTLY.

HAVE CONFIDENCE! IF YOU ARE GOING TO THROW A STRIKE THEN THROW IT!

IF YOU ARE GOING TO DO A KICK … THEN KICK! DO NOT PERFORM POOR TECHNIQUES!

IF YOU ARE NOT BLOCKING CORRECTLY YOU WILL FEEL IT. BELIEVE ME.

WHEN YOU GET HIT A GOOD ONE FROM YOUR OPPONENT!

LAST BUT NOT LEAST KNOW YOUR LOCATION. KNOW YOUR LOCATION OF YOUR BLOCKS AND TRIKES IN RELATION TO YOUR OPPONENT.

* LOCATION IS ABOVE FAR THE MOST IMPORTANT COMPONENT OF KNOWING YOUR KATAS!

LEARNING HOW TO CORRECTLY BREATH IS THE OTHER.

AFTER ALL THIS; THEN IT IS TIME TO FOCUS ON THE MOVEMENT OF YOUR HIPS.

HIP ROTATION IS THE ULTIMATE KEY TO THE TRUE POWER OF ALL YOUR TECHNIQUES.

IN THE ARTS WE CALL THIS THE TORK. ONE CAN NOT EXIST WITHOUT THE OTHER.

THE GREATER THE TORK THE MORE POWERFULL YOUR TECHNIQUE WILL BECOME!

ALSO REMEMBER TO KEEP TABS OF YOUR HEIGHT IN RELATION TO YOUR MOVEMENT IN YOUR KATAS.

I.E. / YOU DO NOT WANT TO BE ALL OVER THE PLACE. WHAT WE LIST AS A LOT OF UP AND DOWN MOVEMENT.

KEEP A CONSTANT MOVEMENT AND TRY YOUR BEST TO MAINTAN A LEVEL HEIGHT THROUGH YOUR ENTIRE KATA.

FINALLY TO TRULY UNDERSTAND THE ORGINS OF YOUR KATAS, AND WHAT IT IS YOU ARE TRYING TO ACCOMPLISH YOU NEED TO PRACTICE YOUR KATA AS A BUNKI.

A BUNKI IS THE PRACTICAL APPLACTION OF ADDING UES { ATTACKERS } TO YOUR KATA.

QUALITY OF MATERIAL LEARNED IS EVERYTHING AND QUANITY SHOULD HAVE NO BEARING.

WHAT ALL THIS SHOULD MEAN TO YOU IS THIS … ALL THAT I HAVE DISCUSSED ABOVE IS REALLY GOING TO SINK HOME IF YOU APPLY YOUR SELF TO THESE IDEAS IN YOUR TRAINING.

ANOTHER ASPECT THAT I PERSONALLY LIKE TO DO WHEN PRACTICING MY KATAS IS TO FACE ALL EIGHT POINTS OF POSSIABLE ATTACKS.

SO THIS MEANS THAT I PRACTICE EACH KATA EIGHT TIMES FROM THE EIGHT DIFFERENT DIRECTIONS.

IT DOESN'T MATTER WHERE YOU START. THE ENDING WILL ALWAYS PUT YOU BACK TO YOUR ORGINAL STARTING POINT NO MATTER WHAT DIRECTION YOU BEGIN.

I CALL THIS TECHNIQUE CLOCK WORK. IMAGINE THAT YOU ARE STANDING ON THE FACE OF A CLOCK.

THEN PERFORM YOUR KATAS ON EACH HOUR. SO IN THIS PERTINACIOUS WAY YOU WILL PRACTICE YOUR KATAS TWELVE TIMES APIECE.

YOU WILL BE AMAZED IN HOW HARD IT CAN BE JUST BY CHANGING YOUR DIRECTIONS! IT CAN CAUSE GREAT CONFUSION.

BUT THIS IS GREAT. LIKE I SAID … IT IS A MIND THING.

BY PRACTICING IN THIS MANNER IT REALLY WORKS YOUR MIND, AND THE PERFORMANCE OF YOUR KATAS WILL STRENGTHEN TO THE HIGHEST POINT.

THE ONLY EXCEPTION TO THE ABOVE RULE WOULD BE IN THE ART OF KUNG - FU. THE MAJORITY OF THE TIME YOU ALMOST ALWAYS END SLIGHTLY FROM YOUR ORGINAL STARTING POINT.

IT'S THE BEAUTY OF THAT ART.

SO REMEMBER YOUR GOAL IN THIS EXERCISE? TO START AND TO FINISH YOUR KATAS IN YOUR ORGINAL STARTING POINT.

GOODLUCK!

"" WORKING WITH KAITI ON SET OF THE ART OF DEFENSE NOV 14TH 2010 ""

HOW TO PRACTICE WITH A WEAPON :

BEFORE YOU EVEN CONSIDER ADDING A WEAPON TO YOUR TRAINING I STRONGLY BELIEVE THAT YOU HAVE TO BE AT LAST A 5TH KYU. { GREENBELT }

ANYTHING BEFORE THIS IS NOT ACCEPTED BY ME, BECAUSE A WEAPON IS SERIOUS!

ALSO I DO NOT BELIEVE THE MATURAITY LEVEL IS HIGH ENOUGH BEFORE THIS LEVEL IN THE HANDLING OF A WEAPON!

BY FAR THE MOST IMPORTANT RULE IS NO CHILDREN TO BE TAUGHT WEAPONS! NEVER.

WHEN THE TIME DOES COME FOR A STUDENT TO LEARN A WEAPON KNOW THE CORRECT ORDER OF LEARNING.

WOODEN WEAPONS BEFORE BLADED WEAPONS!

 YOU SHOULD ALWAYS START WITH THE STAFF. THEN IN MY PROFESSIONAL OPNION FOLLOW THIS REGIME:

ESCRIMA STICKS ~ TONFA ~ NUNCHAKU ~ SIA ~ KAMA ~ KNIFE ~ SWORD ~ MANRIKIGUSARI ~ MULTIPLE WEAPONS { MIX & MATCH }.

NEXT YOU HAD BETTER KNOW AND UNDERSTAND THE TERM OF A WEAPON, AND WHAT IT MEANS!

IN MARTIAL ARTS THE USE OF A WEAPON IS REFERRED TO AS AN EXTENSION OF THE ARM.

WHEN IT DOES COME TIME FOR THE STUDENT TO LEARN BLADED OR THE USE OF MULTIPLE WEAPONS WHICH BY THE WAY SHOULD BE INTRODUCED SLOWLY OVER A PERIOD OF TIME IT SHOULD BE IN THE DAN LEVELS!

NOW THAT WE ARE CYRSTAL CLEAR ON THIS TOPIC LETS MOVE TO THE PRACTICING PORTION OF USING A WEAPON.

FIRST ALL THAT I MENTIONED AS FAR AS YOUR EMPTY HANDED KATAS ALSO APPLIES TO YOUR WEAPON KATAS.

{ BLOCKS ~ STANCES ~ STRIKES ~ LOCATION ~ BREATHING ~ LOOKING ~ MOVEMENTIN RELATION TO HEIGHT ~ ETC! }

HOWEVER; NOW YOU ALSO NEED TO ADD AWARNESS TO THE EQUATION. YOU KNOW BEING AWARE OF YOUR SURROUNDINGS.

BEING IN TUNE TO WHATS AROUND YOU BEFORE YOU GET STARTED!

{ PEOPLE ~ OBJECTS ~ ENOUGH SAID! }

REMEMBER YOU NEED TO HAVE THE PROPER SPACE FOR THE PRACTICING WITH A WEAPON! THE EXTENSION OF ARM.

YOU DO NOT WANT TO INJURY ANYBODY INCLUDING YOURSELF!

OK NOW BEFORE YOU ARE TAUGHT A KATA WITH A WEAPON YOU NEED TO KNOW THE FOLLOWING INFORMATION:

YOU NEED TO LEARN ALL THE POSSIABLE BLOCKS, AND STRIKES THAT CAN BE ACHIEVED WITH YOUR WEAPON OF CHOICE.

SO I LIKE TO PUT TOGETHER A SYSTEM OF A KATA FOR EACH WEAPON.

1ST A KATA USING ONLY BLOCKS. 2ND A KATA USING ONLY STRIKES.

NEXT YOU NEED TO LEARN SELF DEFENSE FOR YOUR WEAPON USING THE FORMULA OF THE EIGHT POINTS OF ATTACK.

{TOP OF HEAD ~ LEFT & RIGHT SIDE OF HEAD ~ LEFT & RIGHT SIDE OF MID SECTION ~ LEFT & RIGHT SIDE OF LOWER SECTION ~ UNDERNEATH}

AFTER THIS NOW YOU ARE READY TO LEARN MY KATA FOR THE WEAPONS I PRACTICE.

SO NOW YOU WILL BE READY TO LEARN A TRADITIONAL WEAPON KATA.

IN MY BOOK A STUDENT IS NOT READY TO LEARN A WEAPON KATA IF HE DOESN'T KNOW EVERYTHING THERE IS TO KNOW ABOUT THAT WEAPON!

ONCE HE OR SHE DOES LEARN ALL THAT I HAVE STRESSED ABOUT THE KNOWLEDGE, AND THE USE OF THE WEAPON INCLUDING ITS PRATICAL PRIMARY FUNCTION THEN THEY ARE TOTAL PREPAIRED!

IS THERE ANYTHING ELSE LEFT? WHY YES THERE IS…

TO REALLY ADVANCE AND STRENGTHEN YOUR WEAPONS KATA YOU NOW NEED TO PUT IT INTO THE APPLICATION OF A BUNKI.

USE EMPTY HANDED UKES TO YOUR EXTENSION OF ARM. NEXT ADD A WEAPON VS. WEAPON.

THIS IS REALLY FUN TO DO, BUT AGAIN ONLY AFTER YOU FULLY UNDERSTAND ALL THE PRINCIPLES OF THE WEAPON THAT YOU ARE PRACTICING AND LEARNING.

* THE BEST AND MOST PRACTICAL WEAPON TO VS ALL OTHER WEAPONS WHEN PRACTICING IS THE STAFF!

*** *FOOTNOTES FOR KATAS* ***

KATAS ARE A FORMAL EXERCISE. THEY ARE O A MARTIAL ARTIST WHAT FLOOR EXERCISES ARE TO A GYMNAST.

HOWEVER; WHEN KATA IS PRACTICED AS A BUNKI IT IS CALLED A FORMAL APPLICATION!

IN THIS APPLICATION THE BEAUTY IS IN THE EYE OF THE STUDENT!

WHAT THIS MEANS IS THAT EVERYONE HAS DIFFERENT OPINIONS OF THE INTERRUPTION OF THE KATA WHEN APPLIED INTO BUNKI.

FOR EXAMPLE / NOT ALL THE TECHNIQUES IN A KATA MAKE PERFECT SENSE IN APPLICATION FORM.

THE REASON FOR THIS IS ELAPSED TIME AND THE LOSS OF INFORMATION.

WHEN THESE KATAS CAME FROM THE GREAT TEMPLES CENTURIES AGO THE COMMUNICATION BREAK DOWN BEGAN.

THE GRANDMASTERS PASSED THEIR KNOWLEDGE ONTO THEIR STUDENTS, WHO BECAME THE MASTERS.

THEN THESE MASTERS PASSED THEIR KNOWLEDGE ONTO THEIR STUDENTS, WHO BECAME THE SENSEI.

EACH TIME THE INFORMATION WAS PASSED ALONG IT SLOWLY LOST PERTINENT APPLICATION AS TO TECHNIQUES THAT WERE PLACED WITHIN THESE KATAS!

THIS THEORY IS MUCH RELATED TO WHAT IN TODAYS SOCIETY WE CALL THE GRAPEVINE.

THIS IS WHY WE ASK QUESTIONS, AND IF YOU DO NOT THEN YOU SHOULD.

IN THESE AREAS OF CONCERN YOU AS THE STUDENT NEED TO INTERRUPT THE VIEW YOU HAVE OF THE INFORMATION GIVEN TO YOU TO WORK WITH.

THIS REFLECTION OF YOUR OPINION OF WHAT IS HAPPENING WITH THE TECHNIQUES WHICH MAKE UP THE KATA IS WHAT I CALL THE TRUE BEAUTY.

IT IS HELD IN YOUR MIND, AND IT IS WHAT YOU VISUALIZE THREW YOUR EYES TO MAKE PERFECT SENSE OF THE BUNKI.

A TRUE MARTIAL ARTIST KNOWS THAT THE ANSWERS ARE NEVER WRONG FROM ONES INTERRUPTION OF A BUNKI.

IN THE PRESENT TIME WHICH IS THE TIME WE NOW LIVE IN WE CAN HELP CHANGE THESE FLAWS.

WITH THE TECHNOLOGY WE POSSESS IN MULTI MEDIA OPTIONS WE CAN MAKE PERMANENT RECORDS FOR CENTURIES TO COME.

IT IS CALLED A DVD LIBRARY.

ALSO THREW THE USE OF OUR COMPUTERS WE CAN WRITE ALL OF OUR INFORMATION DOWN AND PUT IT INTO THE HARD DRIVES, AND WRITE THIS ONTO A DISK FOR BACKUP PURPOSES.

THEN WHEN NEEDED WE CAN PRINT THE INFORMATION OUT, AND PLACE THIS INTO HARD BINDERS.

THIS IS A COUPLE OF WAYS THAT WE CAN PRESERVE THE INFORMATION WE CURRENTLY HAVE NOW.

I AM MORE THAN SURE THAT IN THE NEAR FUTURE THE TECHNOLOGY WE POSSESS WILL ALLOW US TO INCORPORATE EVEN BETTER WAYS TO PRESERVE KNOWLEDGE!

<u>PREPARING FOR COMBAT :</u>

THE FIRST STEP IN PREPARING FOR COMBAT IS TO ALWAYS EXPECT THE UNEXPECTED!

NEXT YOU NEED TO LEARN HOW TO READ YOUR OPPONENT. WHAT ARE THE FACIAL GESTURES?

{ HAPPY ` SAD ` BLANK ` IN DIFFERENT ` ANGRY ? }

NEXT WHAT DO THE BODY GESTURES TELL YOU?

{ CALM ` TENSE ` EXCITED ` NERVOUS ? }

THEN BE AWARE OF THE SURROUNDINGS YOU ARE IN, AND WHAT IS GOING ON THERE.

{ INSIDE ` OUTSIDE ` PUBLIC ` PRIVATE ? }

BEING ABLE TO REALIZE THESE SIGNS MAY SAVE YOUR LIFE SOMEDAY, AND ALSO YOU WILL BE ABLE TO TELL A LOT ABOUT THE INTENTIONS OF OTHERS.

NEVER EVER UNDER ESTIMATE ANYBODY EVEN IF YOU THINK THAT YOU KNOW THEM!

BECAUSE SOMEDAY YOU MAY BE SURPRIZED! IS THERE ANY REASON TO EXPECT A CONFRONTATION?

THE VERY NEXT STEP YOU NEED TO DO IS REMAIN CALM! DO NOT PANIC NOR SHOW SIGNS OF IT.

BEFORE YOU DECIDE TO DO ANYTHING RASH LOOK FOR SOLUTIONS TO THE POSSIABLE ROBLEM.

REMEMBER YOU NEVER KNOW WHO IS WHO, OR WHO THEY ARE WITH!

I CALL THIS LESSON: *"" LEARNING TO READ THE FENCE. ""*

ABOVE ALL PLEASE KEEP THIS IN MIND DO NOT GET CAUGHT WITH YOUR HANDS IN YOUR POCKETS!

WHAT I MEAN BY THIS IS IF YOU HAVE A GUT FEELING ABOUT A SITUATION THEN GO WITH IT.

KEEP LEVEL HEADED, AND YOUR HANDS SHOULD ALWAYS BE UNRESTRICTED AVAILABLE FOR DEFENSE WHEN THE NEED IS APPARENT!

* YOU ARE NOT ABLE TO DO THIS IF YOUR HANDS ARE NOT FREE.

DON'T SECOND GUESS YOURSELF EVER! IF YOU FEEL A CERTAIN FEELING ABOUT A CIRCUMSTANCE IT IS FOR GOOD REASON!

AGAIN I STRESS THE FACT; ALWAYS LOOK FOR A WAY OUT FIRST THAT IS PEACEFULL.

THE BIGGER MAN CAN ALWAYS WALK AWAY! THERE IS NO SHAME IN THIS.

ONLY RESORT TO YOUR TRAINING IF THERE ARE NO OTHER OPTIONS AVAILABLE!

WHEN IT COMES TO THE SAFETY OF FAMILY, FRIENDS, OR YOURSELF YOU NEED TO DO WHAT IT IS YOU HAVE TO.

AS FAR AS THE LAW IS CONCERNED; ONLY USE THE FORCE THAT IS REQUIRED TO NEUTRALIZE THE SITUATION UNTIL THE PROPER AUTHORITIES ARRIVE!

TO SPELL IT OUT FOR YOU: "" *IF THEY FALL TO THE GROUND YOU STOP AND MAINTAIN CONTROL TO THE POLICE ARRIVE!* ''

"" *IF THERE IS A WEAPON INVOLVED ... YOU HAVE NO CHOICE! THEN WHAT EVERY HAPPENS MAY THE OUTCOME BE FAVORABLE TO YOU. DO WHAT YOU NEED TO, AND MAKE SURE THAT IT WILL NOT HAPPEN TO SOMEONE ELSE!* ""

AGAIN I CALL THIS READING THE FENCE. SOME PEOPLE WHO ARE VERY GOOD AT THIS TECHNIQUE REFER TO IT AS RIDING THE FENCE.

SO PICTURE YOURSELF BEING SEPERATED BY A FENCE. YOUR ON ONE SIDE, AND SOMEONE ELSE IS ON THE OTHER.

IF THE OTHER PERSON CROSSES OVER THAT FENCE THEY HAVE NOW INVADED YOUR PERSONAL SPACE!

I.E. A CONFRONTATION IS GOING TO TAKE PLACE. BE READY!

NOW LETS TALK A LITTLE BIT MORE ABOUT YOUR PERSONAL SPACE...

WHEN ANOTHER PERSON IS SO CLOSE TO YOU THAT THEY CAN REACH OUT AND TOUCH YOU THEN IT IS PERSONAL!

THEY ARE TO CLOSE TO YOU.

FOR MOST PEOPLE THIS IS REALIZED WHEN IT COMES DOWN TO THE FACIAL AREA. I HAVEN'T FOUND ANYONE TO DATE 10 / 26 / 2010 THAT LIKES ANYBODY NEAR THEIR FACE!

UNLESS IT WAS SEXUAL OF COURSE. THIS SPACE IS VERY PERSONAL!

HERE IS THE UNDERLINING FACTOR … NEVER BE THE FIRST ONE TO ACT OUT.

WHEN YOU ARE IN DANGER FROM AN ATTACK THEN YOU REACT!

AS STATED BEFORE … WITH ENOUGH FORCE TO RESOLVE THE PROBLEM AT HAND.

YOU NEED TO DETERMINE WHAT IT IS THAT IS NEEDED TO COMPLETE YOUR SELF DEFENSE.

IS IT A MATTER OF LIFE OR DEATH? WHAT EVER YOU DO … THE REASONS FOR THE CHOICE YOU MAKE HAS TO BE CLEAR!

{ EMPTY HANDED OR WEAPON INVOLVED? }

THEN AFTER YOU MAINTAIN THE CONTROL, AND THE PROPER AUTHORITIES HAVE TAKEN OVER LEAVE.

DO THIS AS FAST AS YOU CAN! THERE IS NO REASON FOR YOU TO HANG AROUND FOR ANY PERIOD OF TIME.

WHAT I HAVE DISCUSSED WITHIN THESE PARAGRAPHS APPLIES TO ALL ASPECTS OF LIFE.

BOTH INSIDE CLOSED DOORS, AND OUT IN THE STREETS!

NOW LETS TALK ABOUT PREPARING FOR COMBAT IN A CONTROLED SETTING. THE DOJO.

TRAINING FOR COMBAT IN THE DOJO IS COMPLETELY DIFFERENT.

HERE YOU LEARN TO PERFECT YOUR TECHNIQUES. THEN PUT IN COUNTLESS HOURS OF WHAT I LIKE TO CALL CORE TRAINING.

YOU SHOULD BE SPARRING AT EVERY WORKOUT. TO START AND FINISH THE NIGHT.

INBETWEEN THE TWO YO SHOULD BE WORKING YOUR BASICS WITH SEVERAL DIFFERENT STUDENTS!

THE MORE THE BETTER. PERSONALLY I ALWAYS PERFER TO WORK WITH EVERYONE WHO IS BIGGER THAN ME.

WHY IS THIS? BECAUSE IT IS VERY GOOD FOR YOU! SIMPLE… THE MORE YOU WORK WITH DIFFERENT BODY TYPES:

{ SHORT ` TALL ` MUSCULAR ` BROAD ` ETC… }

THE BETTER YOU WILL BECOME, BUT AFTER WORKING WITH HUGH PEOPLE THE SMALLER ONES ARE EASIER TO HANDLE.

NOW YOU WILL BE BETTER ADAPT TO CONQUER ANY OPPONENT! NO MATTER WHAT THEIR PERSUASION MAY BE.

NEXT YOU NEED TO WORK YOUR CARDIO! HIT THE HEAVY BAG, THE SPEED BAG, JUMP ROPE, AND DO ROAD WORK. RUN…

THE HEAVY BAG WILL DEFINE YOUR STRENGTH IN ALL YOUR STRIKES. HAND AND FEET.

CARDIO WILL INCREASE YOUR STAMINA, AND THE SPEED BAG WILL DEVELOP YUR HAND TO EYE COORDINATION.

ALONG WITH THE ROAD WORK ALL THIS WILL HELP SPEEDUP YOUR BODY SYSTEMS!

PUTTING IN MY OWN PERSONAL TOUCH TO THE TWO TYPES OF COMBAT TRAINING TOGETHER I LIKE TO CALL SHAKING THE TREE.

IF YOU ARE GOING TO STRIKE SOMEONE THEN LEARN TO HIT HARD! MAKE IT COUNT.

YOU NOT ONLY NEED TO WORK THE HIPS FOR TORK, BUT YOU ALSO NEED TO CONDITION OUR HANDS AND FEET TOO.

I DO THIS BY PRACTICING THE FOLLOWING TECHNIQUES:

{ STRAIGHT PUNCH ` KNIFE HAND ` THRUST PUNCHES ` INSIDE & OUTSIDE CRESCENT KICKS ` & ROUNDHOUSE KICKS AGAINST A TREE. }

THIS BUILDS UP YOUR SKIN INTO THICK HARD SPOTS. BY HITTING THE TREE!

HENCE MY PHRASE: *"" SHAKING THE TREE "*"

THE TREE IS A SOLID MASS. IF YOU CAN MAKE IT MOVE … { SHAKE } THEN THINK WHAT THIS WILL DO TO A HUMAN BEING?

THE BODY HAS GIVE TO IT, OR YOUR GOING TO BREAK BONES! FOR SURE.

SO IF YOUR GOING TO STRIKE THEN AGAIN MAKE IT COUNT! JUST LIKE I SAID BEFORE. MAKE THEM REMEMBER YOU.

WHAT MAKES ME LAUGH IS THIS … WHEN I ASK A STUDENT IF THEY HAVE EVE BEEN IN A REAL FIGHT BEFORE?

THE ANSWERS AND ALL THE STORIES THAT I GET ARE UNBELIEVABLE! SO I WILL JUST CUT TO THE ABSOLUTE TRUTH.

DURING A REAL FIGHT IF IT LAST ANY LONGER THAN TWENTY SECONDS THAN SOMETHING IS WRONG!

TWENTY SECONDS IS LIKE AN ETERNITY! WHAT EVER YOU NEED TO DO IT SHOULD BE ACCOMPLISHED WITHIN THIS TIME PERIOD!

AH … YES; AND IT HURTS TO GET HIT. NO MATTER HOW TOUGH YOU MAY THINK YOU ARE.

SO PLEASE DO KEEP THIS IN MIND! IN A FIGHT THERE ARE NO REAL WINNERS.

JUST SOMEONE WHO WAS BETTER PREPARED THAN THE OPPOSITE.

"" NEW YORK CITY 2010 ""

THE DIFFERENCES BETWEEN THE DOJO AND THE STREET :

IN THE DOJO WE START OUR OFFICAL MARTIAL ARTS TRAINING. IT IS HARD WORK, AND ABOVE ALL A DEDICATION TO DISCIPLINE!

DURING OUR PRACTICES WE INCORPRATE MANY SELF DEFENSE APPLICATIONS ALONG WITH DRILLS FOR SPARRING.

THE UNDERLINING FACTOR IS THE PRIMARY PRINCIPLE OF LEARNING HOW TO DEFEND YOURSELF, AND OTHERS.

IN DOING THIS WE TRAIN RATHER HARD, AND PUT OUR SPIRITS TO THE TEST!

HOWEVER IN HE DOJO WE DO NOT GO FULL THROTTLE AGAINST ANOTHER STUDENT!

BECAUSE IF YOU INJURE YOUR TRAINING PARTNERS WHO WILL YOU BE ABLE TO TRAIN WITH? NO ONE!

THIS IS WHY WE CALL IT PRACTICE. SAVE ALL THE REST FOR THE STREET WHEN THE TIME ARISES.

WE RESPECT ONE ANOTHER AT ALL TIMES,   FOR THE ACTIONS WE PARTAKE IN THE BENEFIT OF OUR TRAINNG IN THE ARTS.

HOW DO WE PERFORM THIS? WELL IT IS CALLED LEARNING HOW TO PULL A PUNCH.

I DIDN'T SAY DO NOT HIT THEM… BUT WHAT I AM SAYING IS THERE IS NO REASON TO HURT THEM.

YOU NEED TO MAKE CONTACT EACH TIME YOU TRAIN! IF YOU DON'T YOUR ONLY HURTING YOURSELF IN THE LONG RUN.

YES ACCIDENTS DO HAPPEN NOW AND THEN. IT GOES WITHOUT SAYING.

WE HAVE TO REMEMBER THAT MARTIAL ART TRAINING IS A FULL CONTACT SPORT, AND SOMETIMES PEOPLE GET CARRIED AWAY IN THE ADRENALIN FACTOR.

THIS IS WHY YOU NEED TO PERFECT THE ART OF SELF CONTROL IN YOUR STUDIES!
ALSO IN OUR TRAINING WE FOLLOW THREW WITH A FINISHING BLOW TO END ALL TECHNIQUES.

NOW AS FAR AS TAKING OUR TRAINING ONTO THE STREET REMEMBER NEVER START ANY TROUBLE.

BUT IF TROUBLE FINDS YOU OR SOMEONE IN YOUR CARE THEN THERE IS NO HOLDING BACK! LET EVERYTHING GO.

WHEN THIS POINT COMES TO PLAY YOU NEED TO ALWAYS KEEP A LEVEL HEAD, AND BE AWARE OF WHATS GOING ON ALL AROUND YOU.

AS I HAD MENTIONED EARLIER ON BEING AWARE IS VITAL IN A STREET SITUATION!

YOU DO NOT KNOW ANYTHING ABOUT YOUR WOULD BE ATTACKER, OR WHO HE MAY BE WITH NOT TO MENTION WHAT THEIR BACKGROUNDS OR INTENTIONS MAY BE.

* REMEMBER YOUR TRAINING! NO MATTER WHAT. YOU ARE THE PERSON WHO IS IN CONTROL.

THE ONLY DIFFERENCE BETWEEN THE DOJO AND THE STREET IS THIS …

ONCE YOU PUT YOUR ATTACKR TO THE GROUND AND MAINTAIN CONTROL YOU MUST STOP!

THERE IS NO FINISHING BLOW! THE LAW IS WITH YOU UNTIL YOU PROCEED TO CONTINUE AFTER THIS POINT WITHOUT JUST CAUSE.

"" **<u>SELF DEFENSE</u>:** IS DEFINED AS / *AN ACT OF DEFENDING YOURSELF OR LOVED ONES WITH THE NECESSARY MEANS FOR SURVIVAL, AND THE WELFARE OF THEIR WELL BEING!* ""

THE ONLY TIME YOU MAY CONTINUE AFTER THE POINT OF GOING TO THE GROUND IS ….

WHEN THERE IS A WEAPON INVOLVED, AND YOU DO NOT HAVE ANY OTHER OPTIONS BUT TO FOLLOW THREW TO THE END!

SIMPLY PUT INTO PERSPECTIVE "" *YOU DID WHAT YOU HAD TO DO WHEN IT BECAME NECESSARY TO DO SO!* ""

PLEASE TAKE NOTE AS LONG AS NO WEAPON IS INVOLVED AFTER YOU BRING YOUR ATTACKER DOWN THERE IS NO REASON FOR YOU TO BE HANGING AROUND.

PERIOD! GATHER UP YOUR THINGS OR THE PEOPLE WHO ARE WITH YOU, AND LEAVE.

A.S.A.P!

YOU DO NOT NEED TO BE INVOLVED IN ANY MORE CONFRONTATIONS.

TRUST ME. IT IS IN YOUR BEST INTERESTS.

THESE ARE THE DIFFERENCES AND THE RULES OF ENGAGEMENT OF CONFRONTATIONS BETWEEN THE DOJO, AND THE STREETS.

ONE IS FOR PRACTICE …

THE OTHER IS FOR SURVIVAL!

"" THE BALANCE OF POWER IS IN YOUR HANDS ""

"" SELF - CONTROL IS YOUR DOMAIN! / M.P.F. ""

THE MANY PRACTICES OF THE MARTIAL ARTS TODAY :

WITHIN THE WORLD OF MARTIAL ARTS THERE ARE MANY SYSTEMS FOR WHICH YOU MAY STUDY.

THEY COVER A VAST AMOUNT OF CULTURE WITH THEM ALONG WITH THE KNOWLEDGE OF THEIR HISTORIES. BOTH PAST AND PRESENT.

AS FOR ME I WILL FOREVER BE A TRADITIONALIST! THE ARTS HAVE BEEN AROUND FOR CENTURIES, AND FROM THIS I FIND MY COMFORT.

HOWEVER IN THE STUDING OF THE MARTIAL ARTS IN OUR CURRENT SOCIETY THERE ARE TWO MAIN FOCUSES WHICH DRAW MUCH ATTENTION AS WELL AS BIG MONEY.

THE FIRST BY FAR IS THE DEVELOPMENT OF THE { MMA }. THIS IS THE MIXED MARTIAL ARTS.

THE GROWTH OF THIS CONCEPT HAS BECOME EXTREMELY POPULAR. IT SEAMS THAT ALMOST EVERY STREET CORNER IN THE CITIES HAS A GYM SETUP FOR MMA!

I DO LIKE THIS CONCEPT. ACTUALLY VERY MUCH SO, BUT WE NEED TO REMEMBER THAT MOST OF THESE GUYS ARE NOT FROM A MARTIAL ARTS BACKGROUND.

YES SOME OF THEM ARE. IN MY OPNION THEY ARE THE ONES WHO STAND OUT OF THE PACK AS FAR AS TRUE SKILLS AND THE REAL SPIRIT OF THE WARRIOR.
BUT THE REST ARE JUST THE NEXT STEP EVOLVING FROM THE BOXING GAME.

I BELIEVE THAT THESE PEOPLE SHOULD BE EXTREMELY CAREFUL WHEN IT COMES TO THE PRO FIGHTERS.

BECAUSE FOR ONE I BELIEVE THEY HAVE A FAR BETTER OVER ALL CARDIO PROGRAM COMPAIRED TO THE MMA TRAINING.

SECOND BECAUSE I ALSO BELIEVE THAT THE ONLY THING THAT KEEPS THEM CIVILIZED IS THE REF IN THE CENTER OF THE RINGS FOR WHICH THEY FIGHT.

LETS REMEMBER MOST OF THESE FIGHTERS COME FROM THE STREETS. THEY ARE THE REAL THING. MEAN AND NASTY WITHOUT ANY DOUBT!

IF THEY COULD GET AWAY WITH IT I AM SURE THEY WOULD LOVE TO TAKE IT TO THE MAT.

SO IN MY OPNION THIS MAKES THEM QUITE A WORTHY OPPONENT TO ANYONE.

I FOR ONE WOULD LOVE TO SEE A MATCH UP CHALLENGE BETWEEN A HIGH RANKED BOXER IN HISPRIME AGAINST AN MMA ATHLETE IN HIS!

LOOKING BACK FROM MY CHILDHOOD MY GRANDFATHER AND UNCLE WERE BIG TIME FANS OF THE SPORT.

MY UNCLE STILL IS! I CAN REMEMBER STAYING UP LATE ON A SATURDAY NIGHT TO WATCH THE FIGHTS WITH THEM.

THERE IS ONE MAN… THAT I WILL ALWAYS REMEMBER. JUST TO LOOK AT HIM WAS SCARY!

THAT MAN WAS THE LEGEND ROBERTO DURAN. HE WAS AN ANIMAL. COULD YOU PICTURE HIM IN THE MMA RING?

IT WOULD BE AWESOME! I JUST CAN'T HELP BUT WONDER HOW A MAN OF HIS TALENTS BACK IN THE DAY WOULD COMPARE TO THE MEN OF THE UFC TODAY?

THIS I WOULD HAVE LOVED TO HAVE SEEN.

IF ONLY THE BIG MATCH UP BETWEEN DURAN AND BENNY " THE JET " WOULD HAVE TOOK PLACE WAY BACK IN THE EARLY SEVENTIES ALL THE QUESTIONS OF TODAY MIGHT HAVE BEEN SETTLED!

I THINK THEY SHOULD TAKE ONE UFC FIGHTER, AND ONE PRO BOXER LIKE I SAID THAT ARE BOTH IN EQUAL PRIMES AT THE TOP OF THEIR GAMES, AND MAKE IT HAPPEN.

WHO WOULDN'T WANT TO SEE SUCH AN EVENT?

WE WOULD HOWEVER HAVE TO COME UP WITH A NEW NAME FOR THIS MATCH UP AS FAR AS A CATEGORY.

IT WOULDN'T BE CONSIDERED UFC, NOR PROBOXING. SO LETS CALL IT PIT FIGHTING!

BECAUSE WE ARE PITTING TWO GREAT TYPES OF FIGHTERS AGAINST ONE ANOTHER TO DO BATTLE.

WELCOME TO THE PIT! ARE WE READY? …

THE SECOND BIG MONEY GRABER FOR POPULARITY IS THE AEROBIC KICKBOXING.

I DO THINK THIS DOES HAVE ONE GREAT QUALITY. AND THAT BEING THE CARDIO PORTION OF THE ROUTINE.

AS FAR AS KICKBOXING IF YOU REALLY THINK THAT A CLASS OF THIS NATURE IS GOING TO MAKE YOU SOME KIND OF BAD ASS THEN I FEEL VERY SORRY FOR YOU!

THE FIRST GUY EVEN WOMAN FOR THAT MATTER THAT YOU RUN INTO THAT HAS JUST SOME BACKGROUND IN FIGHTING IS GOING TO DESTROY YOU.

SO AGAIN IN MY OPNION IF YOU ARE LOOKING TO GET A REAL GOOD CARDIO WORKOUT YOU WILL FIND IT HERE.

I MYSELF HAVE TRIED IT FROM TIME TO TIME JUST TO BREAK THINGS UP A BIT. IT REALLY DOES BOOST YOUR CARDIO PERFORMANCE.

IT IS ALSO A GREAT FILL IN FOR ROAD WORK FOR A CHANGE IN YOUR TRAINING, AND IT IS FUN.

BUT AS FAR AS LEARNING ANY FIGHTING SKILLS IT'S A JOKE!
THE ONLY OTHER THING YOUR GOING TO FIND IS A LOT OF VERY PRETTY WOMEN.

YES I CAN SEE YOU POSSIABLE LEARNING A LITTLE KNOWLEDGE OF SELF DEFENSE, BUT NOTHING CLOSE TO MARTIAL ARTS TRANING!

SO IN CONCLUSION BETWEEN THE TWO MOST POPULAR ATTRACTIONS IN THE MARTIAL ARTS TRAINING TODAY MMA IS THE BETTER CHOICE.

BUT IF YOU WANT THE REAL DEAL NOTHING IS GOING TO BEAT OUT OLD FASHION MARTIAL ARTS TRAINING!

JUST TAKE A LOOK AT THE UFC FIGHTERS BACKGROUNDS; THE FIGHTERS THAT FOR THE MOST PART DO THE BEST HAVE TRADITIONAL MARTIAL ARTS TRAINING UNDER THEIR BELTS!

"" THE GRACIES ~ GSP ~ THE LITTLE DRAGON ""

NOW I AM NOT TALKING ABOUT WHAT IS REFERED TO TODAYS MMA OR GRAPPLING.

THE STUDY OF MARTIAL TRAINING HAS BEEN AROUND FOR CENTURIES!

IT CAN BE TRACED BACK ALL THE WAY TO THE DAYS OF THE SILK TRADING BTWEEN INDA AND CHINA.

SO WHY CHANGE SOMETHING THAT HAS WORKED JUST FINE ALL THESE YEARS WITH A CHEAPER VERSION?

TO TRAIN IN TRADITIONL MARTIAL ARTS WILL MAKE YOU WELL ROUNDED AND COMPLETE WITHIN YOURSELF.

IT TEACHES YOU ALL THE BASICS THAT YOU NEED TO BUILD YOUR FUNDAMENTAL FOUNDATION WITH.

THEN IT TOUCHES BASE WITH ALL THE OTHER TOPICS YOU NEED TO COMPLETE YOUR TRAINING!

{ STRIKING ~ GRAPPLING ~ JUJITSU ~ BOXING ~ FOOTWORK ~ BREATHING }

IF WE DECIDE TO PUT YOU TO THE GROUND THEN WE WILL, BUT WHY WOULD WE EVER NEED TO TAKE YOU TO THE GROUND?

WE ARE STRIKERS! MULTI STRIKERS. NOT WRESTLERS. AGAIN GET THE JOB DONE.

DO NOT PLAY AROUND WITH FOOLISH HEAD GAMES! BECAUSE THEN YOU WILL BECOME THE VICTIM.

THESE ARE MY VIEWS TO THE THOUGHTS THAT ARE BEING PRACTICED IN SOCIETY AS WE LIVE IT TODAY.

THE YEAR 2010

"" ARUBA 2010 ""

THE TWO KINDS OF BLACKBELTS :

SAD BUT TRUE THE SHODANS OF TODAY ARE NO WAY WHAT THEY WERE IN THE YEARS PAST!

THE FIRST TYPE OF BLACKBELTS ARE THE ONES WHO WORK HARD! EACH AND EVERYDAY.

THEY TEACH… THEY TRAIN FULLY IN THE STUDY OF THEIR ART, AND THEY HELP OTHERS WHO ARE IN NEED THAT CAN NOT HELP THEMSELVES!

THESE SHODANS SET GOALS IN THEIR LIFE AND FOLLOW THE RULES TO ACHIEVE THOSE GOALS.

THEN AFTER THEY COMPLETE THAT GOAL THEY FIND A NEW TASK TO COMPLETE.

ALWAYS MOVING FORWARD IN LIFE WITH A POSITIVE OUTLOOK.   TO THEM TRAINING IS NOT CONSIDERED EXERCISE, BUT A WAY OF LIFE!

THE SECOND TYPE OF BLACKBELTS ARE THE ONES WHO FORGOT WHO THEY ARE, AND WHERE THEY CAME FROM!

THEY HAVE STRAYED FROM THE PATH OF THEIR TEACHINGS.

THEY BECOME SELF ABSORBED WITH RECEIVING RESPECT, BUT HAVE ACTUALLY FORGOTTON HOW TO EARN THE RESPECT OF THEIR PEERS!

RESPECT IS NOT A TITLE THAT IS GIVIN TO YOU. IT IS A CLASS THAT YOU EARN!

TO THESE SHODANS MARTIAL ARTS IS A HOBBY AT BEST! THIS IS WHAT IS SAD.

"" THE WORD CAN'T ISN'T IN MY MEANS! ""

THE PROBLEM WITH SHODANS TODAY :

IN MY TRAINING I HAVE TAKEN NOTIC THAT A MAJORITY OF THE SHODANS HAVE INDEED FORGOTTON WHAT IT IS TO BE A BLACKBELT.

NOT TO MENTION HOW THEY GOT THERE IN THE FIRST PLACE!

WHEN IT COMES TO CLASS TIME THEY ARE NOT INTERESTED IN WORKING OUT ANYMORE.

WORSE THAN THAT WHEN IT COMES TIME FOR DRILL WORK THEIR TECHNIQUES ARE WEAK. NO HEART AT ALL!

THE ONLY THING THEY ARE INTO AS IT SEEMS TO ME IS: *"" I AM A BLACKBELT THERE IS NO NEED FOR ME TO WORKOUT ANYMORE. ""*

OR ...

"" JUST SHOW ME RESPCT! AND WHEN IT COMES TO SELF DEFENSE THEN I WILL SHOW YOU SOMETHING. ""

WELL THIS IS TOTAL BULL SHIT! THIS IS WHY WHAT EVER I EXPECT OF MY STUDENTS I DO IT WITH THEM 100% NO MATTER WHAT!

IF YOU LET ALL YOU USED TO DO JUST GO ... THEN YOUR SKILLS AND TECHNIQUES WILL SUFFER TREMENDOUSLY!

THERE IS NO EXCUSE FOR BEING LAZY. IF YOU WANT TO BE RESPECTED THAN EARN THAT RESPECT. DO NOT DEMAND IT!

THE UNDERBELTS LOOK UP TO US. DON'T TEACH THEM BAD HABBITS! DO THE RIGHT THING. KEEP TRADITION!

ALIVE IN YOU AND YOUR STUDENTS. ALWAYS AND FOREVER.

NOT ONLY DO YOU NEED TO KEEP WORKING OUT, BUT YOU HAD BETTER GET YOUR EGO BACK IN CHECK. FAST!

JUST BECAUSE YOU RECEIVED YOUR RANK OF SHODAN DOESN'T MEAN THAT YOUR BETTER THAN ANYONE ELSE. YOU TOO NEED TO KEEP WORKING HARD.

ON THE REALITY OF SCOPE YOUR TRAINING HAS JUST ONLY STRTED AT SHODAN!

ALL THE PRETTY COLORS YOU EARNED PREVIOUSLY WHAT I MENTIONED BEFORE AS POSITIVE REINFORCMENT WAS JUST PRACTICING TO BE A STUDENT OF THE MARTIAL ARTS!

NOT TRAINING! YOU HAVE NO CLUE TO WHAT REAL RAINING IS YET.

IF YOU WANT TO BE CONSIDERED A TRUE BLACKBELT THAN KEEP TRAINING AS YOU DID BEFORE WHEN YOU WANTED TO BECOME THE SHODAN.

PLUS YOU HAD BETTER START WORKING EVEN HARDER NOW!

BECOMING A SHODAN IS A PRIVILEG NOT AN AUTOMATIC RESPECT APPROVAL!

YOU STILL I CAN'T STRESS THE FACT ENOUGH … EARN THE PRIVILEGE IN MY BOOK!

I PRAY FOR ALL OF YOU THAT MY WORDS HAVE SUNK IN!

THE CIRCUIT YEARS :

THESE WERE SOME OF THE BEST YEARS IN MY MARTIAL ART CAREER. I REFER TO THEM AS PLAYING THE POINT GAME.

WAS IT FUN? THIS IS A QUESTION THAT IS FREQUENTLY ASKED TO ME…

HELL YES! IT WAS AN AWESOME PERIOD OF MY LIFE. IT TAUGHT ME HOW TO PUSH MY LIMITS TO ACHIEVE WHAT OTHERS TOLD ME COULD NEVER BE DONE!

BACK THEN AND STILL TODAY IT IS KINDA LIKE A MISSION IN LIFE FOR ME TO DISPROVE THE NEGATIVITY OF OTHERS.

THIS IS WHAT I DO BEST! BEATING ALL THE ODDS. A TRUE UNDERDOG.

BEING ABLE TO WATCH AND LEARN NEW CREATIVE THINGS FROM OTHER MARTIAL ARTISTS IS A GREAT WAY TO EXPAND ONES MIND.

THEN BY PUTTING MY HARDWORK TO THE TEST SO I COULD FIND OUT WHO WAS THE BEST OF THE BEST?

DURING ALL THESE YEARS THERE IS ONE ASPECT THAT I WANT TO BE KNOWN.

THAT IS EVERY TIME I ENTERED THE RING FOR A KATA OR A WEAPON KATA I ALWAYS PERFORMED SOMETHING DIFFERENT!

IT WAS TRULY AMAZING TO SEE ALL THE SAME PEOPLE ALWAYS DOING THE SAME KATAS. THEY NEVER CHANGED IT UP.

THE ONLY TIME THEY DID CHANGE IF AT ALL WAS FOR THE NEXT YEARS TOURNAMENTS.

TO ME THIS WAS NOT CONSIDERED A TOURNAMENT. IT WAS BORING MOST OF THE TIME.

SO WHEN THE DAY CAME TO TRAVEL THE WORLD, AND BECOME A REPRESENATIVE OF THE UNITED STATES ON TEAM AMERICA IT WAS A GREAT EXPERIENCE FOR ME!

BECAUSE EVEN THOUGH I CAME ACROSS A FEW PEOPLE FROM DIFFERENT COUNTRIES OVER AND OVER AGAIN …

THREW THE YEARS THEY TOO HAD SOMETHING NEW EACH TIME WE FACED OFF AGAINST ONE ANOTHER.

THIS IS WHY I CONSIDER THE WORLD GAMES THE BEST OF ALL TOURNAMENTS!

THESE WERE WITHOUT ANY QUESTION THE BEST OF THE BEST THAT IS OFFERED BY EACH COUNTRY.

THIS IS WHAT MADE IT SPECIAL TO ME, AND THE THRILL WAS AN ALL TIME RUSH THREW MY VEINS!

LOOKING BACK IT REALLY SHOULDN'T HAVE MATTERED IF YOU WON OR LOST, BUT THAT YOU HAD THE NUTS TO GIVE IT A TRY!

WHEN YOU LEAVE THE UNITED STATES AND TRAVEL TO OTHER COUNTRIES FOR SPORT IT IS A WHOLE NEW STAGE.

THE PEOPLE ARE DIFFERENT… THE SETTINGS ARE DIFFERENT … AND SOMETIMES THE RULES ARE VERY DIFFERENT!

THEIR WERE PLENTY OF TIMES THAT I LEFT THE SPARRING RINGS TO GO GET PATCHED UP AT THE LOCAL EMERGENCY ROOM.

IT WAS LIKE A RITUAL. IN OTHER COUNTRIES IT IS SCARY! YOU TRY TO MAN IT OUT IF YOU KNOW WHAT I MEAN.

BUT BACK IN THE STATES … BROKEN BONES IN MAINE, STICHES IN MASS, TORN MUSCLE IN RI, AND THE LIST IS TO LONG TO LIST THEM ALL.

BUT NOW REACHING THE BIG FOURTY MARK COMING IN MAY I KNOW EXACTLY WHAT DAD USED TO TELL ME ABOUT KNOWING WHEN THE BAD WEATHER IS A BREWING.

THE MULTIPLICATION OF THE INJURIES HAS CAUGHT UP WITH ME! ESPECIALLY THE ONES THAT ARE ASSOCIATED WITH THE FEET, KNEES, SHOULDERS, AND ALONG WITH MY JOB THE NECK.

SOMEDAYS ARE REAL BAD, BUT I KEEP PLUGGING ON.

IT IS THE MOST AWESOME FEELING IN THE WORLD OF PAIN TO TAKE THAT FIRST STEP OUT OF BED IN THE MORNING, AND HAVE SUCH A SHOOTING PAIN RUNNING UP FROM YOUR FOOT TO YOUR SPINE!

THIS BRINGS A SINGLE TEAR THAT RUNS DOWN FROM MY EYE TO MY CHIN. TRYING NOT TO WAKE MY WIFE OR SON.

THIS IS NO FUN AT ALL! SO WHY DO WE STILL DO IT? FOR ME IT'S THE LOVE OF CONTINUING THE LIFE I HAVE CHOOSE TO LEAD.

BECAUSE I LOVE WHAT I DO, AND NOTHING IS GOING TO KEEP ME FROM DOING WHAT I HAVE A PASSION FOR.

LIVING THE MARTIAL WAY! ... ...

AS FOR THE SANCTIONS I FOUGHT IN THE {N.A.S.K.A.} / NORTH AMERICAN SPORT KARATE ASSOCIATION.

THE KRANE ASSOCIATION, IPPONE, AND THE {W.O.M.A.A. } / WORLD ORGANIZATION OF MARTIAL ARTS ATHLETES THREW ALL MY YEARS OF TOURNAMENT FIGHTING.

THESE TOURNAMENTS TOOK ME TO THE FOLLOWING PLACES IN THE UNITED STATES AND ABROAD WHICH LEAD TO SOME TYPE OF COMPETITION OR RAINING FOR A COMPETITION.

" MAINE - VERMONT - NEW HAMPSHIRE - MASS - RI - CT - NEW YORK - PA - DELAWARE - MARYLAND - GEORGIA - CALIFORNIA - AUSTRALIA - IRELAND - HAWAII - MEXICO - AND FLORIDA. ""

I FOR PERSONAL REASONS DECLINED THE FOLLOWING OFFERS DUE TO FAMILY.

" SPAIN - GERMANY - AND COSTA RICA. "

WITHOUT ANY DOUBT IN MY MIND I HAD NOT ONLY WITNESSED AMAZING FEATS BUT I HAD ALSO MADE SOME GREAT FRIENDSHIPS ALONG THE WAY THAT I STILL HAVE TODAY.

I KEEP IN TOUCH VERY CLOSELY WITH IRELAND AND AUSTRALIA STILL.

GREAT FRIEND ARE EVERYWHERE IN MY LIFE. IT IS MY HONOR TO HAVE THEM NOT ONLY IN MY LIFE, BUT THE LIVE OF MY FAMILY AS WELL.

ALL FOR ALL MY STATS WERE EIGHTYONE WINS - TWO LOSSES - AND ONE DISQUALIFICATION FOR THE USE OF EXESSIVE FORCE.

NOT A BAD RUN AT ALL, BUT IT WAS TIME TO MOVE ON.

ONE ASPECT THAT NEEDS TO BE ADDRESSED AS FAR AS TRAINING IN THESE CIRCUITS:

THIS IS FOR LOCAL TOURNAMENTS WHICH I CONSIDER ANY TOURNAMENT WITHIN THE BORDERS OF THE UNITED STATES ALL YOU NEED IS ROUGHLY AROUND TWO TO MAYBE THREE MONTHS OF TRAINING TIME TO BE PROPERLY PREPARED.

HOWEVER; ANY TOURNAMENT THAT YOU LEAVE THE COUNTRY FOR I.E. THE WORLD GAMES IT IS A WHOLE DIFFERENT BALL OF WAX!

IF YOU TRAIN THE SAME WAY THAT YOU DO FOR LOCAL TOURNAMENTS PLEASE DO NOT EVEN BOTHER TO TRY THE BIG LEAGUES!

BECAUSE YOU WILL BE IN FOR A TREMENDOUS RUDE AWAKENING!

FOR THIS CALIBER OF EVENT I USED TO TRAIN FOR TEN MONTHS OUT STRAIGHT! SEVEN DAYS A WEEK.

FOR AS MUCH TIME AS MY MIND, AND MY BODY WOULD ENDURE.

I HAD TO GIVE UP SO MANY THINGS IN MY PRIVATE LIFE.

I MISSED OUT ON ALL KINDS OF FAMILY TIME THAT CAN NOT BE REPLACED! NOT BY PICTURES OR HOME MOVIES. NOTHING!

LOOKING BACK NOW I HAD WHAT IT TOOK THEN, AND I STILL DO TODAY!

BUT WAS IT IS IT … WORTH IT? YES AND NO!

ALL THE TRAINING AND THE REWARDS IT BRINGS TO ME IS WORTH IT, BUT ALL THE TIME THAT I LOST WITH MY WIFE TAMMY, AND MY SON MASON WHEN HE WAS LITTLE ESPECIALLY JUST THEM …

WAS AND IS NOT WORTH ANYTHING! LIFE WITHOUT FAMILY IS NOT LIVING AT ALL.

IT TOOK ME A LONG TIME TO FIGURE THIS OUT. IF I TEACH YOU NOTHING AT ALL IN THIS BOOK AT LEAST REMEMBER THIS LESSON.

THEN ON THE ELEVENTH MONTH I WOULD JUST RELAX AND TAKE IN ALL THE TRAINING I HAD AND DO FUN THINGS WITH MY FAMILY!

NEXT ON THE TWELFTH MONTH I WOULD WAKE UP THE DAY BEFORE IT WAS TIME TO LEAVE, AND THINK ONLY ONE THOUGHT …

AND THAT THOUGHT WAS; "" *I AM NOT GOING TO COME HOME EMPTY HANDED! I SPENT TO MUCH TIME AND ENERGY PREPARING FOR THIS. I WANT TO REPRESENT MY COUNTRY AS ONE OF THE BEST!* ""

ON THAT VERY NEXT MORNING MY FAMILY AND I WOULD HEAD TO THE AIRPORT.

LET THE GAMES BEGIN!

DURING THIS PERIOD OF TIME OF ALL MY WINNINGS THAT I HAVE BEEN FORTUNATE TO ACCLAIM IN MY CAREER OF TOURNAMENT YEARS, BY FAR THEY ARE ALL THE MEDALS FROM THE WORLD GAMES!

ALSO LET IT BE KNOWN THAT I NEVER LOST A WORLD GAME EVER! I ATTENDED SIX IN A ROW OVER SIX YEARS TIME, AND I WON SIX YEARS IN A ROW!

BEFORE I DECIDED MY TIME WAS OVER, AND I RETIRED WHILE I WAS ON TOP.

AUSTRALIA

TWO GOLD AND TWO SILVER

THE UNITED STATES OF AMERICA

TWO GOLD (TWO SEPARATE OCCASSIONS)*

IRELAND

THREE SILVER

HAWAII

ONE GOLD - FOUR SILVER - AND FOUR BRONZE

MEXICO

ONE GOLD - THREE SILVER - AND TWO BRONZE

MARTIAL ARTS AND POLITICAL VIEWS :

THE WORLD IN WHICH WE LIFE HAS A SOCIETY THAT IS TURNED COMPLETELY UPSIDE DOWN!

IT IS A DAME SHAME THAT A PERSON HAS TO BE PONDED AS IN REFRENCE TO THE GAME OF CHESS DUE TO HIS OUTLOOK ON PHILOSOPHY IN TRAINING, IN RELATION TO PROGRESS!

NOW THAT IS A MOUTH FULL INDEED, BUT WHAT IT STANDS FOR IS FAR TO TRUE! WHETHER IT IS SAID ALOUD, OR SHOWN IN ACTIONS.

WHEN I TRAINED AT THE NEW ENGLAND KARATE ACADEMY UNDER SHIHAN ALAN D ' ALLESSANDRO, AND EXPRESSED MY FEELINGS OF OUTLOOK IT WAS HELD AGAINST MY PROGRESS OF ADVANCEMENT!

SO I LEFT. FLAT OUT AND SIMPLE. WHY SHOULD I STAY SOMEWHERE THAT I AM NO LONGER RESPECTED?

WHEN I TRAINED WITH SHIHAN WAYNE MELLO HE ONCE TOLD ME THAT ALAN WAS A GOOD MAN, BUT HE HAD A LOT OF GROWING UP TO DO!

IF YOU WANT TO TRAIN WITH ME YOUR MORE THAN WELCOME TOO. SO I DID.

THEN WHEN ALAN STARTED TO PROMOTE BIG TOURNAMENTS WAYNE WAS IN FULL WITH HIS STUDENTS IN ATTENDANCE FOR THEM.

HOPING THAT IN RETURN ALAN WOULD REPAY HIM WITH HIS ATTENDANCE AT HIS.

SO LIKE WISE ALAN BECAME TO WAYNE WHAT WAYNE BECAME TO ALAN.

NOW IT IS ONLY MY DEDUCTIVE CONCLUSION OF OPNION THAT ONE HAND FEEDS THE OTHER FOR SUCCESSFUL FUND RAISING FOR THESE LOCAL TOURNAMENTS.

AN OF COURSE THIS MAKES PERFECT BUSINESS SENSE IN RELATION TO PROFITS.

HOWEVER; HOW DOES IT PLAY INTO ROLE WITH THE TRAINING OF ME?

THIS IS A QUESTION THAT STILL HAUNTS MY MIND AS FAR AS THE TRUTH!

WELL TO MY BELIEF IT MEANS: *"" HEY MIKE I LIKE YOU, AND YOU ARE A GOOD GUY. YOUR SKILLS ARE GOOD, AND YOU HAVE STRONG MORALS. BUT IF I PROMOTE YOU I MAY LOOSE MONEY DURING TOURNAMENT SEASON? ""*

THIS IS WHAT I THINK IT MEANT. I CALL THIS MARTIAL ART POLITICS!

ITS NOT RIGHT, BUT HOW COULD YOU EVER PROVE IT? AGAIN THIS IS ONLY MY BELIEF OF EVENTS THAT OCCURRED WHILE BETWEEN THESE TWO MASTERS.

NEITHER ONE EVER ACTUALLY CAME STRAIGHT UP TO ME AND SAID: "" "".

BUT AS YOU READ ON AND IF YOU HAVE READ MY OTHER BOOK LIMELIGHT TO THE DEVILS PARADISE YOU WILL SEE THAT MY THOUGHTS OF REASON WERE IN FACT DEAD ON!

NOW BACK TO THE STORY AT HAND. NOT TO GET AHEAD OF MYSELF.

I RESPECT BOTH MASTERS. HOWEVER; YOU HAVE TO WONDER WHY YOUR ALWAYS PASSED UPON, AND ONE WHO IS NOT EVEN HALF SKILLED AS YOU MOVES ON?

THE THINGS THAT MAKE YOU SAY HMMMMMMMMMMMMMMMMMM!

THAT'S WHY I TAKE MY JOURNEY ALONE, AND ONLY TEACH PRIVATELY TO THOSE WHO DESERVE THE CHANCE!

MY TRADITIONS, AND MY TRAINING ARE TAUGHT BY MY LIFES EXPERIENCES!

IF AND WHEN I DO HAVE THE CHANCE TO TKE PART IN A WORTHY TRAINING SESSION I EMBRACE IT FOR ALL IT HAS TO OFFER ME.

THEN I TAKE IT. DEFINE IT .. WORK IT ... AND RE - SHAPE IT INTO MY PERSONAL KNOWLEDGE OF STUDIES.

HERES ANOTHER PRIME EXAMPLE OF MARTIAL ARTS AND POLITICES!

IN THE YEAR 2004 I BECAME A CERTIFIED JUDGE FOR THE KRANE AND NASKA TOURNAMENT CIRCUITS.

ONE DAY DURING JUDGING I WAS PULLED ASIDE BY THREE OTHER JUDGES OUT OF FIVE OF US IN THE RING.

I WAS THEN ASKED: "" *HEY MIKE WHY ARE YOU GIVING THIS GUY SUCH A LOW SCORE? AND THE OTHER GUYS A MUCH HIGHER SCORE?* ""

"" *DON'T YOU KNOW WHO THIS GUY IS? THAT HE IS A TOP SEED?* ""

MY REPLY WAS THIS: "" *YES I DO KNOW WHO HE IS AS WELL AS WERE HE IS PLACED! HOWEVER; THIS IS A KATA DIVISION. NOT A GYMNAST MEET.* ""

THEY THEN SAID: "" *WHAT?* ""

SO I TOLD THEM I DO NOT CARE ABOUT HIS NAME OR HIS SEEDING! I DO CARE ABOUT HIS PERFORMANCE ON BASICS!

YES HIS GYM SKILLS WITH ALL THE FLIPS AND TRICKS ARE AWESOME! BUT HIS BASICS ARE WAY UNDER PAR!

THE STANCES WERE WEAK. HIS TECHNIQUES THAT APPLY TO MARTIAL ARTS WERE WEAK. WE ARE HERE TO JUDGE MARTIAL ARTS ARE WE NOT?

NOW ALL THE OTHER GUYS BASICS AND THEIR ATTENTION TO DETAIL: { STANCES - STRIKES - BREATHING - LOCATION IN REFRENCE TO THEIR BODY } WERE FANTASTIC!

AND THATIS WHAT I AM HERE TO JUDGE! WELL THEY OVER RULED ME.

BECAUSE IT AFFECTED OR SHOULD I SAY WOULD HAVE AFFECTED HIS RATINGS!

HE WAS GOING TO LOOSE TO A KNOWBODY, AND HIS POINT COUNT WOULD GO DOWN.

BIG DEAL! GET USED TO IT. IF HE DESERVED IT FINE. BUT IF HE DIDN'T THEN LEARN FROM IT!

WHEN I WAS RANKED IN THE TOP THREE PLACES FOR MY DIVISIONS OF KATA - WEAPONS - AND KUMITE IN BLACKBELT MAGAZINE WHAT I EARNED IS WHAT I EARNED.

I DIDN'T CRY ABOUT IT. UNDER THE KRANE AND NASKA LISTINGS FOR YEARS IF I LOST I LOST. I TOOK FROM IT AND LEARNED FROM IT.

IT MADE ME A BETTER MARTIAL ARTISTS, AND KEPT MY EGO AT BAY.

EVEN THOUGH I ONLY LOST TWICE OUT OF EIGHTYFOUR TIMES.

THE OTHER TWO TIMES SOMEONE ELSE WAS THE BETTER MAN. I DIDN'T COMPLAIN ABOUT IT.

SO ON THIS CERTAIN DAY AT THE DUNKIN D'S CENTER IN PROVIDENCE RI I WALKED RIGHT OUT THE DOOR, AND NEVER WENT BACK AGAIN.

BUT FIRST I WENT UP TO ALL THE OTHER MEN IN THE DIVISION I WAS JUDGING, AND EXPLAINED TO THEM THE SITUATION AT HAND.

THAT THEY WERE ALL GOOD MARTIAL ARTISTS BUT GOING UP AGAINST A SUPERSTAR ON THE RISE THEIR CHANCES FOR FAIR PLAY WERE SLIM TO NONE!

THE OTHER GUY WAS GOING TO WIN HAND DOWN. WITH OR WITHOUT ME AS A JUDGE.

WHY DID I DO THIS? BECAUSE IT IS A MATTER OF PRINCIPLE! AND WHAT WAS GOING ON WAS WRONG!

BUT THREE TO ONE, AND ONE NO CONTEST, AND ALL OF IT POLITICAL!

LETS SAY THAT THIS GUY IN QUESTION I HAVE SEEN ON TV SEVERAL TIMES THREW THE YEARS, AND HE IS STILL AN AWESOME GYMNAST.

BUT AS FOR HIS MARTIAL ARTS …   THEY ARE STILL IN NEED OF IMPROVEMENT!

THERE IS NO NEED TO MENTION HIS NAME. IT WOULD UP SET TO MANY SO CALLED STARS.

IF YOU FOLLOW THE GAME AND WERE AROUND BACK DURING THIS TIME IT ISN'T HARD TO FIGURE OUT WHO I MAY HAVE BEEN TALKING ABOUT.

COMING TO TERMS :

AT THIS PHASE OF MY LIFE I WAS RANKED IN THE TOP THREE SPOTS IN MY DIVISIONS IN THE WORLD.

COVERING SPORT KARATE IN THE FIELDS OF KATA - WEAPONS - AND KUMITE.

FROM THE TIME PERIOD OF LATE 1998 TO MID SPRING OF 2004.

IT WAS DURING THIS TIME TAMMY AND I WERE BLESSED WITH OUR SON MASON DOUGLAS FARADAY!

HE WAS BORN ON MARCH 2ND IN THE YEAR 2001. LIFE WAS CHANGING FAST FRO ME NOW, AND THE STRESS OF PERFORMANCE WAS STARTING TO TAKE ITS TOLL!

I HAD THREE EVENTS IN MY LIFE THAT HAD BROUGHT ME TO MY REASONS FOR RETIREMENT FROM THE CIRCUIT.

THE FIRST ONE WAS TAKING A BAD BEATING IN KILLARNEY IRELAND DURING THE WORLD GAMES IN 2002.

I WAS IN THE BRIZILIAN JU JUITSU DIVISION. THIS WAS PRETTY MUCH LIKE THE MMA OF TODAY.

MY OPPONENT WAS A STUDENT OF THE GRACIE FAMILY. OF ALL PERSONS I COULD HAVE FACED IT WAS ONE WHO STUDIED WITH THE FOREFATHERS OF THIS STYLE.

THESE GUYS ARE THE ONES WHO INVENTED THIS TYPE OF FIGHTING SO RIGHT AWAY I KNEW I WAS IN BIG TROUBLE, AND A BATTLE WAS IN STORE FOR ME.

IN THE FIRST ROUND OF THREE PROABLE THE FIRST FIFTEEN SECONDS OR SO I WAS ALREADY SPITTING OUT BLOOD, AND HAD A CUT ON MY FACE UNDER MY EYE!

IN THE SECOND ROUND I FOUND MYSELF TRYING TO GET UP OFF THE GROUND A LOT! WITH HIS LEGS WRAPPED AROUND MY NECK AND USING MY ARM AS A ROWING PADDLE!

THEN I TOOK A TERRIABLE BLOW TO THE SIDE OF MY LEFT KNEE THAT WAS INCREDITABLE!

IT SENT MY LEVEL OF PAIN TO AN ALL TIME NEW HIGH. FOR SURE!

SO I THINK YOU GET THE FULL PICTURE NOW? RIGHT. IT WAS ONE DAY THAT I WILL NEVER FORGET!

THE THOUGHTS THAT WERE RUNNING THREW MY HEAD AS THIS GUY JUST REALLY DID WHAT HE WANTED, AND ALL I COULD DO WAS HANG ON...

THE REST OF THIS DIVISION WAS ABOUT THE SAME.

BUT IN THE END BEING THICKHEADED RATHER THAN SMART HAD PAID OFF.

I WAS ABLE TO HOLD ON IN THERE, AND ACTUALLY TOOK HOME THE SILVER MEDAL FOR THE GOOD OLD U.S.A!

THE GUY FROM BRAZIL TOOK THE GOLD OF COURSE. HE WAS THE BETTER MAN AND HAD A LOT OF CLASS.

I RESPECTED THAT FACT. HE WASN'T THE ONLY MAN DURING THESE GAMES EITHER.

IN THE REGULAR FIGHTING DIVISION I HAD ANOTHER EXPERIENCE FOR WHICH I WAS TEARING THREW MY OPPONENTS UNTIL I CAME ACROSS A MAN FROM SCOTLAND WALES.

THE ONLY DIFFERENCE BEING I KEPT UP BETTER WITH HIM. BUT HE WAS MUCH FASTER THAN I.

MOVING ON AS THE DAY WAS WINDING DOWN, AND I GOT BACK TO OUR ROOM THE PAIN IN MY KNEE WAS BEGINNING TO BE UNBEARABLE!

MY WIFE WAS EXTREMELY UNHAPPY WITH ME TO SAY THE LEAST.

I WAS TOLD FLAT OUT IN NOT SO MANY GOOD WORDS THAT THIS WAS THE LAST TIME!

WELL I STAYED IN THE ROOM FOR A COUPLE OF DAYS, WHILE ATTEDING DINNER ONE OF THOSE NIGHTS THE TEAM DOCTOR WAS CONSIDERING SENDING ME TO THE HOSPITAL TO TAKE A CLOSER LOOK AT MY KNEE.

IT WAS NOT IMPROVING AND IT WAS LOOKING NASTY. { SWOLLEN AND BLACK}

IT WAS AT THIS TIME TAMMY PULLED ME ASIDE AND SAID: "" *NEVER AGAIN! NOT THIS TYPE OF DIVISION. YOU HAVE A FAMILY NOW TO THINK ABOUT! SO YOU HAD BETTER START.* ""

LIKE I EXPLAINED BEFORE WHEN YOU LEAVE THE COMFORT OF YOUR HOME AND YOUR COUNTRY IT IS A VERY SCARY EXPERIENCE.

NOT TO MENTION A SERIOUS WAKE UP CALL!

NUMBER TWO HAPPENED AT A LOCAL TOURNAMENT IN PROVIDENCE RI. IF I CAN REMEMBER CORRECTLY IT WAS IN THE YEAR 2003.

BEFORE THE GAMES BEGAN I WAS IN THE LOCKER ROOM AS USUALLY, BEFORE HAND GETTING READY.

THEN THIS GUY CAME IN WITH A REALLY BIG MOUTH AND BAD ATTITUDE.

HE WAS SAYING OUT LOUD AND VERY CLEARLY HOW HE WAS HOPING TO FIGHT SOME OF THE TOP SEEDS.

TOP SEEDS ARE THOSE WHO ARE HIGHLY RANKED IN THE SPORT, AND IF YOU WANT TO MAKE A NAME FOR YOURSELF YOU NEED TO BEAT THEM.

HE THEN WENT FUTHER ALONG AN EXPLAINED HIS INTENTIONS OF HURTING THEM REAL BAD IN THE RING, SO YOU GUESSEDIT THAT HE COULD AKE A NAME FOR HIMSELF ON THIS DAY.

HE EVEN HAD A PRINT OUT OFF THE INTERNET OF THE NAMES OF THE TOP SEEDS IN HIS DIVISIONS.

OF COURSE I WAS ONE OF THOSE NAMES. IT WAS IN THIS MOMENT A WEIRD BONE CHILLING FEELING WENT DOWN MY SPINE!

WHEN I HAD LEFT HOME THAT MORNING MASON AND TAMMY WERE STILL IN BED, AND THE NIGHT BEFORE I PROMISED THEM THAT WHEN I GOT BACK WE WOULD GO DO SOMETHING FUN TOGETHER.

THEN IT HIT ME... LIKE A BRICK! HAVING A FAMILY IS FAR MOREIMPORTANT THAN GOING TO THE HOSPITAL FOR SERVICES JUST BECAUSE I WANTED TO PROVE MYSELF TO THE WORLD OF MARTIAL ARTS.

THE NAME OF THE GAME IN A TOURNAMENT IS SUPPOSED TO BE ABOUT SKILL AND CONTROL. NOT GOING FOR BLOOD!

YES MOST OF THE TIME IT DOES GET WAY OUT OF CONTROL, BUT I NEVER HAD TO WORRY ABOUT BEING ABLE TO PLAY WITH A SON BEFORE!

BECAUSE BEFORE IT WAS JUST TAMMY AND I. THE OLY THING I DID HAVE TO BE CONCERNED WITH WAS BEING ABLE TO GOTO WORK AND SUPPORT US.

HAVE A CHILD IN THE PICTURE NOW DIDN'T COMPARE IN ANY DEGREE!

I GREW TO REALIZE THAT PERHAPS MAKING MY FAMILY HAPPY AND ENJOYING LIFE WITH THEM WAS MORE IMPORTANT TO ME THAN THE LIMELIGHT!

BUT ONCE AGAIN I MANAGED TO PLACE IN THE TOP THREE ON THIS DAY TOO. IN FACT I TOOK FIRST AND SECOND PLACES.

MY FINAL DECISION CAME ABOUT SOMETIME IN 2004, BUT REALLY I HAD ALREADY SEEN THE LIGHT AND THE ERROR OF MY WAYS WITH FAMILY.

I JUST WASN'T QUITE READY TO ACCEPT IT JUST YET.

NOW AS FAR AS THE WORLD GAMES ARE CONCERNED I HAD NEVER LOST ONE YET.

AND ON THE NATIONAL CIRCUIT I ONLY HAD TWO LOSSES AND ONE "DQ" FOR THE USE OF WHAT WAS LABELED EXCESSIVE FORCE.

I WAS MUCH YOUNGER BACK THEN AND HAD LESS INJURIES TOO.

BUT NOW I THOUGHT I AM NOT GETTING ANY YOUNGER. HOWEVER; THE SPORT OF KARATE AND THE GAMES WERE GETTING HARDER AND HARDER STILL.

IF I RETIRED NOW I COULD NOT ONLY GO OUT ON TOP, BUT STILL HAVE GOOD HEALTH ALONG WITH THIS DECISION AS WELL.

IT WAS AT THIS TIME IN MY LIFE THAT I TOOK A STEP BACK AND I SAID TO MYSELF:

"" I DO NOT NEED AN MORE TROPHIES OR MEDALS! ... THEY DO NOT DEFINE ME AS A PERSON OR AS A MARTIAL ARTIST. IT IS MY ACTIONS AND WORD OF HONOR THAT MKES ME WHO I AM... ""

I HAD FOUGHT SO HARD FOR SO LONG IT WAS TIME FOR A CHANGE IN MY LIFE, AND I FELT AS THOUGH I HAD NOTHING MORE TO PROVE TO ANYBODY!

NOT EVEN MY SELF. I HAD BEAT ALL THE DD THAT WERE STACKED AGAINST ME FOR YEARS, AND I HAD PROVED ENOUGH!

IT WAS TIME TO LET SOMEONE ELSE HAVE THE CHANCE TO REIGN. SO I RETIRED FROM THE TOURNAMENT PORTION OF MY MARTIAL ARTS CAREER.

JUST BECAUSE I WANT TO STOP DOING SPORT KARATE DOESN'T MEAN I CAN'T TRAIN ANYMORE.

SO MANY PEOPLE GET FIXATED ON THE TOURNAMENT TRAINING THAT THEY NEVER LEAVE IT.

IN THIS FACT THEIR MARTIAL ARTS TRAINING AS FAR AS ADVANCEMENT REALLY SUFFERS.

ALL THE GLORY AND THE HYPE OF THIS LEADS TO FALSE HOPES OF STARDOM!

THEY REALLY NEVER LEARN ANY MORE KNOWLEDGE OF TRUE MARTIAL ARTS TRAINING, BECAUSE THEY ARE FAR TO BUSY CAUGHT IN THE LOOP.

YOU KNOW THE REAL REASON WE BEGAN IN THE FIRST PLACE WAS NOT TO BE TOURNAMENT HEROS BUT TO LEARN A DISCIPLINE OF CULTURE.

THIS IS WHAT HAD BEEN LOST ALONG THE WAY. THEY JUST WANTED TO BE IN MAGAZINES AND TRY ANYTHING TO LAND THE BIG BUSINESS TV GIG!

YES IT WOULD BE VERY COOL, BUT NOT MANY ARE ABLE TO DO IT!

AND THE ONES THAT ARE LUCK ENOUGH TO MAKE IT HAVE TROUBLE LIVING IN THE REALITY OF SCOPE.

IT IS HARD TO HANDLE THE RESPONSIBILITY THAT IS ASSOCIATED WITH THESE DREAMS.

THEY ONLY LEARN NEW TRICKS TO IMPRESS THE JUDGES FOR ANOTHER VICTORY.

FOR ME IF I FOUND MYSELF IN A BRAWL AT THE LOCAL WATERING HOLE I WOULD MUCH RATHER HAVE A GUY WITH ME THAT COULD THROW A GOOD BLOCK AND FOLLOW IT UP WITH A PUNCH.

INSTEAD OF THE GUY WHO WAS THE FANCY GYMNAST DOING ALL KINDS OF FLIPS AND RELATED STUFF!

I WOULD BECOME TO CONCERNED THAT THEY MIGHT HIT THEIR HEAD ON SOMETHING AROUND THEM, AND THEN I WOULD HAVE TO TAKE CARE OF THEM PLUS EVERYONE ELSE.

FOR THOSE OF US THAT HAVE BEEN THEIR YOU KNOW EXACTLY WHAT IT IS THAT I AM TALKING ABOUT HERE!

SO I DID. THEN INSTEAD OF PREPARING FOR TOURNAMENTS ALL THE TIME I SPENT MORE TIME ON REQUIRMENTS IN MY TRAINING FOR ADVANCEMENT.

AS WELL AS QUALITY TIME MUCH NEEDED DUE TO NEGLECT WITH MY FAMILY!

SO THEN COMES AN END OF ONE ERA, AND THE BEGINNING OF ANOTHER IN MY LIFE …

I HAD FINALLY GREW UP AND TOOK RESPONSIABLITY. IT IS JUST TOO BAD IT TOOK ME SO LONG TO REALIZE THIS FAULT!

""ABOARD THE JOLLY PIRATE; NOTHING IS BETTER THAN FAMILY TIME! ""

"" ARUBA 2010 ""

SOME OF MY FAVORITE QUOTES :

" " MY TOP TEN LIST " "

FUCK THE MAN!

A HAPPY LIFE IS A HAPPY LIFE!

HE WHO SHEDS MORE SWEAT DURING PRACTICE SHEDS LESS BLOOD ON THE BATTLE FIELD!

GO BACK AND DO IT AGAIN!

ARE YOU MENTALLY CHALLENGED?

STUPIDITY IS AN EPIDEMIC! AND IT IS RUNNING PAMPID AROUND HERE!

A LOSS TODAY IS A WIN TOMMORROW!

GOOD THINGS COME TO THOSE WHO WAIT!

IF YOUR FEET WERE AS FAST AS YOUR MOUTH; YOU WOULD HAVE FINISHED HOURS AGO!

IF FIRST YOU DO NOT SUCCEED, TRY . TRY .. AGAIN!

" " BY: KYOSHI " QUICKSILVER " MICHAEL P. FARADAY " "

KENPO VS. SHOTOKAN :

TO ME THE STUDYING OF THE MARTIAL ARTS IS LIKE PHYSICS. WHICH IS THE SCIENTIFIC STUDY OF ENERGY, MATTER, AND MOTION.

IT POSES VARIABLE EQUATIONS FOR A VAST ARRAY OF SITUATIONS!

WE GAIN **ENERGY** FROM OUR WORKOUTS, AND LEARNING HOW TO CONTROL OUR BREATHING.

THE **MATTER** IS PUTTING OUR BODIES AGAINST THE POWER OF OUR MINDS!

THE **MOTION** IS THE FLUENT MOVEMENT FROM THE POWER OF OUR TECHNIQUES!

OF ALL MY YEARS IN TRAINING I SPENT THE MOST TIE STUDING THE ART OF KENPO FIRST, AND SHOTOKAN SECOND.

THERE ARE SO MANY DIFFERENT STYLES OF MARTIAL ARTS TO CHOOSE FROM.

{ KUNG - FU ~ JUDO ~ TAE KWON DO ~ JIU JITSU ~ TANG SOO DO ~ }

JUST TO NAME A FEW OF THE MANY THAT ARE AVAILABLE OUT THERE.

EVEN IN A LIFE TIME YOU WOULD NEVER BE ABLE TO EXPERIENCE THEM ALL! NOT EVEN CLOSE.

SO IN THE DEFINING OF MY PERSONAL MARTIAL ARTS LEARNING, AND TEACHING I HAVE DECIDED TO COMPARE AND CONTRAST THESE TWO ARTS ONLY.

FIRST LETS TALK ABOUT KENPO. IT IS CHINESE IN NATURE, BUT IS CONSIDERED TO BE AN EVEN MIX OF ACTUALLY SIX DIFFERENT ARTS.

THESE ARTS INCLUDE: *WESTERN BOXING ~ KUNG - FU ~ KARATE ~ JUJITSU ~ JUDO ~ AND KENPO.*

WHAT THEY DO IS DRAW FROM THE BASICS, AND INCORPORATE THE MOVES THAT ARE BEST UTILIZIED INTO WHAT IS CALLED THE KENPO FLOW.

THE KNOWLEDGE OF MOVEMENT WITHIN THE OFFENSE AND DEFENSE OF ONES BODY.

I FELL IN LOVE WITH THIS STYLE, BECAUSE IT NOT ONLY WAS WELL SUITED TO MY BODY, BUT TOUCHED BASE WITH BOXING AND KUNG - FU FOR WHICH I HAD STUDIED FOR A WHILE IN THE YOUNGER YEARS OF MY TRAINING.

IN SHORT THE ART OF KENPO IS DESIGNED TO BE A MULTI - BREAKDOWN OF AN ATTACKER.

WHAT I MEAN BY THIS STATEMENT IS THIS… THIS STYLE USES SEVERAL TECHNIQUES THAT FLOW FROM ONE TECHNIQUE TO ANOTHER TO STOP A WOULD BE ATTACK.

THIS ART IS CONSTANTLY EVER FLOWING AND CHANGING DIRECTION UNTIL THE OUTCOME YOU DESIRE IS ACHIEVED!

FIRST THE BLOCK. THEN PERHAPS A SECOND OR MAYBE MORE. KEEP IN MIND THAT EVERY BLOCK IS A STRIKE AND EVERY STRIKE COULD BE A BLOCK.

THEN MULTIPLE SETUP STRIKES TO PUT THE ATTACKERS BODY IN A FAVORABLE POSITION THAT YOU DESIRE.

LASTLY THE FINISHING BLOW! THIS COULD RANGE FROM A VARITY OF POSSIABLITIES!

FROM STANDING UP TO GOING ONTO THE GROUND. MAYBE A BREAKING MOVE OR PERHAPS A CONTROLED LOCK?

THIS IS UP TO YOU, AND IT MUST FIT THE SITUATION THAT PRESENTS IT SELF TO YOU.

IN THE KENPO SYSTEM THERE IS A LOT TO LEARN. JUST IN WHAT IS CALLED THE NUMBERED SYSTEM THERE ARE THIRTY THREE COMBINATIONS!

THESE FALL UNDER THE MULTI FOOT AND HAND TECHNIQUES. ALSO REFERED TO AS THE KARATE TECHNIQUES.

THEN THERE ARE FIFTEEN KENPO TECHNIQUES. THEY SIMPLIFY THE ABOVE SYSTEM TO A DEGREE FOR THE MULTI HAND TO FOOT RATIO.

BUT IN MY OPINION THEY ARE QUITE UNIQUE IN NATURE AND ARE COMPLETELY DIFFERENT. THAT IS WHY THEY ARE LABELED KENPO TECHNIQUES!

NEXT IS WHAT IS CALLED THE ANIMAL TECHNIQUES. THESE ARE SETS OF USUALLY THREE MULTI TECHNIQUES FOR EACH OF THE FIVE MAIN ANIMALS IN STUDY FROM KUNG - FU PRINCIPLES.

THESE FAB FIVE ARE: *THE TIGER ~ CRANE ~ SNAKE ~ LEOPARD ~ AND DRAGON.*

THEY BEGIN EASY. THEN EVOLVE INTO A MEDIUM AND ADVANCED LEVEL OF SKILLS!

THESE ARE THE KUNG - FU TECHNIUES OF KENPO.

THEN THERE IS THE SECTION OF HOLDS AND GRABS. THESE ARE PUT INTO THE JUJITSU TECHNIQUES.

NEXT UP ARE THE TAKEDOWN AND SWEEPING PORTION OF KENPO. THESE TECHNIQUES FIT UNDER THE JUDO TECHNIQUES.

LAST UP IS WHAT IS CALLED KUMITE, OR THE SPARRING SECTION.

NOT ONLY DOES THIS FALL INTO THE BOXING SECTION, BUT THE INCORPRATION OF AS MANY OF THE OTHER TECHNIQUES FROM THE KENPO SYSTEM THAT YOU CAN WORK INTO YOUR FIGHTING!

THIS TAKES YEARS OF PRACTICE TO ACHIEVE. IT CAN NOT BE LEARNED OVERNIGHT.

NOW LETS DISCUSS THE SHOTOKAN SYSTEM OF MARTIAL ARTS. SHOTOKAN IS A JAPANESE ART.

THE BEAUTY OF THIS STYLE IS SIMPLICITY! WHAT I CALL PURE AND TRUE TRADITION!

THEY HAVE MUCH MORE BASIC TECHNIQUES IN NATURE BECAUSE THEY ARE KARATE ORIENTATED.

IN THE SINGLE ART OF KARATE; THE THEORY IS BASED ON THE ONE WELL DELIVERED STRIKE WHICH REFLECTS EQUAL TO ONE KILL IN THEIR MIND!

NEXT INSTEAD OF LIKE FIFTY DIFFERENT TECHNIQUES THE SHOTOKAN SYSTEM HAS WHAT THEY CALL COBALTS.

IN JAPANESE COBALTS ARE DEFINE AS THE SELF DEFENSE TECHNIQUES. THESE ALTHOUGH FEW IN NUMBERS ARE MEANT TO USE THE THEORY OF BASIC IS BEST.

I LIKE THEM VERY MUCH! THEY HAVE A COUPLE OF COBALTS FOR EACH POSSIABLE SITUATION THAT MAY COME ABOUT AS FAR AS A FIGHT IS CONCERNED.

BASICALLY THE STRUCTURE IS COMPOSED OF A BLOCK FOLLOWED BY A COUNTER STRIKE. THAT'S ALL. NOTHING MORE MOST OF THE TIME.

I FIND THIS TO BE VERY REALISTIC FOR TODAYS SOCIETY. IT SEEMS MORE NATURAL IN MY OPNION. QUICK AND TO THE POINT!

SO HERE ARE THE COMPARISONS BETWEEN THESE TWO DIFFERENT STYLES:

BOTH STYLES OF COURSE HAVE THE SAME COMPONENTS. THERE ARE BLOCKS, STRIKES, SELF DEFENSE, KATAS, SPARRING, AND WEAPON TRAINING.

ALSO BOTH STYLES ARE GREAT FOR DISCIPLINE AND CHARACTER BUILDING!

BUT IF I HAD TO PICK JUST ONE, IT WOULD BE KENPO. I REALLY DO ENJOY SHOTOKAN, BUT THE FREEDOM OF MULTI EXPRESSION IS WHAT KENPO IS ALL ABOUT!

I USED TO SAY THAT SHOTOKAN WAS MY PICK. THIS WAS BECAUSE I FEEL INTO A RUT AND NEEDED A BREAK FROM THE COMPLEXITIES OF THE KENPO TRAINING.

HOWEVER; IF YOU ATTEND ONE OF MY SEMINARS AND LOOK DEEPLY INTO WHO I AM AS AN ARTIST THE FLOW OF KENPO RUNS THREW MY VEINS!

IT ALLOWS ME TO BE SIMPLE WHEN NEEDED, BUT ALSO ALLOWS DIVERSITY OF THOUGHT IN TIME OF NEED!

TO SUM THIS STATEMENT UP INTO A SIMPLIER VERSION:

"" THERE WILL MORE OFTEN THAN NOT BE PERIODS OF TIME THAT A SIMPLE BLOCK AND STRIKE WILL NOT BE ENOUGH! DURING THIS PHASE HAVING THE KNOWLEDGE OF MULTIPLE SKILLS IS REQUIRED. ""

"" ALWAYS KEEP MOVING FORWARD! NEVER GO BACK. ATTACK THE EYES, THROAT, GROIN! TAKE THE SPACE OF YOUR OPPONENT AND HAULT HIS ATTACK. ""

YES IN SHOTOKAN THERE ARE LIMITED TECHNIQUES IN NUMBER. THIS IS GREAT FOR QUICK DIRECT INSTANCES.

SHOTOKAN IS POWERFUL. IT IS ALSO DOWN TO EARTH AND SIMPLE IN NATURE.

IN KENPO THERE ARE NOT ONLY SIMPLE TECHNIQUES THAT REFLECT THE SAME OUTCOME, BUT THERE ARE SO MANY DIFFERENT TECHNIQUES OF MULTI DEFENSE TACTICS!

IT IS THIS WHICH I BELIEVE TO BE THE BEST DEFENSE BECAUSE YOU CAN SUBDUE YOU ATTACKER NOT ONLY DIRECTLY, BUT INDIRECTLY AS WELL!

BY KNOWING THE MECHANICS OF THE HUMAN BODY. MAKING THE BODY MOVE IN THE WAY THAT YOU DESIRE IT TO, TO CONTROL THE SITUATION THAT IS PRESENTED.

THIS IS ALSO GREAT FOR MULTIPLE ATTACKERS! REMEMBER IN SHOTOKAN WE FOCUS ON ONE WELL DELIVERED STRIKE FOR ONE PERSON AT A TIME.

IN KENPO YOU TRAIN FOR MULTI DEFENSE AS THE MAJORITY OF YOU TRAINING!

AGAIN THERE IS NOTHING WRONG WITH LEARNING EITHER STYLE. BOTH ARE AWESOME IN THEIR OWN WAY.

TO ME KENPO AT TIMES MAY BE AN OVERLOAD OF INFORMATION, BUT IT IS LIKE SECOND NATURE TO ME.

IN A FIGHTING SENSE YOU NEED TO REACT FAST AND PERCISE! ALSO BECAUSE OF THE SOCIETY WE LIVE IN TODAY THE ONE ON ONE VERSION OF FIGHTING IN NO LONGER HONORED!

IT IS USUALLY TWO OR THREE ONTO ONE! IN THIS THEORY IT IS ABSOLUTE THAT YOUR SKILLS IN SELF DEFENSE MEET THE DEMAND.

KENPO WILL DO THIS FOR YOU. IT WASN'T UNTIL I TOOK A STEP BACK AND FULLY COMPARED THESE TWO STYLES OF COMBAT BEFORE I TRULY UNDERSTOOD WHAT IT WAS I WAS SEARCHING FOR.

IN ENDING THIS CHAPTER LET THIS BE KNOWN…

IT IS UP TO YOU TO DECIDE WHICH STYLE FITS YOUR PERSONALITY.

THEN THE AMOUNT OF EFFORT THAT YOU PUT INTO THE TRAINING YOU DO WILL CONCLUDE THE ACHIEVEMENT YOU GET OUT OF THAT TRAINING!

BEAUTY IS IN THE EYE OF THE BEHOLDER.

ANY STYLE THAT YOU MAY CHOOSE TO TAKE PART IN WHETHER IT BE KENPO, SHOTOKAN OR ANOTHER DISCIPLINE OF THE ARTS IT ALL COMES DOWN TO THE SAME PRINCIPLE.

BASICS AND MORE BASICS! THE BETTER YOUR FOUNDATION… THE MORE EFFECTIVE YOUR TECHNIQUES WILL BECOME!

PUT IN THE REQUIRED EFFORT AND NOT ONLY WILL YOUR SKILLS GROW, BUT YOU WILL AS WELL.

IT IS THIS MANNER OF THOUGHT THAT WILL SEPARATE YOU FROM ALL THE OTHERS.

THIS IS THE DIFFERENCE BETWEEN THE COMMON MARTIAL ARTIST AND THE KNOWLEDGABLE MARTIAL ARTIST!

TRAINING WITH SENSEI GIAQUAINTO :

MY TRAINING WITH SENSEI JOHN WAS A LOT OF FUN, BUT HAD MANY MEMORABLE VALUES THAT WERE LEARNED!

HE HAD ME DOING SOME ABSOLUTELY CRAZY WORKOUTS! I COMPARE HIM TO THE MOVIE THE KARATE KID.

BUT IN THIS INSTANCE IT WASN'T A MOVIE IT WAS REAL LIFE. MY LIFE.

ONE OF MY MOST MEMORABLE WORKOUT EXPERIENCES WITH HIM WAS USING THE WHEELBARROW!

HE HAD A DRIVEWAY THAT WAS LIKE A SKI JUMP. IT WAS VERY LONG AND HAD A HUGH DROP.

AT THE BOTTOM OF THIS HE HAD SEVERAL LARGE ROCKS IN VARIABLE DIMENSIONS OF SHAPE.

THEY WERE ALL PLACED HERE FROM THE CONSTRUCTION OF HIS NEW POOL THAT HE HAD PUT IN.

WELL WHAT I HAD TO DO WAS THIS… I HAD TO RUN FROM THE TOP DOWN TO THE BOTTOM.

THEN I HAD TO FILL THE WHEELBARROW UP TO THE TIPPY TOP, AND THEN RUN UP THE STEEP SLOPE WITH ALL THE ROCKS!

NEXT I HAD TO DUMP ALL OF THEM OUT, AND THEN START OVER AGAIN.

ONCE ALL THE ROCKS WERE RE - LOCATED TO THE TOP PORTION OF THE DRIVEWAY NEAR THE STREET LEVEL I THEN NEEDED TO BRING THEM ALL BACK TO THE BOTTOM AGAIN!

ALL THIS WAS TO BE DONE UNTIL COMPLETED. PLUS YOU WERE NOT ALLOWED TO DROP ANY OF THE ROCKS.

JUST TO LET YOU KNOW SOME OF THESE ROCKS WEIGHT WAS TOUGH TO ACCOMPLISH IN LIFTING!

ALL IN ALL ON THIS DAY THIS EXERCISE TOOK ME ABOUT THIRTY MINUTES TO COMPLETE.

AND WHEN I SAY THIRTY MINUTES I MEAN THIRTY TOTAL MINUTES WITH NO STOPPING!

THEN AT THE END SENSEI JOHN WOULD COUNT ALL THE DROPPED ROCKS BETWEEN POINT A TO POINT B.

THIS IS WHERE THE PUNISHMENT WOULD COME INTO PLAY. THIS WOULD EQUAL ALL THE DROPPED ROCKS TIME SETS OF THREE FOR TEN TOTAL SETS.

LETS JUST SAY IT WAS EXTREMELY PAINFUL! AFTER ALL THIS WHAT WOULD YOU THINK WE DID NEXT?

WE REPEATED THE WHOLE SEQUENCE OVER AGAIN. THAT'S WHAT WE DID!

FOR MY PUNISHMENT I HAD TO CRANE HOP ACROSS SEVERAL RAILROAD TIES THAT WERE PLACED IN A REAL MESSED P PATTERN.

FOR THOSE WHO DO NOT KNOW WHAT CRANE HOPPING IS … IT IS WHEN YOU JUMP AS FAR AS YOU CAN LANDING ON ONE LEG, AND THEN USING THAT SAME LEG REPEAT BUT LAND ON THE OPPOSITE LEG!

THE REP FOR THIS WAS ALSO THREE SETS OF TEN. BOTH FRONTWARDS AND BACKWARDS!

IF YOU FELL DURING THIS PUNISHMENT SECTION OF EXERCISE, THEN YOU WOULD RECEIVE ANOTHER PUNISHMENT THAT WAS FAR WORSE THAN THIS!

TO SAY IN THE LEAST THIS WAS A TOTAL LEG STRENGTHENING AFTERNOON WHICH LASTED FOR HOURS!

ANOTHER ASPECT THAT I REALLY ENJOYED AS I HAVE MENTIONED BEFORE IN MY OWN TYPE OF CLASSES WAS THE FACT THAT SENSEI JOHN LIKED TO USE THE OUTDOORS AS MUCH AS POSSIABLE.

I WOULD SAY THAT DURING THE CASE OF A TOTAL YEAR WE WOULD BE OUTSIDE ABOUT 65 % OF THE TIME.

SENSEI DIDN'T SEEM TO ENJOY THE COLD WEATHER AS MUCH AS THE OTHER SEASONS, BUT WHEN WE DID GO OUTSIDE NEVER THE LESS IT WAS A REAL TREAT AS FAR AS I WAS CONCERNED.

SOMETIMES THE ANSWERS TO ALL HIS OFF THE WALL TRAININGS TOOK ME A FEW DAYS TO UNDERSTAND, BUT IN THE END THE REASONS BECAME CLEAR TO ME.

THEIR SOUL PURPOSE WAS FOR MY PERSONAL BENEFIT WITHIN MY TRAINING FOR THE MARTIAL ARTS!

SENSEI JOHN HAD TAUGHT ME HOW TO CIRCUIT TRAIN AS WELL USING A COMBO OF HEAVY BAG WORK TO THE USE OF WEIGHTS IN DIFFERENT FASIONS.

HE ALSO TAUGHT ME THE LESSON OF HOW TO TAKE A GOOD PUNCH. SEVERAL TIMES OVER MANY YEARS!

BESIDES ALL THIS I ALSO HELPED SENSEI JOHN TEACH A BASIC KARATE SELF DEFENSE CLASS TO LOCAL KIDS AT THE BOYS AND GIRLS CLUB OF AMERICA.

THIS CLUB WAS LOCATED IN DUDLEY MA 01571 AT THE TIME.

ON THIS PROJECT SENSEI AND I TAUGHT THESE CHILDREN MAINLY HOW TO LEARN THE DISCIPLINE OF RESPECT!

NOT ONLY FOR THEMSELVES, BUT FOR OTHERS AS WELL.

WE ALSO USED THE TEACHING OF THE ARTS TO BUILD UP THEIR CHARACTER BY GIVING THEM SOMETHING TO LOOK FORWARD TO A COUPLE NIGHTS A WEEK.

THIS IN THE END GAVE A GREAT FEELING OF ACCOMPLISHMENT FOR EVERYONE INVOLVED.

FOR JUST A LITTLE OF OUR TIME WE WERE ABLE TO WORK WONDERS WITH THESE KIDS WHICH IN TURN WOULD CHANGE THEIR LIFE FOREVER!

BOTH OF US WERE INVOLVED WITH THE BOYS AND GIRLS CLUB FOR THREE YEARS UNTIL OUR CLASS BECAME A BUDGET CUT.

AS FAR AS A TIME SLOT AVAILABILITY FOR OTHER ACTIVITIES WHICH THE BOARD OF TRUSTEES THOUGHT WERE BETTER SUITED FOR THE CHILDREN.

THIS WAS TOO BAD! SOME OF THESE KIDS HAD COME SUCH A LONG WAY FROM THE LETS SAY BAD LIFE STYLE THEY HAD PREVIOUSLY EXPERIENCED IN LIFE.

BOTH FROM HOMES WITH BROKEN FAMILIES AND THE STREET LIFE THAT THEY FELL VICTIM TO EVERYDAY.

FOR EXAMPLE HAVING FEAR OF BEING BULLIED!

HOWEVER HARD WE PROTESTED AND SHOWED PROABLE CAUSE TO EFFECT IN THE NEED FOR OUR CLASS TO CONTINUE YOU JUST CAN'T MAKE A SUIT AND TIE TYPE OF GUY SEE WHAT IT IS THEY DO NOT WISH TO SEE.

AFTER THIS WAS ALL SAID AND DONE JOHN WAS ABLE TO KEEP ONE KID GOING ON THE RIGHT PATH, AND I KEPT ANOTHER ONE ON IT TOO.

WE BOTH DID WHAT WE COULD FOR THEM FOR AS LONG AS THEY WANTED TO LEARN.

BOTH THESE KIDS LASTED ABOUT ANOTHER YEAR OR SO UNTIL THE TRAINING BECAME TO HARD FOR THEM.

WHEN YOU ARE YOUNG YOUR INTERESTS ONLY STAY FOCUSED FOR SO LONG.

IT IS VERY RARE TO FIND SUCH COMMITMENT IN WHAT WE DO WITH ADULTS NEVER MIND KIDS OR TEENAGERS.

THIS IS WHEN HANGING OUT WITH FRIENDS BECOMES MORE IMPORTANT TO YOUR SOCIAL CLASS THEN TRAINING IN THE STUDY OF MARTIAL ARTS!

ACTUALLY JOHN AND I WORK TOGETHER AS LETTER CARRIERS FOR THE UNITED STATES POSTAL SERVICE IN WEBSTER MA 01570 NOW SINCE 1990.

SO WE SEE EACH OTHER ON A DAILY BASIS, AND HE IS LIKE A FAMILY MEMBER TO ME.

THE MAIN REASON FOR ME LEAVING HIS TEACHINGS WAS WE HAD COME TO A POINT THAT HE HAD NOTHING MORE HE COULD TEACH ME.

JUST OUT OF THE BLUE AFTER MANY YEARS OF TRAINING TOGETHER HE TOLD ME THIS:

"" TODAY IS YOUR LAST DAY WITH ME. YOU NEED TO FIND SOMEONE ELSE TO FUTHER YOUR EDUCATION IN THE ARTS, BECAUSE I CAN NO LONGER DO SO! ""

AT FIRST THIS WAS DEVASTATING TO ME! TO HEAR THOSE WORDS FELT LIKE THE WORD HAD CEASED.

HOWEVER; IT HAD BECOME ANOTHER GREAT LESSON IN MY DESTINY FOR MY MARTIAL ARTS TRAINING!

JOHN AND I HAVE TOTAL RESPECT FOR ONE ANOTHER. THIS WILL NEVER CHANGE.

WHEN EVER ONE OF US IS IN NEED THE OTHER COMES TO ASSIST. NO QUESTIONS ASKED NO MATTER WHAT.

THIS IS WHY HE IS MORE LIKE FAMILY TO ME THAN A FRIEND OR A SENSEI.

HE IS WHOM I CONSIDER TO BE ANOTHER BROTHER TO ME!

"" MASTER CHARLES TARR & SENSEI JOHN GIAQUAINTO ""

TRAINING UNDER MASTER ALAN D ' ALLESSANDRO :

EVEN THOUGH AS FAR AS TODAY IS CONCERNED MASTER D' ALLESSANDRO AND I DO NOT GET ALONG I DO OWE HIM MY THANKS.

IF IT WASN'T FOR THIS MAN I WOULD HAVE NEVER BECAME THE MAN I AM THAT STANDS BEFORE YOU TODAY!

THREW THE GRAPEVINE I WAS TOLD I DO NOT EXIST, AND THAT I AM A DISCRACE TO ALL MARTIAL ARTISTS IN HIS WORDS.

IN MY WORDS: *"" TUNNEL VISION IS A SICKNESS THAT SPREADS BIASIED RUMORS AND BELIEFS THAT ARE OPNIONS OF THOSE WHO IN TURN ARE NOT PROPERLY EDUCATED TO SPEAK OF SUCH THOUGHTS. ""*

ALSO JUST OUT OF CURIOSITY I HAD RECENTLY VISITED HIS WEBSITE 11/4/10 AND FOUND OUT THAT MY NAME HAS BEEN REMOVED FROM ALL FAMILY TREES ASSOCIATED WITH THE NEW ENGLAND KARATE ACADEMY.

TO THIS I FIND HUMOR FOR IT ONLY SHOWS THAT ALL THAT IS ABOUT TO BE REVEALED IS TRUE AND IS STRENGTHENED BEYOND ALL REASONABLE DOUBT.

THE WAY THAT I CAME ACROSS MASTER D ' ALLESSANDRO AND HIS SCHOOL N.E.K.A. WAS THREW THE TOURNAMENT CIRCUIT.

IN A PUBLICATION OF THE KRANE TOURNAMENT MAGAZINE THERE WAS A FEATURE ARTICLE ABOUT HIS DAUGHTER.

HER NAME WAS APRIL D ' ALLESSANDRO AND SHE WAS A HOPEFULL TO BECOME AN UP AND COMING SUPERSTAR IN THE SPORT KARATE CIRCUIT.

SO I THOUGHT TO MYSELF THIS IS WHERE I NEED TO TRAIN! SO I CALLED DOWN TO THE DOJO TO SETUP AN INTERVIEW WITH MASTER D ' ALLESSANDRO.

IT DIDN'T LAST LONG BEFORE I WAS ASKED TO START TRAINING RIGHT AWAY, AND WITH THIS I STARTED THAT SAME WEEK WITH HIM.

MR. D ' ALLESSANDRO HAD AN IMPRESSIVE BACKGROUND. HIS TRAINING STARTED WITH A VERY WELL KNOWN MASTER TO THE REGION.

HIS NAME WAS PROFESSOR ROCKY DIRICO. THEN WHEN FOR WHAT EVER REASONS ALAN NEEDED TO MOVE ON PROFESSOR DIRICO INTRODUCED ALAN TO A LEGEND IN HIS TIME.

THIS MAN WAS THE LATE AND WELL RESPECTED WORLDWIDE PROFESSOR AND GRANDMASTER NICK CERIO!

THIS WAS ALANS BIG BREAK INTO HIS TRAINING. IT WAS UNFORTUNATE THAT HIS TRAINING WAS CUT SHORT.

THIS WAS DUE TO THE UNTIMELY PASSING OF PROFESSOR CERIO. THIS WAS TRULY A GREAT LOSS TO THE MARTIAL ARTS COMMUNITY!

PERHAPS IF HE WERE STILL ALIVE TODAY THINGS WOULD HAVE BEEN QUITE DIFFERENT AS FAR AS MASTER D ' ALLESSANDROS TRAIN OF THOUGHT.

HOWEVER; ALANS TRAINING WAS NONE THE LEAST EXTENSIVE AND VERY CHALLENGING FOR ME WHILE IT LASTED.

THIS THEN OPENED THE DOORWAY FOR HIM TO BE ACCEPTED BY ONE OF PROFESSORS HIGH RANKING STUDENTS.

THIS MAN WAS MASTER DON RODRIGUES, AND IT WAS JUST RECENTLY THAT MR RODRIGUES RECEIVED HIS APPOINTMENT TO GRANDMASTER SHIP!

THIS IS AN APPOINTMENT WELL DESERVED! GOING BACK TO GRANDMASTER RODRIGUES AND ALANS TRAINING …

I STRICKLY REMEMBER A CONVERSATION LONG AGO WHERE IT WAS MENTIONED BY MASTER D ' ALLESSANDRO THAT THE MAIN REASON FOR DON ACCEPTING HIM AS A STUDENT WAS DUE TO HIS CONNECTION TO PROFESSER CERIO.

TODAY EVEN THOUGH ALAN AND I DO NOT COMMUNICATE, BECAUSE OF OUR DIFFERENCES ON THE CONCEPTS OF MARTIAL ARTS I STILL OWE HIM RESPECT.

ALSO TO KEEP IN REFRENCE TO ABOVE INFORMATION … ALAN IS STILL UNDER GRANDMASTER RODRIGUES DIRECTING OF TRAINING. 11/07/10

EVEN THOUGH HE DOESN'T AGREE WITH ME OR MY IDEAS IN AND FOR THE ARTS I STILL RESPECT HIM.

ALL THAT THIS MAN HAS ACCOMPLISHED SHOULDN'T BE TAKEN LIGHTLY. HE IS A GREAT MAN WHO DESERVES THE RESPECT FROM HIS PEERS!

YES I MAY SOUND A BIT REDUNDANT ABOUT THIS ISSUE OF TRAINING WITH MASTER D ' ALLESSANDRO?

IT IS JUST VERY HARD TO BELIEVE THAT PEOPLE WHO YOU DO LOOK UP TO AT ONE TIME OR ANOTHER CAN BE SO DECEITFUL!

MARTIAL ARTS IS COMMON KNOWLEDGE FOR ALL WHO SEEK ITS TRADITION TO FIND!

IT IS WHAT YOU YOURSELF PUT INTO YOUR TRAINING THAT MAKES THE DIFFERENCES!

AS FAR AS ALAN IS CONCERNED TO ME ... HE HAD TAUGHT ME A LOT ABOUT MYSELF.

BOTH INSIDE AS WELL AS OUT. IT IS MY ONLY WISH THAT SOMEDAY HE REALIZES HIS MISTAKES IN LIFE SO HE TOO CAN BE THE BEST HE CAN!

WE ALL MAKE MISTAKES IN LIFE. IT IS HOW WE LEARN FORM THEM AND ADAPT FROM THEM IN THE NEXT SITUATION THAT MY REFLECT IN WHOLE OR A PORTION OF OUR LAST MISTAKE.

FOR SOME PEOPLE THIS IS HOWEVER IMPOSSIABLE TO ACCOMPLISH.

MOVING ON HERE ARE SOME OF MY MANY THOUGHTS OF MY TIME SPENT WITH MASTER D ' ALLESSANDRO AND HIS TEACHINGS…

FOR MY EXTENSIVE TRAINING IN WEAPONS I HAD LEARNED SUM STRONG VALUES FROM ALAN.

THESE WERE APPLIED TO MY CONCEPTS OF THE FOLLOWING WEAPONS:

" STAFF ~ ESCRIMA ~ & KAMAS "

IT WAS BECAUSE OF THIS TRAINING I WAS ABLE TO SELF TEACH MYSELF THE REST OF THE WEAPONS THAT I PRACTICE TODAY.

" NUNCHAKU SINGLE & DOUBLE ~ SIAS ~ SWORD ~ CHAIN "

AS FAR AS MY ULTIMATE LESSON UNDER HIM IT IS WITH OUT DOUBT MY FIRST TEST FOR SHODAN!

SHODAN IS THE PROPER TERM AND FIRST OFFICAL GRADED RANK OF BLACKBELT. WE CALL ALL THESE LEVELS THE DAN RANKS.

THIS LESSON WILL BE FOREVER WITH ME! IT WAS BECAUSE OF THIS SINGLE ACT THAT MADE ME WHO I AM TODAY.

THANK YOU MASTER D ' ALLESSANDRO FOR THIS. IT WAS OUTSTANDING!

ANOTHER ASPECT I REALLY ENJOYED WITH ALAN WAS HIS SELF DEFENSE DRILLS.

HE HAD SO MANY TO TEST EACH SKILL THAT YOU WERE CURRENTLY LEARNING.

BUT OUT OF ALL OF THEM MY FAVORITE ONEWAS CALLED THE GAUNTLT!

I REFER TO THIS EXERCISE AS THE ZIPPER EFFECT!

THIS WAS A GREAT TRAINING DRILL. ESPECIALLY WHEN WE HAD A CLASS OF FIFTEEN OR MORE, AND MOST OF THE CLASS CONTAINED DAN RANKS!

IN THIS DRILL IT SIMULATED THE EFFECT OF WALKING DOWN AN ALLY WAY.

YOU NEVER KNEW WHO WAS GOING TO ATTACK YOU, OR IF THEY MIGHT HAVE A HIDDEN WEAPON AT HAND!

IT COULD HAVE BEEN STAGGERED, OR IT COULD HAVE BEEN EVERYONE WHO ATTACKED YOU!

THAT WAS THE BEAUTY. YOU JUST NEVER KNEW.

YOU WERE ASKED TO LEAVE THE ROOM. THEN ALAN WOULD PICK WHO WAS TO ATTACK AS WELL AS HOW TO ATTACK.

IT WOULD CONTAIN: FRONTAL AND BACK ATTACKS, PUNCHES OF VARIOUS PLACEMENT OR KICKS, AND SOMETIMES EITHER A KNIFE, BAT, OR GUN.

THIS EXERCISE WAS A HEART POUNDING EXPERIECE TO THE EXTREME!

THE MAIN REASON FOR MY LEAVING ALAN AND THE N.E.K.A. SCHOOL WAS DUE TO THE FOLLOWING:

WHEN I EXPRESSED MY OWN IDEAS FOR MY OWN SCHOOL, AND THE TIME CAME FOR ME TO ASK ALAN HIS OPINION OF THE PACKED I HAD WORKED ON FOR YEARS IT DIDN'T GO OVER WELL AT ALL!

AFTER THIS IT SEEMED LIKE EVERY OPPORTUNITY THAT CAME ALONG FOR ME TO ADVANCE IN MY TRAINING …

WHAT EVER IT MAY HAVE BEEN? WAS SIDE STEPPED.

I HAD FALLEN INTO THE CRACKS, AND I FELT LIKE THE BLACKSHEEP OF THE FAMILY ALL OF A SUDDEN.

AND FOR WHAT? … ALL BECAUSE I HAD EXPRESSED MY INTEREST FOR MY OWN SCHOOL!

FOR EXAMPLE: ALAN WROTE HIS FIRST BOOK. IT IS CALLED " *SELF - DEFENSE FOR MEN, WOMEN, AND CHILDREN.* "

IN THIS BOOK HE SPOKE ALL ABOUT HIS PRACTICAL SELF DEFENSE TECHNIQUES.

ALONG WITH STEP BY STEP PHOTOS USING VARIOUS BLACKBETS AND A FEW UNDERBELTS TOO.

THEN HE TALKED A LITTLE BIT ABOUT TERMINOLOGY AND THE MARTIAL ARTS.

TO ME THE BEST PART OF THE WHOLE BOOK WAS THE CHAPTER OF ABOUT THE AUTHOR.

THIS WAS VERY INTERESTING WERE AS THE REST WAS NOT OF INTEREST TO ME. DON'T GET ME WRONG IT WAS GOOD, BUT VERY BASIC.

THAN AGAIN THIS WAS THE WHOLE IDEA ANYWAYS. IT IS GEARED TO THE NOVICE.

ALSO IN HIS BOOK THERE WAS A CHAPTER TITLED " *WORDS FROM NEKA STUDENTS.* "

IN THIS SECTION THERE WERE PASSAGES WRITTEN BY BLACKBELT STUDENTS.

ALL THESE PASSAGES WERE ABOUT OUR INSTRUCTOR ALAN, AND THE NEKA SCHOOL IN GENERAL.

THE FUNNY PART ABOUT THIS IS THAT EVERY BLACKBELT IN THE SCHOOL EVEN THE TEENS HAD A PASSGE WRITTEN AND DOCUMENTED IN THIS BOOK.

EXCEPT FOR ME OF COURSE. MY THOUGHTS WERE NEVER ASKED NOR INCLUDED.

DID THIS BOTHER ME? WELL WOULDN'T IT BOTHER YOU? OF COURSE IT DID!

I WAS ONE OF THE SENIOR BLACKBELTS, AND INSTRUCTOR WHEN NEEDED TOO.

I WAS ALWAYS BEING ASKED TO TAKE OVER THE CLASSES.

ESPECIALLY WHEN ALAN WAS PREPARING FOR HIS NEXT DAN RANK WITH GRANDMASTER RODRIGUES.

HE TOOK AT THE TIME ALL THE OTHER ADULT BLACKBELTS TO DON PLACE OUT IN WARWICK RI TO HELP HIM TRAIN FOR HIS OWN ADVANCEMENT.

NEVER ONCE DURING THIS PERIOD OF TIME WAS I EVER THANKED FOR MY SERVICES OF TEACHING OR EVEN CONSIDERED TO GO WITH THEM.

NOT EVEN ONCE. IT WAS ALSO DURING THIS TIME PERIOD THAT I WAS A MEMBER OF THE UNITED STATES TEAM.

TEAM AMERICA, AND I WAS TRAVELING ALL OVER THE WORLD!

AND EACH AND EVERY TIME, AND WHEN I SAY EVERY I MEAN EVERY TIME I HAD AN INTERVIEW I MADE IT PERFECTLY CLEAR THAT ALAN D ' ALLESSADRO WAS MY SENSEI.

ALSO THAT I TRAINED AT THE NEKA SCHOOL AS WELL. THE DOJO AND ALANS NAME WERE LISTED IN FULL EACH TIME.

AS WELL AS THE CREDIT OF MY SUCCESS! WELL LETS SAY IT WAS ANOTHER HARD LESSON THAT I LEARNED!

I NEVER SHOULD HAVE DONE THAT. ESPECIALLY AFTER ALL THAT HAD HAPPENED AND WAS CURRENTLY GOING ON!

BUT I THOUGHT AT THE TIME IT WAS BEST TO REMAIN LOYAL. UNTIL I COULD FIGURE OUT WHAT MY NEXT MOVE WAS GOING TO HAVE TO BE?

ANYWAYS; THIS WOULD NEVER HAPPEN TO ME AGAIN! I WAS GOING TO MAKE SURE OF IT.

ALTHOUGH I HAVE TO THINK … ALAN MUST HAVE BEEN THINKING OF ME TO SOME DEGREE?

BECAUSE HE DID INCLUDE ONE PICTURE OF ME IN HIS BOOK.

THIS PICTURE CAN BE FOUND ON PAGE NINTYONE. IT IS LISTED AS: " *FROM LEFT: ALAN D ' ALLESSANDRO, MIKE FARADAY, AND APRIL D ' ALLESSANDRO / MARCH 2000.* "

THIS PICTURE WAS FROM AN AWARDS CEREMONY WHERE HIS DAUGHTER WAS INDUCTED INTO THE KRANE CIRCUITS WOMENS HALL OF FAME!

ON THIS SAME DAY, I WAS AWARDED TOO. I WAS NAMED BY KRANE AND LISTED IN THE BLACKBELT MAGAZINE CIRCUIT SECTION AS:

NUMBER ONE IN THE NATION FOR MY DIVISION IN KATA, WEAPONS, AND KUMITE. ALSO FOR THE SAME IN THE STATE OF MASS AS STATE CHAMPION.

SOMEDAY I WOULD LIKE TO BE NOMINATED INTO THE HALL OF FAME TOO.

THIS WOULD BE A GREAT ACHIEVEMENT, FOR WHICH I WOULD BE EXTREMELY PROUD OF TO SAY THE LEAST!

I ACTUALLY JUST DO NOT EVEN KNOW ANYMORE?

WHAT DOES IT TAKE TO EVEN GET AWARDED THIS HONOR? IS IT BASED ON HARD WORK AND ACHIEVEMENT LIKE IT SHOULD BE! … ?

OR MAYBE IS I JUST ANOTHER POLITICAL PART OF THE MARTIAL ARTS TODAY?

WITH ALL THAT I HAVE ACCOMPLISHED IN LIFE, IN MY TRAININGS, DURING MY TOURNAMENT YEARS, AS WELL AS THE TEACHING TO OTHERS, I HAVE NEVER ONCE HAD ANYBODY PUT ME UP FOR SUCH AN HONOR.

MAYBE THIS IS BECAUSE I MAKE TO MANY WAVES OF QUESTIONING OF CERTAIN PEOPLES INTEGRITY?

IT ALWAYS DID SEAM FUNNY TO ME THAT BEFORE ALL THIS DRAMA SO TO SPEAK I WAS ONE OF THE STUDENTS THAT WAS ASKED TO HELP OUT IN EVERYTHING.

ALL OF THE TIME. BUT NO MATTER HOW MUCH I WAS IN WONDERMENT I KNEW THAT STRIKE THREE HAD OCCURRED, AND IT WAS CLEARLY TIME TO MOVE ON.

I HAD TAKEN ALL THAT WAS GOING TO BE OFFERED UNTOME, AND NO MORE WAS GOING TO BE FURNISHED!

AT THIS POINT ALL I WAS DOING WAS WASTING MY TIME AS FAR AS MY TRAINING.

ALL THE FRIENDSHIPS HAD BEEN ENDED AT THE NEKA DOJO EXCEPT FOR MY ONE TRUE FRIEND MR. TARR.

WHEN THINKING OF THE PAST NOW PERHAPS THE MAIN REASON FOR ALAN AND MY CLASH THAT ENDED EVERYTHING WAS BECAUSE WE ACTUALLY WERE QUITE ALIKE IN MANY WAYS!

"" OUR STRIVE FOR ACHIEVEMENT AND BEING STRONGLY OPINIONATED? ""

AT THIS TIME IF THE CHANCE DID EVER PRESENT ITSELF FOR ME T WORK WITH ALAN AGAIN I WOULD.

I JUST DO NOT EVER SEE THIS HAPPENING THOUGH. NOT EVER…

ALSO LET THIS BE KNOWN: IF IT DID HAPPEN I WOUDN'T WANT TO SPEND ANY MONEY IN TRAINING WITH HIM AGAIN!

BUT RATHER I WOULD LIKE TO BE A SPECIAL GUEST OR INVITED TO AN EVENT TO AID IN THE TRAINING OF HIS STUDENTS.

THIS WOULD BE FINE, AND I WOULD ENJOY THIS VERY MUCH.

WHO KNOWS … ? SOMETIMES IN LIFE DIFFERENCES ARE PUT ASIDE TO MAKE WAY FOR A BETTER TOMORROW.

TRAINING WITH SENSEI TARR :

IRONICALLY WORKING WITH MR TARR IS ENLIGHENING! THE PART THAT IS SO IRONIC IS THAT MR TARR STILL TRAINS UNDER MASTER D' ALLESSANDRO TO THIS DAY.

SO I SUPPOSE IF YOU THINK ABOUT THE SITUATION WHEN I AM WORKING WITH SENSEI TARR IN AN ESSENSE I TOO WOULD BE STILL TRAINING UNDER ALAN AS WELL.

HOW FUNNY IS THIS? HOWEVER; THE ENLIGHTENMENT OF THIS IS THAT SENSEI TARR TODAY HAS HIS OWN IDEAS AS WELL.

IN HIS TRAINING AND FOR THE TRAINING OF THE STUDENTS THAT HE IS IN CHARGE OF THREW THE NEKA SCHOOL.

THESE CONCEPTS ARE VERY INTERESTING IN THEORY TO ME, AND THEY ARE ALSO ALL HIS OWN TECHNIQUES!

ANOTHER THING IS THAT THEY ARE COMPLETELY DIFFERENT FROM MY OWN VIEWS.

SO TOGETHER WE MAKE NOT ONLY A GREAT STUDENT TO TEACHER VISA VERSA, BUT AN AWESOME TEAM AS WELL! THIS IS WHAT IT SHOULD BE ABOUT.

SENSI TARR AND I WORK TOGETHER AS MUCH AS WE CAN IN LIFE TODAY.

BOTH IN THE MARTIAL ARTS AND SIDE BY SIDE AS LETTER CARRIERS FOR THE POSTAL SERVICE.

WHEN HE NEEDED HELP I WAS ABLE TO GET HIS FOOT INTO THE DOOR.

I LOVE THE DRILL HE HAS DEVELOPED FOR WHAT WE CALL COME - ALONG TECHNIQUES. ALSO CALLED JUJITSU.

HE ALSO HAS SOME VERY INTERESTING AS WELL AS EFFECTIVE GROUND TECHNIQUES TOO!

WHAT I LIKE THE MOST IS THAT ALL THESE TECHNIQUES HE HAS DEVELOPED HIMSELF!

AND FOR THIS I AM PROUD OF HIM. IT SHOWS HIS ABILITY TO BREAK AWAY AND THINK ON HIS OWN.

ABOVE ALL THE PART I LOVE MOST OF ALL ABOUT CHUCK IS … HE IS DOWN TO EARTH!

I ENJOY WATCHING HIM DEMONSTRATING HIS MATERIAL, AND THEN TRYING IT OUT!

WHEN EVER WE HAVE THE CHANCE TO WORK TOGETHER I FEEL A GREAT FEELING OF WISDOM.

THIS IS VERY REFRESHING. A HUGH CHANGE COMPARED TO OTHER TEACHERS THAT I HAVE ENDURED THREW THE YEARS!

FOR THIS I ALSO APPLAUD HIM. HE HAS BECOME A GREAT INSTRUCTOR, AND WHEN HIS TIME ARRIVES HE WILL MAKE A FINE MASTER OF THE MARTIAL ARTS.

SINCE I FIRST WROTE THIS BOOK IN THE FIRST PRIVATE EDITION BACK IN 2009 SENSEI TARR IS ACTUALLY GOING BEFORE A NEWLY DEVELOPED PANEL CONSISTING OF TEN GRANDMASTERS NEXT MAY 2011.

ON THIS DAY HE WILL BE TESTING FOR HIS GODAN WHICH ONCE COMPLETED WILL MAKE HIM A YOUNG MASTER!

I BELIEVE IN HIM AND WILL BE HELPING HIM PREPARE FOR THIS GREAT SUCCESS IN THE MONTHS TO COME.

TIME PERIOD NOW IS 11 / 08 / 10. JUST SO YOU READER DO NOT GET CONFUSED.

JUST TO NAME A COUPLE OF THE GRANDMASTERS THAT ARE GOING TO BE PRESENT ON THIS NEWLY DEVELOPED PANEL:

THEY ARE GRANDMASTER DON RODRIGUES AND GRANDMASTER GEORGE PESARE.

IT IS MY STRONG BELIEF THAT WITHOUT SENSEI TARR AND HIS CLEAR VISIONS INTO THE ARTS THE N.E.K.A. SCHOOL WOULDN'T BE THE SAME.

IN MY OPINION THE ENROLLMENT TO THIS SCHOOL WOULD WITHER! THEY ARE INDEED LUCKY TO HAVE HIM!

SENSEI TARR AND I PROGRESSED THREW THE RANKS TOGETHER AT THE NEW ENGLAND KARATE ACADEMY.

CHUCK AT THAT TIME WAS THREE LEVELS AHEAD OF ME BACK IN THE MIDDLE NINTIES.

WE BECAME GOOD FRIENDS AND STUCK TOGETHER EVER SINCE.

HE NOW FEELS THE SAME WAY I DID BACK THEN BEFORE I LEFT THE N.E.K.A. SCHOOL.

HE SEES EVEN MORE TODAY THAT IS UNFAIR AND NOT JUST THEN I DID WHEN I WAS IN ATTENDANCE.

HOWEVER; HE STILL FOR HIS OWN REASONS FOR WHICH HE HAS REFERED TO ME IN CONFIDENCE ISN'T READY TO PART WAYS JUST YET.

SO WITH HIS REQUEST FOR HIS WISHES I RESPECT THEM, AND WILL NOT MENTION THEIR STRUCTOR

CHUCK AND I HAVE LONG WANTED TO OPEN UP OUR OWN DOJO TOGETHER.

WE HAVE TALKED ABOUT THIS FOR YEARS NOW. THE ECONOMY TODAY IS JUST NOT STABLE ENOUGH TO TAKE ACTION.

FIRST WE WOULD HAVE TO GET AN INVESTOR TO GET STARTED, BUT MORE THAN THIS THERE ARE SOME MANY DOJO OUT THERE WE WOULD HAVE TO FIGHT TO GAIN ENROLLMENT INTO OUR SCHOOL!

WE BOTH STRONGLY BELIEVE THAT OUR SCHOOL WOULD BE MORE OF A BENEFIT TO THE TRAINING OF THOSE WHO WOULD BE INTERESTED.

HOWEVER WASTING MONEY INTO A NEW BUSINESS FOR WHICH WE CAN HAVE NO PROMISES FOR AS TO SUCCESS TO THE RATIO OF PUPILS IS ONE ASPECT WE CAN NOT AFFORD AT THIS PRESENT TIME!

WE WISH WE COULD. WE ALSO JOKE ABOUT HOW THE CLASSES WOULD BE TAUGHT.

CHUCK CALLES ME THE HARD MASTER AND I CALL HIM THE SOFT MASTER.

THIS IS BECAUSE WHEN IT COMES TO OUR TRAINING I PERFER AND TAKE PRIDE IN GOING DOWN THE ROAD LESS TRAVELED!

CHUCK UNLIKE ME PEFERS CLASSES TAUGHT INSIDE AND DOESN'T LIKE MY HARD WORKOUTS OR TRAING REGIME.

HE SAYS IT IS OK ONCE IN A WHILE BUT NOT EACH AND EVERY CLASS.

THIS IS GOOD BECAUSE HE WILL TAKE THE TIME TO TEACH THE KIDS FOR WHAT I DO NOT BELIEVE IN.

MAIN REASON BEING THAT MY CLASSES ARE GEARED FOR HARD TRAINING FOR THE WORLD WE LIVE IN TODAY.

WE MAKE AN EXECELLENT YING AND YANG COMBINATION. HOPEFULLY ONE DAY OUR DREAM WILL COME TRUE!

OUR SCHOOL WOULD OFFER TWO DIFFERENT TYPES OF TRAINING.

SENSEI TARR WOULD TEACH HIS VERSION OF KENPO AND MINE WOULD BE MY SYSTEM OF TAIKYOKUKEN KEN SHO RYU.

CHUCK HAS NO PROBLEMS WITH MY TEACHING METHODS. HE JUST THINKS I AM TOTALITY CRAZY!

WITH MY PRIVATE GROUP AND ALL THE HARSH WEATHER TRAINING.

EARILER ON I HAD MENTIONED THT MY WIFES UNCLE DENY WAS LIKE A BROTHER TO ME, AND THAT HE WAS ONE OF THREE.

WELL CHUCK IS NUMBER TWO, AND ALSO MENTIONED AGAIN SENSEI JOHN IS NUMBER THREE.

CHUCK AND I ARE CONSTANTLY LEARNING FROM ONE ANOTHER EVERYDAY.

IT IS ALWAYS A GREAT PLEASURE IN LIFE TO HAVE AT LEAST A FEW PEOPLE YOU CAN TRUST IN. CHUCK IS ONE OF THESE VERY FEW!

NOW IF I HAD TO NARROW DOWN ONE EVENT I WILL TRULY NEVER FORGET IN MY TRAINING WITH CHUCK IT WOULD BE WHEN HE TESTED ME FOR MY FORTH DAN IN HIS STYLE OF KENPO!

IT WAS A DAY TO REMEMBER. I WAS GIVEN A FIVE WEEK NOTICE. THEN I WAS TOLD BE READY! THIS WAS IT.

NOTHING MORE AND NOTHING LESS.

WHEN THE DAY CAME SENSEI TARR SHOWED UP WITH ANOTHER ONE OF HIS STUDENTS.

HIS NAME WAS ARITIAN. HE WAS FROM BRAZIL, AND HE WAS ALMOST HALF MY AGE.

I HAD WORKED WITH HIM NOW AND THEN, BUT I REALLY DIDN'T KNOW MUCH ABOUT THIS YOUNG MAN.

EXCEPT HE WAS VERY FAST AND QUITE LIMBER!

THIS TEST TOOK FOUR AND ONE HALF HOURS TO COMPLETE. NO BREAKS AND CONSTANT AGRESSION.

WE PERFORMED A LOT OF FREE STYLE TECHNIQUES, AND LOTS OF REVIEW OF MANY BASIC STRIKES.

THEN I HAD TO DO MY ON KATAS AND EXPLAIN THEM IN DEEPTH IN THE BUNKI APPLICATION.

NEXT WE DID SOME OPEN HANDED SPARRING WITH JUJITSU. HOWEVER THE BEST WAS AT THE END.

WE ENGAGED ONE ANOTHER WITH WEAPONS! FIRST WE DID THE STAFF VS. STAFF. THIS IS SENSEI TARRS FAVORITE WEAPON!

THEN WE USED THE STAFF AGAINST THE KAMA, SIA, ESCRIMA STICKS, AND LAST MY FAVORITE WEAPON THE NUNCHAKU!

EACH SEGMENT WAS DONE IN THE FOLLOWING WAY:

" *BLOCKING ~ STRIKING ~ THEN SELFDEFENSE!* "

IT WAS ONE AWESOME DAY AND A GREAT TEST! I LOVED IT. THIS YOUNG MAN REALLY MADE IT HARD FOR ME.

SENSEI TARR EXPLAINED HIS REASON FOR THIS WAS TO SEE HOW FAR AN OLDER MAN COULD GO AND KEEP UP WITH THE YOUNGER MAN.

THIS WAS PROFOUNDLY AN EXEMPLARITY WAY TO TEST MY ABILITIES! FOR THIS I THANK YOU SENEI TARR.

THIS WAS ANOTHER GREAT MEMORY FOR ME. MR TARR IS ALL ABOUT WHAT A TRUE MARTIAL ARTIST SHOULD STRIVE TO BECOME!

HE IS WELL ROUNDED AND HAS COMPASSION FOR HIS STUDENTS. HE PUTS ALL OF THEM FIRST EVEN BEFORE HIS OWN NEEDS. ALWAYS!

I WANT IT TO BE REALIZED AND KNOWN OR THE RECORD THAT I REFER TO SENSEI TARR AS A MASTER OF THE ARTS ALREADY.

STRONGLY DUE TO THE FACT THAT I KNOW THE TRUTH OF HOW HIS CONTINUED FRIENDSHIP WITH ME HAS COST HIM GREATLY ON HIS ADVANCEMENT IN HIS TRAINING WITH ALAN!

MASTER D ' ALLESSANDRO IS VERY LUCKY TO STILL HAVE SENSEI TARR IN HIS TREE, AND I HOPE HE KNOWS IT?

"" MASTER CHUCK TARR & SENSEI JOHN WORKING IT OUT ... ""

TRAINING WITH MASTER WAYNE MELLO :

SHIHAN WAYNE MELLO HAS HIMSELF JUST RECENTLY ATTAINED HIS 7TH DEGREE BLACKBELT IN THE ART OF SHOTOKAN KARATE!

HE BEGAN HIS TRAINING IN THE LATE 1970'S UNDER THE INSTRUCTION OF HANSHI JOHN ALMEDIA.

TODAY SHIHAN MELLO CONTINUES TO TRAIN, INSTRUCT, AND STILL COMPETE IN THE WORLD OF MARTIAL ARTS.

HE IS A MEMBER OF THE I.P.P.O.N.E. CIRCUIT AND WIDELY KNOWN THROUGHT THE PROFESSIONAL KARATE CIRCUIT TOO.

MASTER MELLO IS ALSO THE VICE PRESIDENT OF ALMEDIA'S INTERNATIONAL KARATE ASSOCIATION.

ALSO REFERED TO AND KNOWN AS { A.I.K.A. }

MASTER MELLO HAS COMPETED IN MANY NATIONAL AS WELL AS INTERNATIONAL KARATE TOURNAMENTS, AND HOLDS NUMEROUS IMPRESSIVE TITLES!

HE CURRENTLY OWNS AND OPERATES HIS DOJO; MELLO'S MARTIAL ARTS CENTER.

THIS IS LOCATED IN THE TOWN OF OXFORD MA 01505.

BESIDES ALL THIS MASTER MELLO IS THE PROMOTER OF THE AREAS FAMOUS TOURNAMENT FOR MANY YEARS!

IT IS CALLED THE WORCESTER CLASSIC. THIS TOURNAMENT IS KNOWN TO BE ONE OF THE MOST IF NOT THE CLASSIEST IN THE LOCAL AREA.

MR MELLO IS BELIEVED TO BE ONE OF THE MOST KNOWLEDGEABLE INSTRUCTORS AROUND REGARDING THE TRAINING OF THE ART OF TRADITIONAL JAPANESE SHOTOKAN KARATE!

AND I FULLY AGREE TO THIS STATEMENT WHICH IS POSTED ON HIS INTERNET WEB SITE.

THIS INFORMATION CAN BE READILY FOUND VIA FACEBOOK LISTED UNDER MELLOS MARTIAL ARTS CENTER.

TRAINING WITH WAYNE WAS AN UPLIFTING EXPERIENCE! I REALLY ENJOYED THE STUDING OF THE ART OF SHOTOKAN!

I KNEW WAYNE FROM WAY BACK ACTUALLY EVEN BEFORE I HAD MET ALAN.

WHILE I WAS COMPETING IN THE I.O.P.P.O.N.E. CIRCUIT AS WELL.

I JUST NEVER SOUGHT HIS TRAINING UNTIL THE SUMMER OF 2001. SO I COULD GET SOME INSIGHT INTO HIS ART WHICH WOULD HELP ME LATER ON IN THE WORLD GAMES.

I HAD CALLED HIM ON THE PHONE ONE DAY OUT OF THE BLUE TO SEE IF HE REMEMBERED ME?

AND HE DID. SO I THEN ASKED HIM IF HE WOULD HELP ME PREPARE FOR THE NEXT WORLD GAMES THAT I WAS TAKING PART IN?

THIS WAS GOING TO BE IN IRELAND. KILLARNEY IRELAND TO BE PERCISE.

HE SAID YES. *" BUT WHAT ARE YOU LOOKING FOR HE ASKED? "*

I SAID: *" I WANTED TOLEARN THE POWER AND THE BEAUTY OF JAPANESE TRADITIONAL KATAS. "*

AND I KNOW THAT YOU ARE THE BEST AROUND FOR THIS!

SO WE STARTED. WAYNE TOOK ME IN WITHOUT QUESTION.

WE WORKED PRIVATELY A COUPLE OF TIMES A WEEK FOR ABOUT NINE MONTHS.

IT WAS IN THIS TIME PERIOD THAT MR. D ' ALLESSANDRO FOUND OUT I WAS GOING TO WAYNE FOR PRIVATE INSTRUCTION.

WELL THIS TOO DIDN'T WIN ME ANY PRIVILEGES AT N.E.K.A! BUT ALAN DIDN'T STUDY SHOTOKAN.

HE TAUGHT AND STUDIED KENPO. BOTH ARE VERY DIFFERENT!

ALAN HAD THEN BECOME OBSESSED WITH THE FACT THAT I WAS SHARING SECRETS OF KENPO WTH WAYNE!

JUST ANOTHER THING I COULDN'T BELIEVE.

WAYNE WAS AND TO THIS DAY IS NOT THAT KIND OF MAN! IT IS WAY BENETH HIS STANDARDS.

THIS WAS UNTIL I FOUND OUT HIS THOUGHTS AS TO ME GOING TO GRANDMASTER VAN CLIEF A FEW YEARS LATER!

THIS HAS NO REVELATION TO THIS BOOK RIGHT NOW. HOWEVER; IN MY NEXT BOOK TO COME AFTER " *LIMELIGHT TO THE DEVIL'S PARADISE* " *IT WILL.*

I JUST WANT TO PUT THE THOUGH INTO THE WORKS TO HOOK YOU THE READER IN LATER.

BELIEVE ME IT WAS A SHOCK TO ME! I NEVER INTENDED THE ORDER OF MY BIOS TO GET PUBLISHED IN THE WAY THEY DID.

BUT IN DOING SO IT LEAD TO THE REVISE OF THIS BOOK AND HAS BECOME A WELL SUITED COMPLIMENT.

BESIDES I LIKE HOW TRUE LIFE IRONY PLAYS A REVOLVING ROLE OF HIDDEN PASSAGE. AS FAR AS I AM CONCERNED IT MAKES FOR A GREAT READ!

THE BEST PART OF ALL MY WRITINGS AGAIN IS THE FACT NO MATTER HOW STRANGE THING FALL INTO PLAY....

THEY ARE ALL TRUE, AND HAVE HAPPENED IN THE COURSE OF MY LIFE. IT JUST DOES GOTO SHOW YOU HOW FAR SOCIETY HAS GONE FOR THE WORST!

GETTING BACK ON TRACK THIS IS WHY IN 2004 AFTER BEING ON MY OWN FOR A COUPLE OF YEARS NOW...

I WENT TO TRAIN WITH MASTER MELLO AND HIS CREW FULL TIME.

ALSO DURING THIS TIME I WAS STILL DOING MY OWN THING WITH MY PRIVATE STUDENTS AND WORKING WITH SENSEI TARR ON THE SIDE.

I WAS VERY BUSY TO SAY THE LEAST. I DO NOT THINK EVERYONE REALIZED HOW MANY TASKS I WAS PERFORMING OR WITH WHO.

BUT I MANAGED TO KEEP EVERYTHING IN ITS PERSPECTIVE AND CONTINUE THREW!

NOW MY FIRST NIGHT AT MELLOS MARTIAL ARTS CENTER IS ANOTHER GREAT STORY IN MY TRAINING!

EACH SECTION OF YOUR LIFE CONTAINS A FAVORITE MEMORY. IN MY TIME AT MELLO'S THIS IS INDEED THE ONE.

I HAD TALKED TO SHIHAN MELLO THE NIGHT BEFORE I WAS SUPPOSED TO START.

JUST TO MAKE SURE EVERYTHING WAS COOL, AND HE KNEW I WAS STILL COMING.

SO WHEN I GOT TO HIS DOJO THE NEXT EVENING, AND HE WASN'T THEIR … THIS IS HOW IT PLAYED OUT.

FIRST OF ALL MASTER MELLO NEVER MENTIONED THE FACT TO HIS INSTRUCTORS THAT I WAS GOING TO BE COMING OVER AT ALL.

SO THE HEAD INSTRUCTOR THAT WAS IN CHARGE THAT EVENING WHO WAS A VERY HUGH MAN ASKED IF HE COULD HELP ME?

BUT HE SAID IT IN A MANNER WHICH WOULD LEAVE MOST PEOPLE TO WALK RIGHT BACK OUT THE DOOR THEY CAME INTO. KNOW WHAT I MEAN?

I TOLD HIM SURE. THEN I EXPLAINED TO HIM ABOUT THE CONVERSATION MASTER MELLO AND I HAD THE DY BEFORE.

THE PROBLEM HERE WAS THE FACT THAT FOR ALL THE YEARS I TRAINED PRIVATELY WITH WAYNE NOBODY HAD EVER SEEN ME.

WE PRETTY MUCH GOT TOGETHER VERY EARLY IN THE MORNING HOURS.

THIS INSTRUCTOR THEN TOLD ME OK THEN GO GET DRESSED! SO I DID.

WHEN I CAME OUT WEARING MY BLACKBELT WITH ALL MY STRIPS ON IT I RECEIVED THE STARE DOWN.

THERE WERE TWENTY PUPILS THERE THAT NIGHT JUST LOOKING AT ME!

BUT THIS DIDN'T BOTHER ME MUCH. THEN THE HEAD GUY CAME BACK UP TO ME AND SAID:

"" ARE YOU SURE YOU WANT TO PLAY TONIGHT? … ""

MY REPLY TO HIM CLEAR AND PERCISE WAS YES I DO. SO HE SAID TO ME NEXT:

"" THE WHOLE NIGHT WE ARE GOING TO BANG! "'

IN THE DAYS THAT FOLLOWED THIS NIGHT AND THE EVENTS I NEVER ASKED WAYNE IF THIS WAS MY AUDITION OR NOT?

BUT I STRONGLY BELIEVE THAT IT WAS! LETS SAY IT WASN'T THE EASIEST OF NIGHTS FOR ME, BUT I MADE IT THREW JUST FINE.

I HAD ALSO ON THIS NIGHT GAINED THE RESPECT OF THOSE TWENTY STUDENTS FOR WHAT I THEY THOUGHT WAS GOING TO BE A BEAT DOWN.

I DID THE BEST I COULD AND MADE IT THREW. THIS IS ALL THAT COUNTED IN MY MIND.

AFTER TWENTY ROUNDS WITH EACH PERSON THERE FOR TWO MINUTES APIECE WITH A THIRTY SECOND REST INBETWEEN WAS QUITE THE WORKOUT!

I WAS NOW CONSIDERED TO BE ONE OF THEM. A MEMBER OF THE SHOTOKAN FAMILY.

THIS WAS NOT ONLY AN INTERESTING NIGHT, BUT WAS JUST LIKE OUT OF A COMIC BOOK.

THE NEXT DAY I WAS REAL SORE! TO SAY THE LEAST! BUT YET I ALSO FELT GREAT FOR SURVIVING THIS TASK PUT BEFORE ME.

THE VERY NEXT CLASS I WENT TO THE SAME TWENTY GUYS WERE THERE AS WELL AS WAYNE, AND I WAS ASKED:

"" SO YOU ACTUALLY CAME BACK FOR MORE ...? "" THIS WAS SPOKEN BY ONE DONNY OLESKI, AND WAYNE MELLO.

I SAID WITH A SMILE: *"" YES! ""* THEN THEY BOTH SAID OK THAN YOUR COOL WITH US.

AND THAT WAS THAT, AND SO BEGAN MY FULL TIME TRAINING IN THE ART OF SHOTOKAN.

WHILE UNDER SHIHAN MELLOS DIRECTION TWO OF MY SKILLS HAD GREATLY IMPROVED.

THE FIRST ONE WAS MY KICKING. I HAVE TROUBLE WITH MY FEET ACTUALLY DUE TO A CONDITION CALLED PLANTERS FOOT!

THIS IS DUE TO ALL THE YEARS OF POUNDING THE ROUTE AS A LETTER CARRIER.

THEN WITH MY KNEES RESULTING AGAIN FROM ALL THE POUNDING EACH AND EVERYDAY.

I ONCE WORE A PEDOMETER TO WORK TO SEE HOW FAR I ACTUALLY WALKED IN THE COURSE OF A WORKDAY.

FROM THE TIME I LEFT MY FRONT DOOR UNTIL THE TIME I CAME BACK HOME I HAD MEASURED A DISTANCE OF 14.7 MILES.

NOW TIMES THAT AT FIVE DAYS A WEEK FOR TWELVE MONTHS A YEAR!

SO YES TIME IN AND TIME OUT I DO HAVE PROBLEMS WITH KICKING. IT SEEMS TO ALWAYS BE WHEN I LEAST APPERICATE IT TOO!

LIKE WHEN FILIMING DVDS! ALTHOUGH WITH THIS PROBLEM MY KICKS DID GROW STRONGER AND FASTER TOO!

THE SECOND WAS IN MY KUMITE. ALSO REFERED TO AS SPARRING. WE SPARRED EACH AND EVERY CLASS WITH NO EXCEPTIONS!

THIS IS HOW WE STARTED AND ENDED ALL CLASSES. ALL OF THE TIME!

ONE OF THE HARDEST CLASSES WE DID ONCE A MONTH WAS A TOTAL SPARRING CLASS.

IN THIS CLASS THERE WAS NO SPECIFIC ENDING TIME TO THE NIGHTS TRAINING.

IT WORKED LIKE THIS: EVERYONE IN ATTENDANCE THAT EVENING LINED UP AGAINST THE WALL.

THE FIRST TWO WENT OUT INTO THE CENTER OF THE FLOOR, AND SPARRED FOR TWO MINUTES.

THEN THE FIRST GUY FROM THE LINE STAYED IN FOR THE REMAINDER OF THE BODIES LEFT UP AGAINST THE WALL!

WHILE THE SECOND WENT BACK TO THE END OF THE LINE. EACH PERSON DID THIS UNTIL WE WENT THREW THE WHOLE CLASS!

BETWEEN EACH FIGHT YOU WERE LUCK TO GET A ONE MINUTE REST.

IF YOUR FIGHT WASN'T MOVING ALONG FAST ENOUGH YOUR BREAK WAS CUT TO THIRTY SECONDS!

WE ALL HAD THIRTY SECOND BREAKS AFTER A WHILE. THIS IS NO EASY TRAINING TO UNDER GO.

THIS TYPE OF DRILL REALLY SHOWED YOU WHERE YOU STOOD! ESPECIALLY IN THE CARDIO DEPARTMENT.

IF YOU DIDN'T LEARN THE MEANING OF DRIVE AND HOW TO DIG DEEP DOWN WITHIN YOURSELF THEN YOU WOULD NEVER MAKE IT THREW THIS CLASS!

WAYNE WAS A TRUE MASTER. A TRADITONAL MARTIAL ARTS MASTER AT THAT!

HE TOLD YOU WHAT HE THOUGHT, AND WHY ALL THE TIME SO YOU COULD WORK TO IMPROVE YOU FAULTS.

THIS WAS GREAT! CONSTRUCTIVE CRITIQUING IS WHAT MAKES FOR A GREAT MASTER.

HE NEVER TALKED DOWN TO YOU, BUT HE DID MAKE HIS POINTS TO YOU UNDERSTOOD FOR THE BETTERMENT OF YOUR TRAINING!

IT WAS TRAINING FIRST FRENDSHIP SECOND. HOWEVER AS FAR AS ADVANCEMENT WAS CONCERNED I WAS NEVER ASKED.

NOT EVEN AFTER YEARS OF TRAINING WITH MASTER MELLO. THEN I DO HAVE TO SAY AFTER ABOUT TWO YEARS MAYBE A LITTLE BIT MORE I WAS ADDRESSED AS A SEMPI.

IN JAPENESE AND THE TRAINING OF SHOTOKAN A SEMPI IS REFERED TO AS A BLACKBELT INSTRUCTOR.

EVEN THOUGH I NEVER FORMALLY TESTED FOR RANK IN THIS SYSTEM.

I HAD LEARNED ALL I WAS SUPPOSED TO FROM WHITE LEVEL TO SHODAN LEVEL, BUT I WAS NEVER GRANTED A TESTING OPPORTUNITY.

MY BELIEF WAS THIS WAS DUE TO WHAT I HAD REFERED TO AS MARTIAL ART POLITICS.

I MAY BE WRONG ABOUT THIS FACT WHO KNOWS? ALTHOUGH WHEN I LEFT WAYNE IT WAS ON WHAT I THOUGHT WAS GREAT TERMS.

I WAS TOLD THAT WHEN EVER I WANTED TO COME TRAIN AGAIN JUST TO WALK THREW THE DOOR.

MY RESPONSE TO THIS WAS: "" THANK YOU SHIHAN MELLO FOR EVERYTHING, AND I WILL. ""

HOWEVER I HAVE SO MUCH ROLLING THREW MY MIND ABOUT LIFE THAT I NEED TO STOP MY TRAINING WITH YOU FOR NOW.

BUT WHAT I DIDN'T TELL HIM WAS THAT I WAS GOING BACK FULLY TO MY OWN BELIEFS AND KEEP WORKING WITH SENSEI TARR TOO.

I DO REMEMBER THOUGH ONE NIGHT NOT TOO MUCH BEFORE I MADE THIS DECISION, AFTER I HAD TAUGHT ONE OF MY SPECIAL CLASSES FOR HIS STUDENTS…

WAYNE HAD PULLED ME ASIDE AND SAID TO ME THESE WORDS:

"" MICHAEL … … IF YOU WANT TO BECOME A TRUE MASTER IN THE MARTIAL ARTS THEN YOU NEED TO STICK WITH ONE STYLE OF TRAINING! ""

SO PERHAPS REALLY WAYNE DID KNOW WHAT WAS GOING ON IN MY MIND?

BY TELLING ME THIS. MAYBE HE WANTED ME TO FIGURE IT OUT FOR MYSELF?

BUT IF I COULDN'T DO IT, AND WASN'T READY YET TO MAKE THIS TOUGH DECISION I WOULD STILL BE WELCOME INTO HIS HOUSE.

SO AGAIN I SAY TO HIM … YOU ARE A GREAT MASTER! MANY THANKS TO YOU FOR ALL YOUR TEACHINGS TO ME.

I HAVE NO PROBLEM SENDING ANYBODY TO MR MELLO FOR TRAINING.

IN FACT WHEN I AM APPROACHED, AND ASKED ABOUT HOW I TEACH IF THEY ARE NOT INTO THE WAY I GO ABOUT MY TRAINING OR IF THEY ARE KIDS I SEND THEM TO HIS DOJO!

THAT IS UNTIL RECENT EVENTS FOR WHICH WILL NOT BE REVEALED UNTIL MY NEXT BOOK WHICH TAKES PLACE AFTER THE LIMELIGHT BOOK.

MY TYPE OF TRAINING IS NOT FOR CHILDREN! PLEASE DO COME TO ME WHEN YOU ARE AN ADULT AND WANT TO MAKE A SERIOUS COMMITMENT.

UNTIL FEBRUARY OF 2009 I WAS STILL SENDING STUDENTS HIS WAY. WHETHER OR NOT THESE PEOPLE ACTUALLY SIGNED UP OR EVEN TRIED A CLASS I WILL NEVER KNOW.

BESIDES SHIHAN MELLO THERE IS ONLY ONE OTHER WHO IN MY EYES IS UP AND COMING TO THE AREA.

I WILL GET TO THIS PERSON IN THE CHAPTERS AHEAD. I SINCERELY HOPE BOTH WILL CONTINUE IN THEIR PRACTICES OF STRONG TRADITION!

EVEN THOUGH I HAVE A DIFFERENT OPINION OF SHIHAN MELLO THESE DAYS AS FAR AS HIS FEELINGS TOWARD ME THE FACT REMAINS THE SAME.

HIS TRADITIONS OF TRAINING WITHIN HIS ART OF SHOTOKAN ARE THE BEST AROUND, AND SOUGHT AFTER BY MANY IN THE AREA BOTH LOCAL AND FAR.

"" KEEPING IT TRADITIONAL ""

TRAINING WITH MY STUDENT :

AS I HAD MENTIONED BEFORE IN DETAIL KAITI IS AN UNBELIEVABLE STUDENT!

IT DOESN'T MATTER WHAT I THROUGH HER WAY … SHE JUST KEEPS ON COMING BACK FOR MORE!

SHE HAS THE POTENTIAL OF WHAT WE REFER TO AS THE WARRIORS SPIRIT.

HOW FAR SHE DEVELOPS THIS IS UP TO HER? AS FOR NOW SHE IS HEADED ON THE RIGHT PATH.

IT HAS NO BEARING IN LIFE TO HOW LONG THIS MAY TAKE HER. FOR IT COULD TAKE A LIFE TIME.

NEVER THE LESS I BELIEVE IN HER, AND I WILL HELP HER EACH STEP OF THE WAY.

SO RATHER THAN TELLING MY COMPLETE THOUGHTS OF HER TRAINING I HAVE DECIDED TO LET HER TELL YOU IN HER WORDS.

ON TUESDAY EVENING THE TWENTYSEVENTH OF NOVEMBER 2009 BEFORE WE OFFICIALLY STARTED OUR SESSION …

I GAVE HER TEN MINUTES TO WRITE THE FOLLOWING PASSAGE. THE SUBJECT WAS: WHAT SHE THOUGHT OF HER TRAINING WITH ME?

HERE IS WHAT SHE WROTE THIS NIGHT ON THE SPOT WITHOUT HESITATION.

BY : MS. KAITI FLYNN

"" MY INDOCTRINATION INTO THIS LIFESTYLE BEGAN WITH A RESPECT FOR THE REALISM ENCOMPASSED WITHIN THE PRACTICE OF THE ART.

THE PHASE PRACTICE OF THE ART IS SIGNIFICANT, BECAUSE THERE ARE MANY INTERPRETATION'S OF THIS…

INTERPRETATION INVOLVED PRACTICING STRIKES, DOCTRINES, AND FORM OUTDOORS YEAR ROUND IN NEW ENGLAND!

IT INVOLVED PUSH UPS IN THE SNOW, RUNNING WITH ONLY FRIGID AIR IN ONES LUNGS, AND MOST CONTENTIOUS OF ALL …

HUMAN CONTACT! IN OTHER WORDS YOU WERE ACTUALLY MEANT TO STRIKE ONE ANOTHER!

OF ALL THINGS IN A KARATE CLASS.

HOWEVER; ALL OF THESE CUSTOMS SEEMED TO FIT WITHOUT CONTRADICTION IN THE TEACHINGS.

IN THE GREAT AND HONORABLE TRADITION OF ACIENT ARTISTS WE WOULD WORK FOR IT! WE WOULD EARN IT!

THE CATLYST FOR MY UNDERSTANDING OF WHY WE CONDUCTED OURSELVES THIS WAY CAME IN TWO PARTS:

THE FIRST WAS WHEN OUR SENSEI { MR. FARADAY } TOLD US HOW BLACKBELTS BECAME BLACKBELTS LONG BEFORE KARATE CLASSES COULD BE ATTENDED BY ANYONE IN A SUBURAN SRTIP MALL.

AN INDIVIDUAL BEGINS WITH A WHITEBELT, AND THEY ONLY BECAME A BLACKBELT WHEN DIRT, SWEAT, AND BLOOD STAINS TURNED THEIR ONCE WHITEBELT BEYOND REPAIR!

ANOTHER PART OF MY UNDERSTANDING CAME WHEN IN A PERTICULAR CLASS WE WERE FACED WITH A REAL WORLD SITUATION, AND SENSEI FARADAY STATED THE FOLLOWING:

IF SOMEONE ATTACKS YOU ... YOU WANT TO MAKE SURE THEY CAN NOT ATTACK ANYONE EVER AGAIN. BRILLANT!

AT THAT TIME THE PROCERBIAL LIGHT BULB WENT OFF!

THESE CIRCUMSTANCES ALLOWED A HIGH STRUNG, OPINIONATED FEMALE WITH A PROBLEM WITH AUTHORITY ...

LEARN TO CHANNEL ENERGY, INTO SOMETHING SHE RESPECTED, AND BEGAN TO RESPECT THE WORDS AND ORDERS OF MY SENSEI!

MR. FARADAY " "

UPON READING LATER ON THAT EVENING WHAT MS. FLYNN HAD WROTE ... THE FEELING OF OVER WHELMING JOY HAD WARMED MY HEART!

HERE IS A WOMEN WHO CAME TO ME FROM THE ADVICE OF A FRIEND SHE HAD.

WHEN SHE STARTED TRAINING WITH ME SHE WAS IN AFFECT AFRAID OF HER OWN SHADOW.

NOW SHE HAS BECOME A SELF ASSURED WOMAN! WITH THE CONFIDENCE OF A TRUE WARRIOR!

ONE THING IS FOR SURE. I DO NOT HAVE ANY WORRY ABOUT HER MAKING IT HOME ALONE AFTER A SOCIAL EVENT.

JUST IMAGINE THIS THOUGHT… IF YOUR TEACHINGS OF THE MARTIAL ARTS COULD HAVE SUCH AN IMPACT OF THIS MAGNITUDE IN EVERY STUDENT IN THIS FASHION?

THE POSSIABLITIES WOULD BE BOUNTIFULL!

FROM THE TRAINING THAT I HAD PROVIDED, AND SHALL CONTINUE TO PROVIDE TO NOT ONLY KAITI BUT TO ALL OF THOSE WHO SEEK IT.

"" THE PATH TOWARDS KNOWLEDGE ""

SOME OF MY PERSONAL FAVORITE DRILLS :

{ WORKING OUT }

BEFORE WE GET INTO THE PHRASE OF WORKING OUT I DO BELIEVE THAT STRECTCHING IS VERY IMPORTANT!

IN DOING THIS IT ALLOWS THE MUSCLES TO BECOME WARM AND MORE LIMBER.

THIS LEADS TO NOT ONLY LESS INJURY, BUT IT ALSO HELPS STRENGTHEN THE MUSCLES YOU ARE WORKING ON TOO.

THE ACTUAL BREAK DOWN, AND REBUILDING PROCESS OF THE MUSCLE TISSUE FOR THE AID IN THE PREVENTION OF TRAINING INJURIES.

HOWEVER; IT IS MY BELIEF THAT THIS SHOULD BE DONE ON YOUR OWN TIME.

MY REASON BEING THIS: WHEN THE TIME MAY COME FOR YOU TO DEFEND YOURSELF OR A LOVED ONE THERE IS NO TIME TO STRETCH!

YOU MUST BE READY TO REACT! THERE IS NO TIME FOR ANYTHING ELSE.

SO DURING MY TRAINING THIS IS MY REASON OF BEING AS TO THIS TOPIC.

YOU CAN NOT ASK AN ATTACKER TO WAIT FOR YOU! BECAUSE YOU DIDN'T PREPARE FOR DEFENSE BY STRETCHING.

"" REMEMBER WHEN WARMING UP NEVER BOUNCE! THIS WILL CAUSE SMALL TARES IN THE MUSCLES THAT OVER TIME WILL CAUSE MORE DAMAGE THAN GOOD. KEEP A STEADY PRESSURE AND HOLD FOR ABOUT THIRTY SECONDS. THEN STRETCH A LITTLE MORE AND REPEAT. THIS IS THE PROPER WAY TO WORK AND WARM UP YOUR MUSCLES. ""

THE DRILLS! :

10 / 10 / 10

MY TEN - TEN - TEN WORKOUT BEGINS LIKE THIS: FROM A FIGHTING STANCE USING BOTH LEFT AND RIGHT SIDE FORWARD I DO EVERY …

BLOCK / STRIKE / & KICK THAT I KNOW IN SETS OF TEN. THEN I FALL TO THE GROUND A.S.A.P!, AND DO TEN PUSHUPS, FOLLOWED BY TEN SITUPS, THEN TEN JUMPING JACKS!

NEXT I REPEAT THE SEQUENCE WITH THE NEXT ONE AND SO ON UNTIL I HAVE GONE THREW ALL BASICS.

TRY THIS FOR AN HOUR.   I GUARANTEE YOU WILL DROP FROM EXHAUSTION!

THREE / TWO / ONE

WITH THIS DRILL I USE THE HEAVY BAG OR A B.O.B. BAG. { BODY OPPONENT BAG }.

THIS DRILL IS DONE IN THE FOLLOWING MANNER: FIRST ROUND THREE MINUTES STRIKING.

LAST THIRTY SECONDS GO FULL OUT ASSAULT CRAZY NO HOLDING BACK!

SECOND ROUND IS FOR TWO MINUTES, AND THEN FOR THE LAST TWENTY SECONDS AGAIN FULL OUT ASSAULT.

LAST ROUND IS FOR ONE MINUTE, AND YES NOW IT IS FULL OUT FOR THE LAST TEN SECONDS!

THIS IS DESIGNED TO BUILD UP YOUR DRIVE TO STAMIGA. AFTER YOU HAVE TRIED THE ABOVE METHOD ADD BLOCKS AND KICKS.

YOU WILL LOVE IT, AND YOU WILL ALSO LOVE WHAT IT DOEST TO YOU!

THE IRON CHAIR

I TRUST EVERYONE HAS HEARD OF THIS EXERCISE? IF NOT IT WORKS YOUR LEGS. TOP TO BOTTOM!

STANDING AGAINST A WALL YOU SIT DOWN UNTIL YOUR UPPER BODY IS IN L SHAPE TO YOUR KNEES. LIKE YOU WERE SITTING AT A TABLE WITH NO TABLE.

KEEP GOOD POSTURE AND FOCUSED. THE BURN IS INCREDITABLE! FOR NO REASON DO YOU MOVE OR STRAY FROM THIS POSITION. WORK IT!

MY PERSONAL BEST EVER TIME IS THIRTYFIVE MINUTES. CAN I DO THIS EACH TIME? NO WE ALL HAVE OUR GOOD DAYS AND OUR BAD.

AN AVERAGE TO STRIVE FOR WOULD BE AT LEAST TEN MINUTES. GOODLUCK.

PUSHUPS

FOR THESE I PREFER THE CHAIN METHOD. IT WORKS BY STARTING AT TEN, AND GOING DOWN TO ONE.

THEN GO BACKWARDS FROM ONE TO TEN. THE KEY IS TO NOT STOP! ONE CONSTANT FLOW OF MOVEMENT.

SHOOT FOR REPS OF THREE IS YOU CAN. IF NOT THEN WORK YOUR WAY UP TO IT.

SITUPS

MY ALL TIME FAVORITE AND THE ONLY ONES I LIKE TO DO ARE UPSIDE DOWN SITUPS.

THIS IS DONE BY SITTING ON A BENCH AND PLACING YOUR FEET UNDER THE CHAIR RAIL.

THEN YOU LAY BACKWARDS OFF THE BENCH. THEN SITUP! AWESOME BURN!

YOUR WHOLE UPPER BODY JUST HANGS OVER THE SIDE, AND YOU HAVE TO USE EVERY MUSCLE IN YOUR STOMACH TO GET UP.

SHOOT FOR THREE REPS OF THIRTY TO FOURTY OR MORE IF YOU CAN?

I CALL THIS STYLE OF WORKOUT HELL NIGHT! I TREAT MY STUDENTS TO THIS ONCE A MONTH FOR AN ENTIRE CLASS PERIOD.

IT HAS BEEN MENTIONED BY ALL THE GREATS … *"" PAIN IS MERELY WEAKNESS LEAVING THE BODY. ""*

SELF DEFENSE DRILLS :

TIME LINE

LINE YOUR CLASS UP IN THE MIDDLE OF YOUR WORKING SPACE. THEN HAVE THEM CLOSE THEIR EYES.

IF THEY OPEN THEM PICK A PUNISHMENT DRILL. NEXT PULL THREE STUDENTS OUT OF THE LINE.

NEXT YOU AND THE LUCKY FIRST THREE WALK AROUND THE OTHERS IN THE LINE. BE AS QUIET AS YOU CAN.

THEN PICK YOUR PREY, AND GRAB THEM FROM ANY ANGLE OR HOLD YOU WISH. YOU CAN ALSO ONCE IN A WHILE PULL THEM RIGHT DOWN TO THE GROUND TOO.

DO THIS FROM BEHIND THEM. THE EFFECT IS MUCH MORE TO BENEFIT FROM!

AT THIS TIME AS SOON AS THEY FEEL YOUR TOUCH… THEY MAY OPEN THEIR EYES.

THEN FOR WHAT EVER SITUATION THEY FACE THEY MUST REACT! THIS CAN BE FROM PULLING OFF A TECHNIQUE, OR SHOWING THE REGAINING OF CONTROL.

IF YOU ARE PULLED DOWN FROM BEHIND? THIS WORKS YOUR SLAPPING OUT TECHNIQUE.

IF YOU DO NOT KNOW IT WELL…. IT WON'T TAKE LONG TO LEARN IT RIGHT! AS WELL AS QUICK.

THIS I FIND TO BE AN AWESOME REACTION TIME DRILL! THIS WILL HELP YOU AND YOUR STUDENTS BE PREPARED.

ADD SOME FUN TO THIS BY CHECKING YOUR HEART RATE BEFORE AND AFTER THE DRILL.

MY STUDENTS LOVE TO DO THIS TO ME! YOUR GOAL AS FAR AS HEART RATE IS TO START AND FINISH WITH THE SAE LEVEL BEAT PER SECOND.

THIS SHOWS CALMNESS IN THE FACE OF DANGER WITH THE ABILITY TO PROCESS THOUGHT!

AFTER A FEW MINUTES SWITCH THE FIRST THREE OUT AND INTO THE MIX, AND PICK NEW STUDENTS TO HAVE SOME FUN.

THIS DRILL NEEDS TO BE SEEN FROM BOTH SIDES OF THE COIN TO THE STUDENT.

THE PUSH

STACKING UP SEVERAL MATS UNTIL YOU REACH A HEIGHT THAT IS EQUAL TO YOUR HEAD LEVEL … SEVERAL FEET OFF THE GROUND.

HAVE ONE STUDENT JUMP UP ON TOP FACE DOWN. MAKE SURE THEIR UPPER BODY IS HANGING OVER THE SIDE.

THEN HAVE ANOTHER STUDENT SIT ON TOP OF THEIR LEGGS TO WEIGHT THEM DOWN.

NEXT ARRANGE ALL THE OTHER STUDENTS IN SOME TYPE OF PATTERN TO ONE SIDE OF THE MATT.

DO THIS WITH AND WITHOUT WEAPONS. NOW PERFORM THIS DRILL AS FOLLOWS:

HAVE THE LEG HOLDER COUNT REPS OF TEN, AND YOU DO INVERTED SITUPS!

WHEN FINISHED WITH YOUR DESERIED REP ROLL OFF THE MATT ONTO THE GROUND LEARNING TO FALL.

ONCE YOU HIT THE GROUND START DOING PUSHUPS FOR THE SAME REP!

THEN HAVE ALL THE OTHER STUDENTS THAT ARE IN THE PATTERN START ATTACKING AS SOON AS THE PUSHUP REPS ARE COMPLETED!

YOUR JOB IS TO FIRST GET OFF THE GROUND A.S.A.P. WHILE BEING ATTACKED, AND THEN MAKE IT PASSED ALL THE OTHER ATTACKERS TO SAFETY!

WHEN YOU MAKE IT TO THE END NOW YOU BECOME THE LEG HOLDER, AND THE LAST ATTACKER BECOMES THE NEXT VICTIM.

THEN KEEP MOVING ALONG UNTIL ALL HAVE HAD THE SAME EXPERIENCE.

THIS DRILL IS ONE GREAT WAY TO END AN EVENING WITH. THIS TOO REALLY PUSHES THE DRIVE BUTTONS!

THESE ARE JUST A FEW OF THE MANY FAVORITE DRILLS I LIKE TO DO.

I CAN'T TELL YOU ALL OF MY MATERIAL, BECAUSE THEN YOU WOULDN'T NEED ME OR BE INTERESTED IN OTHER BOOKS OF MINE TO COME.

SO PLEASE HAVE FUN WITH THE ONES I HAVE SELECTED FOR THIS BOOK.

PLEASE TAKE NOTE… MARTIAL ARTS IS A FULL CONTACT SPORT. BOTH IN EXERCISE OF PERFORMING CERTAIN DRILLS, AND PRACTICE WITH PARTNERS!

THIS ASPECT SEEMS IF TO BE FORGOTTEN BY MANY, AND REMEMBERED FOR FEW.

TAKE ALL OF YOUR TRAINING SERIOUS. THIS DOESN'T MEAN TO KILL YOUR PARTNER EACH TIME YOU PRACTICE EITHER!

THIS IS WHY WE PRACTICE. TO GAIN CONTROL AND LEARN DISCIPLINE OF OUR TOTAL BODY.

TOTAL BODY INCLUDES NOT ONLY OUR MUSCLE OF MATTER, BUT OUR MUSCLE OF MIND AND SPIRIT.

"" IT DOESN'T MATTER IF YOU HAD A GREAT PRACTICE OR A BAD PRACTICE, BECAUSE ALL PRACTICES ARE GOOD, BECAUSE WE DID PRACTICE! ""

" AS IT WAS SAID MANY CENTURIES AGO ALL MARTIAL ARTS BEGAN IN INDIA. "

KNOWING YOUR TERMINOLOGY :

IF YOU ARE GOING TO STUDY THE MARTIAL ARTS THEN YOU SHOULD BE ABLE TO SPEAK KNOWLEDGABLE ABOUT THE TRAINING YOU ENDURE.

IF SOMEBODY COMES UP TO YOU, AND ASKS: "" SO WHAT ARE YOU STUDYING? ""

THEN YOU SHOULD BE ABLE TO AT LEAST TELL THEM A BRIEF DESCRIPTION OF WHAT YOU DO, AND HOW YOU GO ABOUT DOING IT!

PLEASE HAVE THE DECENTNESS OF SPEAKING INTELLIGENTLY AND CLEARLY!

THIS WILL STRENGTHEN YOUR CHARACTER, AND SPEAK WONDERS ABOUT YOUR INSTRUCTOR.

THE FOLLOWING IS A LIST OF TERMS USED IN THE PRACTICE OF MARTIAL ARTS TODAY.

I BELIEVE THESE ARE VERY IMPORTANT FOR ALL OF YOU WHO DO TRAIN ... TO KNOW!

THESE TERMS ARE NOT IN A ~ B ~ C ORDER, BUT RATHER IN A WORKING SENSE OF ORDER TO ME FOR YOU.

ZEN :

"" MEANS ALL TOTALITY. ALL IS ONE, AND ONE IS ALL. ""

YIN & YANG :

TWO PRINCIPLES THAT ARE OPPOSING AND YET COMPLEMEMTARY. ONE CAN NOT EXIST WITHOUT THE OTHER! ALSO REFERED TO AS GOOD AND EVIL.

UKE :

AN ATTACKER USED IN PRACTICE.

TORI :

ONE WHO DEFENDS AGAINST THE UKE.

TE :

MEANS THE HAND.

SOKE :

IS THE FOUNDER OF A SYSTEM OR STYLE.

SHUTO :

MEANING KNIFE HAND TECHNIQUE. EDGE OF OUTSIDE OF HAND.

SHAOLIN :

A YOUNG FOREST.

SHIHAN :

MASTER LEVEL OF AN ART. BEGINS AT GODAN OR FIFTH DEGREE BLACKBELT.

SENSEI :

THE PROPER TITLE GIVEN TO AN INSTRUCTOR OF AN ART. HAS TO BE OF A 3RD DAN { SANDAN } 3RD DEGREE BLACKBELT OR HIGHER IN RANK!

RYU :

A DEVELOPED SYSTEM OF AN ART.

PINION :

MEANING PEACE OF MIND. ALSO PRONOUNCED PINAN. THIS IS A TYPE OF KATA USED FOR UNDERBELT DEVELOPMENT.

OBI :

BELT OR SASH. USED TO KEEP YOUR PANTS UP. ALSO DISPLAYS DEGREE OF RANKING.

MEDITATE :

THE CLEARING OF THE MIND. TO REST.

KYU :

A CLASS RANK GIVEN TO UNDER BLACKBELT. KYU'S GO FROM 10TH TO 1ST. OR WHITE TO 3RD DEGREE BROWNBELT.

KUNG - FU :

MEANS HARD WORK AND GREAT ACHIEVEMENT. THIS IS A CHINESE ART OF CIRCULAR MOVEMENTS THAT INCORPORATES THE MOVEMENTS OF ANIMALS INTO TECHNIQUES. THIS TERM COMES FROM THE SHAOLIN TEMPLE.

KUMITE :

THIS IS FREE STYLE SPARRING! { TO FIGHT }.

KIBA - DACHI :

HORSE STANCE. { FOOT WORK } A FIXED POSITION OF STANCE.

DACHI :

A STANCE IN THE PRACTICE OF MARTIAL ARTS.

KIAI :

LOUD SPIRITED SHOUT! PERFORMED TO NOT ONLY DEPRESS AIR OUT OF THE BODY TO PREPARE FOR IMPACT, BUT TO INSTILL FEAR UPON OPPONENT.

KI :

THE INTERNAL ENERGY FROM WITHIN.

KEN - RYU :

A VERSATILE SYSTEM IN THE ART OF KENPO.

KENPO BOW :

THE SHIELD { HAND } AND THE WEAPON { FIST } ON OVER THE OTHER TO REPRESENT PEACE OVER WAR. THIS IS TO SHOW RESPECT!

KENPO :

THE LAW OF THE FIST. THIS IS A CHINESE PUNCHING ART. KENPO FOCUSES ON USING A CHAIN OF TECHNIQUES RATHER THAN JUST ONE STRIKE TO DISABLE AN ATTACKER.

KATA :

THIS IS A FORMAL EXERCISE. ALSO REFERED TO AS A FORM. THE SHOWING OF BASICS IN A VARITY OF MOVEMENT AGAINST INVISABLE WOULD BE ATTACKERS. { LEARNING HOW TO FIGHT }.

KARATE :

AN OKINAWAN - JAPANESE AGGRESSIVE ART. USES BASIC BLOCKS AND STRIKES TO DISABLE AN ATTACKER. { ONE STRIKE TO EQUAL ONE KILL THEORY }.

JU JUITSU :

A JAPANESE RT OF CLOSED QUARTERED FIGHTING. { JOINT LOCKS, THROWS, CHOKES, STRIKING, & GRAPPLING TECHNIQUES }

JUDO :

A JAPANESE GRAPPLING ART. USES YOUR CENTER OF GRAVITY TO TAKE AWAY YOUR ATTACKERS BALANCE. ALSO REFERED TO AS USING YOUR OPPONENTS OWN FORCE AGAINST THEM. THE WAY OF GENTLENESS. THIS ART ALSO USES PIN & JOINT LOCK TECHNIQUES.

JO :

A SHORT STAFF. USUALLY MEASURING LESS THAN FOUR FEET.

GI :

THE NAME FOR OUR MARTIAL ART UNIFORMS.

THE FIVE ANIMALS OF KENPO :

IN THE ART OF KENPO WE DERIVE OUR KUNG - FU TECHNIQUES BASED UPON WHAT WE LABEL AS THE FIVE ANIMALS. THEY ARE:

THE TIGER "" STREGTH & TENACITY / MEANING HARD HEADED! LOWLAND & ROCKY AREAS OF CHINA ""

THE CRANE "" GRACE & BALANCE. WETLANDS OR RICE PATTIES OF CHINA. ""

THE SNAKE "" FLEXIBILITY & RHYTHMIC ENDURANCE. LOWLAND AREA & WETLAND AREA OF CHINA. ""

THE PANTHER "" SPEED & POWER. BOTH LOW & HIGH LANDS OF CHINA. ""

THE DRAGON "" WISDOM & SPIRIT! CAN BE FOUND IN ALL AREAS HAS NO BOUNDS TO EARTH. ""

IN REFRENCE TO HIGHLANDS I AM SPEAKING OF NORTHERN CHINA, AND WHEN I SPEAK OF LOWLANDS I AM REFERING TO THE SOUTHERN PART OF CHINA.

EVERYTHING IN - BETWEEN IS UP FOR MIGRATION PENDING SITUATIONS OF NEEDS TO ENVIROMENT CHANGES!

THE FIVE RULES :

THESE ARE MY PRINCIPLES OF LIFE IN ALL ASPECTS.

EFFORT "" THE ACT OF HARD WORK! ""

ETIQUETTE "" PUTTING FORTH EXECELLENT MANNERS! THE PRESENTION OF ONES SELF. ""

CHARACTER "" YOUR WORD AND YOUR ACTIONS SPEAK EVERYTHING OF WHO YOU ARE! ""

SINCERITY "" IS A PASSION OF HONESTY AND WELL BEING TOWARD ALL! ""

SELF CONTROL "" THE ACT OF HAVING TOTAL PHYSCIAL AS WELL AS MENTAL CONTROL OVER ALL YOUR EMOTIONS! ""

DOJO :

THE NAME GIVEN TO THE TRAINING HALL OF MARTIAL ARTS. THIS IS WERE EVER YOU MAY CHOOSE!

DO :

MEANING FOR THE WAY.

DAN :

IS AN OFFICAL GRADE OR RANK GIVEN TO THOSE WHO MAKE 1ST DEGREE BLACKBELT & UP.

BUNKI :

THE FORMAL APPLICATION OF A KATA. TO SHOW THE TRUE MEANING OF ALL TECHNIQUES WITHIN A KATA AS SEEN BY THE VIEWER.

BUDO :

THE WAY OF HONORABLE COMBAT IN THE MARTIAL ARTS! A CODE.

BOXING :

THE WESTERN STYLE OF MARTIAL ARTS.

BOJITSU :

THE ART OF THE STAFF.

BO :

ANOTHER NAME FOR A STAFF.

TAIKYOUKUKEN :

JAPANESE NAME MEANING THE ULTIMATE FIST STYLE.

BUDOU :

MEANING FOR THE MARTIAL ART.

TACHIAU :

MEANING GIVEN TO BEAR WITNESS TO AN EVENT.

BODI ;

JAPANESE MEANING THE BODY.

OMOI :

JAPANESE MEANING THE MIND.

MAKEAKI :

JAPANESE MEANING THE COMPETITIVE SPIRIT WITHIN.

KYOUKAN :

TITLE OF JAPANESE INSTRUCTOR.

SEMPI :

JAPANESE NAME GIVEN TO ASSISTANT TEACHER. AN INSTRUCTOR IN TRAINING.

SOUKEI :

MEANS TOTAL! COMPAREABLE TO ZEN; JAPANESE.

HAJIME :

TO BEGIN TRAINING IN JAPANESE FORMAT.

YAME :

TO STOP. JAPANESE TO SUSPEND ALL TRAINING TILL FURTHER NOTICE OR COMMAND.

ARIGATO :

JAPANESE ETIQUETTE TO GIVE THANKS. THANK YOU.

SHOMEN NI RI :

JAPANESE MEANING BOW TO FRONT.

OTAGI NI REI :

JAPANESE MEANING TO BOW TO ONE ANOTHER.

SENSEI NI REI :

JAPANESE MEANING BOW TO TEACHER!

JYODAN :

JAPANESE MEANING UPPER LEVEL OF BODY.

CHUDAN :

JAPANESE MEANING MIDDLE LEVEL OF BODY.

GEDAN :

JAPANESE MEANING LOWER LEVEL OF BODY.

SEIZA :

JAPANESE SYING TO KNEEL DOWN.

KYOSEI :

TO BRING TO FRONT ATTENTION. JAPANESE READY STANCE.

MOKUSO :

JAPANESE MEANING TO MEDITATATE. THE ACT OF CLOSING OF THE EYES & CLEARING OF THE MIND. TO REST IN DEEP THOUGHT OF SIGHT.

COBALTS :

THE SELF DEFENSE TECHNIQUES OF JAPANESE MARTIAL ART.

NUNCHAKUS :

A TRADITIONAL JAPANESE WEAPON. MADE OF WOOD. TWO STICKS OF WOOD BOUND TOGETHER BY ROPE OR CHAIN. ITS PRACTICAL USE WAS THAT TO BANG OR BEAT THE DUST OUT OF RUGS. A MOST POWERFUL WEAPON!

SIA :

A TRADITIONAL JAPANESE WEAPON MADE OF STEEL. RESEMBLE SMALL PITCHFORKS. PROPER LENGTH FOR STUDENT MEASURES FROM TIP OF ONES ELBOW TO PALM OF HAND. PRACTICAL USE IS TO BAIL HAY FOR ONE AND PLANTING AS ANOTHER.

STAFF :

A TRADITIONAL WEAPON MADE OF WOOD. MEASURES IN ENGTH FROM FOUR FOOT TO FIVE FOOT. THE PRACTICAL USE OF THIS IS TO AID IN THE CARRYING OF PAILS OF WATER.

KAMA :

A TRADITIONAL JAPANESE WEAPON. RESEMBLES HALF SIZED SICKLES. THE PRACTICAL USE OF THIS WEAPON IS TO CUT & HARVEST CROPS. SUCH AS SUGAR CANE OR WHEAT.

*** *FOOTNOTE* ***

ALL TRADITIONAL WEAPONS ARE FARMERS TOOLS, AND USED IN THE EASE OF THE WORKDAY. IT WAS WHEN THE TIME ARRIVED TO DEFEND THEIR FAMILIES AND THEIR LAND THAT THESE SIMPLE TOOLS WERE CONVERTED INTO SELF PROTECTION WEAPONS FOR DEFENSE!

AND PRACTICED ACCORDINGLY.

TH JAPANESE BASIC COUNTING SYSTEM :

ICHI / ONE

NI / TWO

SAN / THREE

SHI / FOUR

GO / FIVE

ROKU / SIX

SHICHI / SEVEN

HACHI / EIGHT

KU / NINE

JU / TEN

GRANDMASTER FUNAKOSHI :

OUR FOREFATHER OF THE SYSTEM OF SHOTOKAN KARATE! A JAPANESE ART.

GRANDMASTR ED PARKER :

OUR FOREFATHER OF THE SYSTEM OF KENPO KARATE! A CHINESE ART.

SHIDOSHI GRANDMASTER RON " THE BLACK DRAGON " VAN CLIEF :

OUR FOREFATHER OF THE CHINESE GOJU SYSTEM! THIS SYSTEMS ORIGINS BEGAN IN OKINAWA AND JAPAN BY THE LATE HONORABLE CHOJUN MIYAGI.

{ 1888 ~ 1953 }

AFTER HIS DEATH HIS SUCCESSOR GOGEN YAMAGUCHI WAS DESIGNATED TO CARRY ON THE STYLE OF THIS ART.

IN 1959 ANOTHER GREAT GRANDMASTER NAMED PETER URBAN WHO WAS A DISCIPLE OF GOGEN YAMAGUCHI BROUGHT THIS ART STYLE TO AMERICA.

THEN IN WHAT WAS REFERED TO AS THE YEAR OF THE BEATLES INVASION IN 1964 GRANDMASTER URBAN FOUNDED THE U.S.A. GOJU ASSOCIATION. THIS STEP RE - DEFINED THIS ART.

NEXT BEING A DISCIPLE OF GRANDMASTER PETER URBAN CAME GRANDMASTER RON VAN CLIEF. WHO ON JANUARY 25TH 1971 FOUNDED THE CHINESE SYSTEM OF CHINESE GOJU.

SHIDOSHI RON VAN CLIEF A 10TH DEGREE GRANDMASTER { RED BELT } COMES FROM THE FAMILY TREE OF THE FOLLOWING GRANDMASTER'S:

PETER URBAN ~ FRANK RUIZ ~ MOSES POWELL ~ & LEUNG TING!

THIS NEW SYSTEM OF CHINESE GOJU BRINGS TOGETHER & COMBINES BOTH EASTERN AND WESTERN IDEOLOGIES WITH GOOD OLD 100% AMERICAN INGENUITY!

SHORT STORIES OF TRAINING ROUNDABOUT :

THE PERFECT TIME

FOR YEARS ON END THERE WAS THIS GUY WHO WORKED WITH MY WIFE. SHE HAD A PART TIME JOB WORKING FOR VERY GOOD FRIENDS OF OURS DAVE AND LYNN WANG.

THEY OWN A REASTURANT NAMED YUMMIES CHINESE. IT IS THE BEST CHINESE FOOD AND SERVICE IN THE SMALL TOWN OF WEBSTER MA 01570.

NOW EACH AND EVERYTIME I SAW THIS GUY HE HAD A REALLY BIG MOUTH!

HE WAS ALWAYS SAYING TO ME: "" *SO YOU'RE THE BIG KARATE MAN? YOU DO NOT LOOK LIKE MUCH TO ME! COME ON THEN ... LETS SEE YOUR MOVES.* ""

BUT S USUAL I ALWAYS TOLD HIM THE SAME THING. "" *THIS IS NOT THE TIME OR THE PLACE.* ""

THEN AFTER A FEW MINUTES HE WOULD WONDER AWAY AND GO ABOUT HIS BUSINESS.

THEN CAME THE BIG NIGHT. MY WIFE AND I ARE KNOWN TO HAVE A FEW GET TOGETHERS DURING THE SUMMER ALL THE TIME.

ON THIS ONE PERTICULAR YEAR SHE INVITED EVERYONE TO COME THAT WORKED AT THE CHINESE REASTURANT.

WE HAD A GREAT TIME! WE PLAYED VOLLEYBALL, DID SOME CATCHING UP WITH CONVERSATION, AND ATE AND DRANK ALL KINDS OF GREAT STUFF!

P.S. WE DID A LOT OF DRINKING. IT WAS THE 4TH OF JULY, AND WE CERTAINLY CELEBRATED!

SO LATER ON DURING THIS NIGHT AS THE PARTY WAS WINDING DOWN THEN HERE COMETH THE MOUTH.

I REMEMBER IT WELL. I WAS OUT ON OUR BACK DECK WITH SENSEI JOHN GIAQUIANTO, AND SENSEI CHUCK TARR.

WE WERE TALKING SHOP, AND THROWIG BACK A FEW MORE COLD ONES. THEN THE MOUTH WHOSE NAME WAS JOHN STARTED WITH ME AGAIN!

THIS WAS HIS LUCKEY NIGHT.

IT WAS AT THIS TIME AND POINT I SAID TO HIM … : *"" TONIGHT IS YOUR LUCKEY NIGHT BUDDY! IT IS THE RIGHT TIME, AND THE RIGHT PLACE. ""*

"" I AM FEELING GREAT, AND I AM IN THE PRIVACY OF MY OWN HOME. ""

THEN IT WAS A DIFFERENT STORY. HE THEN SAID: *"" I AM NOT GOING TO BEAT UP ON A DRUNK THAT IS SITTING IN A CHAIR! ""*

"" I WILL FEEL TOO BAD ABOUT IT. PLUS HOW WOULD I EXPLAIN IT TO YOUR WIFE? ""

SO I REPLIED: *"" COME ON HIT ME! ""* BUT HE SAID NO. SO I SAID IT AGAIN.

"" HIT ME! WHATS THE MATTER? YOU HVE TOLD ME HOW BIG AND TOUGH YOU ARE, AND HOW WEAK I AM. HIT ME … ! ""

SO HE FINALLY CAME FOR ME! I THEN STOOD UP AND THREW A FORWARD HIGH BLOCK TO HIS STRIKE.

THEN I SPEARHAND POKED HIM IN THE THROAT. NEXT I REACHED BEHIND AROUND HIS NECK AND CHOKED HIM OUT!

THE NEXT THING YOU HEARD WAS THE LAUGHTER FROM SENSEI JOHN AND CHUCK.

AS THE MOUTH COLLASPED BACKWARDS FALLIG INTO ONE OF MY OUTSIDE DECK CHAIRS IT HAD SMASHED INTO SEVERAL PIECES!

I THOUGHT OH .. NO … ! MY WIFE IS GOING TO BE BIG TIME UPSET WITH ME THIS TIME!

SO I SAID TO MY FRIENDS: *"" HEY THIS GUY IS OUT COLD! WHAT NOW? ""*

THEN JOHN SAID NO PROBLEM. I CAN FIX THIS. JOHNS NEXT MOVE WAS TO PICK UP THE ICE CHEST, AND DUMP ALL THE ICE COLD WATER ALL OVER HIS HEAD!

THEN HE WOKE UP. HE SAID: *"" MIKE I AM SORRY. I WILL NEVER TEASE YOU AGAIN. WHAT HAPPENED? … ""*

THEN CHUCH SAID: *"" YOU HAD YOUR BELL RUN, AND YOUR MOUTH SHUT FOR YOU! ""*

THEN I HELPED HIM UP OFF THE DECK SHOWED HIM THE DOOR, AND SAID ONCE AGAIN … :

"" HEY BUDDY THANKS FOR COMING. BY THE WAY YOU OWE ME TEN DOLLARS FOR THE CHAIR YOU BROKE. SO I CAN REPLACE IT! ""

IN MY TEACHINGS I CALL THIS TECHNIQUES NUMBER ELEVEN. THE LESSON HERE IS THIS…

IF YOU CAN WALK AWAY FROM A FIGHT THEN YOU ARE THE BIGGER MAN.

HOWEVER; IF THE FIGHT KEEPS COMING BACK TO YOU AFTER ALL YOUR EFFORTS TO RE - DIRECT IT THEN FINISH IT!

SO ON THIS FINE 4TH OF JULY EVENING… I DID JUST THAT.

THE BEACH

WHILE ON VACTION DOWN SOUTH VISITING SOME FRIENDS AT MYRTLE BEACH; SOUTH CAROLINA…

I HAD LEARNED A MOST VALUABLE LESSON. FOR WHICH I FIND HARD TO FORGET AT TIMES.

WE STAYED AT OUR FAVORITE HOTEL WHICH WAS ON OCEAN BLVD, AND RIGHT ON THE OCEAN.

ONE EVENING AFTER A LONG DAY OF SIGHTSEEING I HAD DECIDED TO GO DOWN TO THE BEACH, AND DO SOME MOONLIGHT TRAINING TO RELAX.

FIRST I DID SOME BASIC EXERCISES IN THE DUNES. THEN AFTER HEATING UP I WENT DOWN TO THE WATER TO HIT THE WAVES THAT WERE POUNDING ACROSS THE SHORE.

WHILE IN THE SURF I COULD LOOK UP AND SEE OUR ROOM. I COULD ALSO SEE TAMMY WANDERING ABOUT TALKING ON THE PHONE.

SO LIKE I SAID WE WERE REAL CLOSE TO THE BEACH. ANYWAY SOME TIME WENT BY…

AND I STARTED DOING MY KATAS ABOUT WAIST DEEP IN THE WATER. IT WAS PRETTY COOL.

THEN FROM THE DISTANCE I HEARD A VOICE OF A MAN YELLING AT ME FROM ACROSS THE BEACH.

HE WAS AN OLDER GENTLEMAN. HE SEAMED TO BE WHAT I WOULD CONSIDER LOCAL TO THE AREA BY HIS CHARACTER.

HE SCREAMED TO ME … *"" HE STUPID! YOU SHOULDN'T BE OUT THERE AFTER DARK. ITS FEEDING TIME AROUND HERE! ""*

MY RESPONSE WAS: "" O.K. THANK YOU FOR TELLING ME, BUT I AM NOT AFRAID. ""

THEN SOME MORE TIME HAD PASSED. I WAS HAVING A BALL JUST TRYING TO DO MY KATAS AGAINST THE SURF!

THEN … ALL OF A SUDDEN! … THINGS BECAME VERY CREEPY.

JUST LIKE THE SNAP OF A FINGER FAST. SOMETHING HIT MY SIDE! I WAS AFRAID NOW!

REALLY AFRAID! MY HEART WAS POUNDING LIKE THE WAVES. WHAT EVER IT WAS HAD SENT ME FOR ABOUT A TEN FOOT SPLASH.

THIS CARRIED ME FORWARD HEADING ACTUALLY BACK IN TO THE SHORE.

I CALMLY GOT UP, AND PROCEEDED TO THE SANDY BEACH, AND ITS SAFTEY!

WHEN I GOT FULLY OUT OF THE WATER MY WHOLE SIDE OF THE BODY THAT WAS HIT WAS BRIGHT RED IN COLOR.
AND IT BURNED! IT FELT LIKE A MASSIVE SCRAPE. I WAS LUCKY. VERY LUCKY IN DEED!

I HAD BEEN SIDE SWIPED BY A SHARK! I LEARNED A VERY VALUABLE LESSON WITH NATURE THAT NIGHT.

WHEN EVER I GOTO THE OCEAN. NO MATTER WHAT PART OF THE WORLD I MAY BE VISITING I DO NOT GO INTO THE WATER FROM DUSK TILL DAWN!

A.K.A. THE PREFERED FEEDING TIME OF THE SHARKS. RESPECT MOTHER NATURE, AND YOU WILL SEE FAR MORE THAN YOU HAVE EVER BEFORE.

THE LONG BAY RESORT SOUTH CAROLINA; MYRTLE BEACH

THE HARDROCK BOSTON MA

ANOTHER TIME MY FAMILY AND I WERE OUT FOR THE DAY IN BOSTON. GOOD OLD BEANTOWN.

WE HAD LOST TRACK OF TIME FROM OUR ADVENTURES DURING THE DAY. IT WAS SHORTLY AFTER SUPPER TIME NOW SO WE DECIDED TO EAT AT ONE OF OUR FAVORITES.

THE HARDROCK CAFÉ. THE PLACE WAS JAMMED PACK. WE HAD TO WAIT A WHILE TO GET IN, BUT IT IS ALWAYS WORTH THE TIME TO US.

WHILE WE WERE WAITING THEIR WAS THIS MAN WHO YOU COULD SEE CAUSING TROUBLE IN THE SEATING AREA NEXT TO THE BAR.

NONE OF US PAID HIM TO MUCH ATTENTION, BUT I DID TAKE NOTICE OF HIS ON GOING ACTIONS.

BUT WHEN WE WERE SEATED GUESS WHERE OUR TABLE WAS? YOU GUESSED IT CLOSE TO THE ACTION.

FOR DINNER IT WAS MY TWO SISTER IN LAWS NICOLE AND BRANDY, MY BROTHER IN LAW CRAIG AT THE TIME, MY MOTHER IN LAW NANCY ALONG WITH MY WIFE TAMMY AND SON MASON.

NEXT YOU COULD NOT ONLY SEE HOW BAD HIS MANNERS WERE BUT YOU COULD HEAR HIS LOUD VERBAL SPEECH TOWARDS THE OTHER DINERS.

HE PROCEEDED TO OUR TABLE, AND STARTED WITH MY SISTER IN LAW AND MOTHER IN LAW!

THIS GUY WAS RUDE, CRUDE, AND YES DRUNK! THINGS WERE HEATING UP.

I SAID TO HIM: *"" EXCUSE ME ... BUDDY! PLEASE MOVE ALONG! BEFORE THERE IS TROUBLE. ""*

I REALLY THOUGHT BRANDY WAS GOING TO KNOCK THIS GUY OUT! IF NOT HER MY WIFE TAMMY FOR SURE!

BUT HE CONTINUED HIS WAYS. I HAD GIVEN HIM FAR WARNING. BUT STILL LOOKING FOR SOME OPTIONS BEFORE MY DECISION OF ACTION…

I THEN MOTIONED FOR THE BAR TENDER TO COME OVER. HE SAW WHAT WAS GOING ON TOO.
I TOLD HIM CAN YOU PLEASE REMOVE THIS GUY? BECAUSE IF YOU DON'T I WILL.

I RATHER NOT MAKE YOUR NIGHT ANY HARDER BY HAVING TO CALL 911!

THE BAR TENDER WAVED TO THE MANAGER, AND BOTH THANKED US FOR NOT TAKING ACTION BY OURSELFS.

PLUS WE RECEIVED ONE FREE DRINK EACH FROM THE HARDROCK. THIS WAS A NICE GESTURE.

THE LESSON HERE IS LEARN TO READ THE FENCE. WAS IT NECESSARY FOR VIOLENCE TO OCCUR, OR WAS THERE ANOTHER WAY TO APPROACH THE SITUATION?

BEFORE IT WAS TO LATE I HAD MADE THE CORRECT DECISION. I BELIEVE IN THIS CASE MY FAMILY AND I HANDLED THE PROBLEM WELL.

IF YOU CAN WALK AWAY FROM A HEATED MOMENT WITHOUT COMPROMISE OF JUST ACTION THEN YOU ARE THE BETTER PERSON!

THE FAMOUS PEOPLE I HAVE MET :

DURING THE COURSE OF MY LIFE TIME IT HAS BEEN MY PLEASURE TO RUN INTO SOME OF THE NICEST PEOPLE YOU COULD EVER MEET.

TO ME THEY ARE FRIENDS, BUT TO OTHERS THEY ARE CONSIDERED CELEBRITIES.

THESE PEOPLE ACTUALLY TAKE NOT ONLY THE TIME TO SAY HELLO AND CONVERSE WITH YOU FOR A SPELL, BUT ALSO ANSWER ANY QUESTIONS I MAY ASK OF THEM.

SOMETIMES THEY EVEN HAVE QUESTIONS TO ASK OF ME. THIS IS WHAT THE TERM ROLE MODELS SHOULD BE DEFINED AS.

GOOD PEOPLE WHO CARE ABOUT WHATS GOING ON IN THEIR LIFE AS WELL AS THE LIFE OF OTHERS!

WHEN I FIRST HAD MET THE LIST OF CELEBRITIES THAT I AM GOING TO ACKNOWLEDGE NEVER ONCE DID ANY ONE OF THEM EVER ASK ME FOR MONEY TO TAKE A PICTURE OR AN AUTOGRAPH.

THEY ARE FIRST CLASS AND VERY DOWN TO EARTH. I THANK THEM ALL FOR BEING A FRIEND TO ME THEN AND NOW.

SOME I HAVE MET FACE TO FACE. WHILE OTHERS I HAVE HAD THE PRIVILEGE TO TRAIN WITH IN THE STUDY OF MARTIAL ARTS.

AND STILL THERE ARE THE ONES THAT TALK WITH ME BY THE WAY OF FACEBOOK.

THE MORE MODERN STYLE TO CONVERSE AND SHARE THROUGH THE INTERNET.

SOMETIMES THEY WRITE FOR INFORMATION, AND OTHERS WRIE TO ASK HOW THINGS ARE JUST SIMPLY GOING.

FACE TO FACE

WELL MY ALL TIME FAVORITE IDOL IS GRANDMASTER CHUCK NORRIS! I REALLY DO NOT THINK PEOPLE REALIZE HOW MUCH HE HAS ACCOMPLISHED IN HIS LIFE.

YES HE WILL ALWAYS BE KNOWN FOR HIS ROLES IN BIG SCREEN AND TV PRODUCTIONS.

HOWEVER; HE IS THE REAL DEAL. HE WAS THE TOP FIGHTER IN HIS DIVISION FOR YEARS!

HE EVEN HELPED TRAIN THE SPECIAL FORCES FOR OUR COUNTRY AT ONE TIME.

I HAVE HAD THE PLEASURE OF MEETING HIM TWICE NOW IN MY LIFE. BOTH OCCASIONS WERE IN PROVIDENCE RI.

HE IS ONE OF THE FRIENDLIEST PEOPLE I HAVE EVER MET! WHEN HE STARTED UP THE W.C.L. { WORLD COMBAT LEAUGE } HE USED TO SEND ME PROMO STUFF, AND LET ME KNOW WHEN THEY WERE COMING TO THE AREA.

BUT AFTER I WAS UNABLE TO MAKE IT TO THE FIGHTS HE STOPPED SENDING ME STUFF.

I HOPE TO MEET HIM AGAIN IN THE NEAR FUTURE.

ANOTHER FAVORITE OF MINE WHO THROUGH THE YEARS WE HAVE BECOME GOOD FRIENDS IS MS. CYNTHIA ROTHROCK.

HER TOO I HAVE MET IN PROVIDENCE WHILE ATTENDING A MARTIAL ARTS TOURNAMENT.

THIS TOURNAMENT IS NONE OTHER THAN THE OCEAN STATE GRAND NATIONALS.

RUN BY GRANDMASTER DON RODRIGUES AND HIS WIFE MASTER CHRISTINE BANNON RODRIGUES.

CYNTHIA IS VERY KIND AND NICE TO CHAT WITH TOO. HER AND I CONVERSE QUITE OFTEN THREW FACEBOOK.

WE ALSO MEET UP IN ATLANTIC CITY FROM TIME TO TIME AT THE TROPICANA HOTEL AND RESORT.

THEN THERE IS MR. DAVID WECKL. HE IS AN AWESOME MUSICIAN. I MET DAVID WITH MY MUSIC TEACHER JIM KELLY AT THE TIME.

JIM AND DAVE WERE CLOSE FRIENDS, AND ACTUALLY JIM WAS TAKING PRIVATE LESSONS HIMSELF FROM DAVID.

WE HAD MET IN DOWNTOWN BOSTON FOR A PRIVATE INVITE ONLY OCASSION.

TODAY DAVID IS ONE OF THE LEADING INDEPENDENT JAZZ DRUMMERS WHO IS CONSTANTLY BEING SOUGHT AFTER IN THE BUSINESS.

SOME OF HIS CREDITS INCLUDE; WORKING WITH MADONNA, ROBERT PLANT, AND CHICK COREA JUST TO NAME A FEW OF MANY.

ALSO THROUGH STUDING MUSIC WITH JIM I WAS ABLE TO HAVE CONVERSATION WITH NEIL PEART FROM THE BAND RUSH.

"" TOP LEFT W/ DAVID WECKL & BOTTOM RIGHT AUTOGRAPH FROM NEIL PERT. SAYS : MERRY CHRISTMAS MIKE ... NEIL PERT ""

TRAINED WITH

DURING MY MARTIAL ARTS CAREER I HAVE HAD THE PRIVILEGE TO WORK AND TRAIN UNDER MASTER BRUCE SMITH FROM MARYLAND.

HE IS THE HEAD COACH FOR TEAM AMERICA AND A GOOD FRIEND TO MY FAMILY AND I.

TOMMY LEE FROM WASHINGTON D.C. HE IS BECOMING VERY WELL KNOWN FOR HIS ACTIONS IN THE TRAINING OF THE ARTS.

TIME TO TIME I CATCH AN ARTICLE ABOUT HIM IN INSIDE KUNG - FU MAGAZINE.

WE HAD MET WHILE I WAS ON TEAM AMERICA AS WELL, AND IN THESE YEARS HAD FOUND TIME TO STUDY WITH HIM WHILE ABROAD FROM OUR COUNTRY TRAVELLING WITH THE TEAM.

MR. PETER TAZ FROM AUSTRALIA WHO TODAY IS A MASTER IN KENPO. PETER AND I HAD FACED OFF AGAINST ONE ANOTHER IN THE WORLD GAMES IN 2000 DOWNUNDER.

TODAY WE STILL KEEP IN CONTACT ONE WAY OR ANOTHER. HE HAD TAKEN THE GOLD AND I TOOK THE SILVER THAT YEAR.

IN THE INTERNATIONAL SPORT OF KARATE I ALSO HAD THE PLEASURE OF WORKING WITH A COMPETITIVE RIVAL OF MINE FROM GERMANY.

HIS NAME IS MARIO WORZFELD. HIM AND I HAD FOUGHT ON THREE DIFFERENT OCCASIONS.

THEY WERE IN IRELAND ~ HAWAII ~ AND MEXICO. AGAINST HIM I TOOK ONE OF EACH MEDAL A GOLD ~ SILVER ~ AND BRONZE.

HE WAS AN AWESOME COMPETITOR AND EVEN THOUGH IN THE RING WE WERE RIVALS OUTSIDE WE BECAME GOOD FRIENDS AND DID SOME TRAINING TOGETHER.

ANOTHER GREAT MARTIAL ARTIST THAT WAS UP AND COMING WAS JOEL' OTHERO.

HE WAS FROM BROOKLYN NEW YORK. HE WAS IN SOME OF THE MORTAL COMBAT MOVIES.

HE DIDN'T FIGHT TO MUCH. HE WAS VERY BIG INTO THE KATA AND WEAPONS DIVISIONS.

THEN I HAVE WORKED WITH MASTER DANIEL STERLING WHO HAS WON THE SHOW NINJA WARRIOR SEVERAL TIMES RUNNING TOURNAMENT RINGS.

FACEBOOK FRIENDS

ON FACEBOOK I HAVE OVER TWO THOUSAND WELL KNOWN MARTIAL ARTIST THAT KEEP IN TOUCH ON A DAILY TO MONTHLY BASIS WITH ME.

IF YOU ARE INTERESTED GOTO MY PROFILE PAGE AND SCAN MY FRIENDS LIST.

TO TAKE THE TIME TO MENTION THE ENTIRE LIST WOULD TAKE A VAST AMOUNT OF TIME.

BUT JUST TO NAME A FEW THAT MY BE OF INTEREST TO YOU:

ALAN NORRIS ~ BENNY " THE JET " URQUIDEZ ~ CECIL PEOPLES ~ AaRON RICHMOND ~ DON ' THE DRAGON " WILSON ~ CHRISTINE BANNON RODRIGUES ~ FRANK W. DUX ~ JANELL VELA SMITH ~ JOHN HACKLEMAN ~ KATHY LONG ~ MARK DACASCOS ~ SOKE MICHAEL DEPASQUALE JR. ~ MIKE CHATURANTABUT ~ STEVEN SEAGAL ~ JODI BROCKTON ~ AMY LOSEK ~ ANN WOLFE ~ HOLLIE DUNAWAY ~ ANTHANASIA DIAMANTI ~ RACHEL GRANT ~ GRANDMASTER ALAN GOLDBERG ~ ALBERTO CRANE ~ SIFU RITA ROSE PASQUALE ~ JOE LEWIS.

SOMETIMES I GET A HELLO HOWS LIFE TREATING YOU, AND OTHER TIMES I GET INVITED TO ATTEND A SEMINAR THEY ARE PROVIDING.

BUT THE TWO THAT I HAVE REAL HEART TO HEART CONVERSATIONS WITH ABOUT MANY A TOPIC ARE SIFU GRANDMASTER ALAN DACASCOS FROM HAWAII, AND SHIDOSHI GRANDMASTER RON " THE BLACK DRAGON " VAN CLIEF.

IF IT WASN'T FOR SHIDOSHI VAN CLIEF THIS AUTOBIOGRAPHY OF MINE OF SORTS WOULD NEVER HAVE EVOLVED!

SO HE NEEDS TO BE WELL CREDITED FOR PUSHING ME TO TAKE ON THIS TASK! CHIEN; SHIDOSHI FOR ALL YOU HELP.

IT HAS BEEN MY HONOR IN WORKING WITH YOU AND IN THE FUTURE I HOPE FOR MANY MORE.

OTHER FRIENDS IN THE ARTS

THE FOLLOWING LIST IS OF PEOPLE WHO ARE NOT FAMOUS YET, BUT PERHAPS ONE DAY WILL BE.

BRITTANY VICTORIA S. BAKER ~ MASTER MICHAEL BURTON ~ PETER TAZ ~ PROFESSOR ROCKY DIRICO ~ ERIN CENTAURO ~ JACK O' TOOLE ~ JACKIE ELFMAN ~ JAMIE NELSON ~ JOSE MANUEL INFATE PEDRAZA ~ MARINA PEREZ ~ MELISSA GLEICK ~ SENSEI MIKE MILLETT ~ MONICA PINNA ~ RICHARD PAT MARRON ~ SMATHA LIEF ~ SCOTT HOLLAND ~ SUI TI FOX ~ ANGELICA STEIN ~ ANGI STOTT ~ ANGIE WOODLUM ~ BEN AND AMANDA MACK ~ ALEXANDER DE ARAYA ~ ALICA ASHLEY ~ CAROLYN NOYES ~ CHRIS LEE ~ CHRISTOPHER TERRY ~ DJ OLEWSKI ~ EDDIE MARALES ~ ERAY CAKIR.

I HAVE HAD LIBERTY TO WORK WITH JUST ABOUT ALL THE ABOVE ONE TIME OR ANOTHER, AND PERHAPS ONE DAY THEIR TIME WILL COME TOO!

IF THEY SO CHOOSE IT TO BE?

BACK TO CHILDHOOD MEMORIES :

EARLY ON

LOOKING BACK AT MY CHILDHOOD I BELIEVE I CAN PINPOINT SOME OF THE MEMORIES THAT HAS BROUGHT ME TO MY DESTINY TODAY.

IN SOME TYPE OF FORM OR SHAPE OF LIFES EVENTS THESE ARE THE DETERMINING FACTORS OF QUESTION?

FIRST ON MY LIST. WHEN I WAS JUST A LITTLE GUY ABOUT SIX YEARS OLD I BECAME INVOLVED IN SCOUTING.

I WAS A CUB SCOUT UNTIL I TURNED OLDER, AND THEN WENT ON FOR A WHILE INTO THE BOY SCOUTS TOO.

MY TROOP NUMBER WAS 173 AND I MADE IT TO THE RANK OF SECOND CLASS BEFORE I SWITCHED INTO SPORTS FULL TIME.

BEING IN THE SCOUTING PROGRAM FOR MANY YEARS TAUGHT ME TO ALWAYS BE PREPARED!

IT ALSO STARTED THE FOUNDATIONS FOR THE FOLLOWING TRAITS …

RESPECT ~ HONESTY ~ KINDNESS ~ TRUTH ~ COMPASSION ~ TRADITION

THIS IS JUST A FEW OF THE MANY GREAT LESSONS THAT BEING A SCOUT HAD IMPACTED MY LIFE.

NEXT I SPENT A LOT OF TIME PLAYING DIFFERENT SPORTS WITH MY ADOPTIVE FATHER DONALD H. FARADAY.

HE WAS A GREAT MAN! HE WAS ALSO MY GRANDFATHER. BUT I CALLED HIM PAPA. I MISS HIM DEARLY!

PAPA HAD TAUGHT ME THE MEANING OF QUITE A FEW THINGS IN LIFE!

ONE WAS DEDICATION. ANOTHER WAS DETERMINATION! THEN THERE WAS SELF RESPECT, AND HOW TO BE A GOOD SPORTSMAN.

BUT BY FAR THE MOST IMPORTANT LESSON HE BESTOWED UPON ME WAS HOW TO BE A GREAT MAN!

AS FOR THE SPORTS HE TAUGHT ME AND THAT WE PLAYED WHENEVER POSSIABLE HERE IS THE LIST:

BASKETBALL ~ FOOTBALL ~ SOCCER ~ BASEBALL ~ TENNIS ~ BADMITTEN ~ FRISBEE ~ CROQUET ~ AND GOLF.

OUT OF ALL THESE FINE SPORTS I ENJOYED PLAYING BASKETBALL THE BEST, AND POPS FAVORITE WAS GOLF.

I NEVER DID WELL AT GOLF. IT SEEMED THAT I COULD THROW THE GOLFBALL FUTHER THAN I COULD HIT IT WITH THE CLUB!

HOWEVER; I DID WIND UP PLAYING BASKETBALL IN THE TOWN SUMMER LEAGUES FROM THE FOURTH GRADE TILL THE EIGHTH GRADE.

I ALSO PLAYED FOR TWO YEARS IN THE BOYS CLUB LEAGUE TOO.

IN THE PARKS DEPT I WAS AWARDED MOST IMPROVED PLAYER AWARD, AND IN THE BOYS CLUB I WAS AWARDED HIGH SCORER.

I AVERAGED AROUND TEN POINTS PER GAME. THEN IN MY FRESHMEN YEAR IN HIGH SCHOOL I MADE THE FRESHMEN TEAM FOR BARTLETT HIGH SCHOOL.

I HAVE ILL FEELINGS TOWARD THIS YEAR IN LIFE FOR MANY REASONS REVOLVED AROUND THE SCHOOL.

FOR ONE I NEVER GOT TO PLAY A GAME ON THE FRESHMEN LEAGUE, FOR WHICH I WILL GET INTO LATER ON IN THE BOOK.

FOR ANOTHER THE TEACHING STAFF AT BARTLETT HIGH THOUGHT THEY COULD RUN MY LIFE BOTH INSIDE AND OUTSIDE OF THE SCHOOLS WALLS!

WELL THIS DIDN'T GO WELL FOR QUITE AWHILE! UNTIL I FINALLY TOLD THEM A FEW CHOICE THOUGHTS!

THESE THOUGHT HOWEVER DO NOT ALL NEED TO BE DISCUSSED AT THIS TIME.

LET IT BE KNOWN AND ALL INFORMATION CAN BE SEARCH DURING MY SCHOOLING YEARS THAT I DID EXTREMELY WELL IN MY G.P.A. SCORES, AND MADE WHOS WHO AMONG AMERICAN HIGH SCHOOL STUDENTS TWICE!

THIS IS WHAT IS IMPORTANT AND ALL THE REST LOOKING BACK REALLY WASN'T. ALTHOUGHT NOW IT SEEMS TO BE KINDA FUNNY.

FRIENDSHIPS

THEN THERE WAS MY NEIGHBORHOOD FRIENDS. IN EVERYTHING WE DID THE CORE CONSISTED OF THE SAME FOUR GUYS.

THEY WERE JIM BACA, KEVIN ADAMS, JOHN POWERS, AND MYSELF.

WE FOUGHT ALL THE TIME. WE FOUGHT WITH ONE ANOTHER, WE AGAINST ONE ANOTHER, AND WE ALSO FOUHT SIDE BY SIDE AGAINST OTHERS!

GOOD OLD NORMANDY AVE AND THE SURROUNDING BLOCKS WAS OUR NEIGHBORHOOD.

IF SOMEBODY CAME INTO OUR BOUNDARIES TO CAUSE TROUBLE WE TOOK CARE OF IT!

BECAUSE OUR STREET DIDN'T NEED ANY BAD BOYS. WE WERE ENOUGH!

I REMEMBER A FEW THINGS THAT WE DID THAT WERE ODD TO LOOK BACK ON THEM NOW.

SUCH AS WE LIVED ON A DEAD END STREET. ON ONE END THEIR WAS THE PLAYGROUND AND GIRLS SOFTBALL FIELD, AND THE OTHER A GAINT SANDPIT NAMED LEO'S.

THERE WERE ARCES AND ARCES OF JUST SAND. THEN THERE WAS AN OPEN GRASSY FIELD THAT WAS GULLIED.

IN BETWEEN THE TWO THERE WAS A NICE SIZED SWAMP, AND LASTLY THE OLD RAILROAD TRACK THROUGH THE WOODS.

PUT IT THIS WAY... THERE WAS PLENTY OF ROOM TO RAISE HELL BACK THEN! AND WE DID JUST THAT.

WE USED TO DIG THESE HUGH HOLES IN THE SANDPITS. THEN WE MADE TEAMS.

NEXT WE GATHERED UP LARGE ROCKS NOT PEPPLES EITHER, AND VARIOUS SIZED STICKS.

SOME OF THESE ROCKS WERE LIKE THE SIZE OF SOFTBALLS. ALONG WITH APPLES OFF THE APLE TRESS THAT GREW WILD AROUND THE AREA.

LASTLY FROM ALL THE DIGGING IN THE DIRT WE HAD LUMPS OF CLAY. THIS CLAY WAS SOMETIMES PRETTY HARD AS WELL.

WHAT CAME NEXT? … THE WAR OF COURSE! WE HIT EACH OTHER WITH ALL WE HAD.

GETTING HIT WITH THE ROCKS AND APPLES LEFT A SERIOUS MARK. EVEN STITCHES ONCE IN A WHILE.

WHEN ALL THOSE SUPPLIES WERE GONE WE USED THE STICKS TO DEFFEND OUR GROUND FROM ONE ANOTHER.

TO US THIS WAS A DAILY EVENT UNTIL WE GOT INTO GIRLS. WE NEVER WORRIED ABOUT THE CAUSE AND EFFECTS OF OUR ACTIONS.

WELL NOT UNTIL WE COULDN'T STOP THE BLEEDING OURSELFS, OR WHEN WE KNEW WE HAD BROKEN A BONE OR TWO!

WHEN YOU GOT HIT IN THE HEAD WITH A ROCK, AND STILL KEPT COMING THE OTHERS KNEW IT WAS TIME TO RUN!

BECAUSE YOU MEANT BUSINESS AND WERE EXTREMELY PISSED OFF!

AFTER ALL THE AMMO WAS GONE AND THE STICKS WE BUSTED WE STOOD AROUND THE PITS WE DUG AND HAD FIGHTING MATCHES.

WE CALLED THIS KING OF THE HILL. YOU STAYED IN UNTIL YOU EITHER LOST OR WASN'T ABLE TO CONTINUE.

SOMETIMES THESE FIGHTS WERE ONE ON ONE, BUT MOST OF THE TIME IT RESEMBLED A RUMBLE!

ALL THE PUNCHING AND KICKING LEFT BEHIND A LOT OF DAMAGE!

EXPLAINING THIS TO OUR PARENTS NEVER WENT OVER WELL, BUT THE NEXT DAY WE WERE FRIENDS AGAIN.

THEN THERE WAS THE SPORTS WE PLAYED. IT WAS ALWAYS VERY COMPETITIVE!

WE THRIVED ON BEING BETTER THAN EACH OTHER. ESPECIALLY TO SCORE SOME OF THE GIRLS IN THE NEIGHBORHOOD.

FOOTBALL WAS NEVER TWO HAND TOUCH. IT WAS FULL CONTACT AND EATING DIRT!

THERE IS NOTHING LIKE THE SOUND OF BONE SMASHING ON BONE! WHAT A SOUND IT MADE.

THEN IN BASKETBALL IT TURNED INTO STREET RULES BEFORE TO LONG. MANY TIMES THE OLD SAYING OF EAT THE BALL BROUGHT A WHOLE NEW MEANING TO IN YOUR FACE!

MY BEST FRIEND KEVIN

ONE TIME WE DECIDED TO PLAY A GAME OF SOCCER AFTER SUPPER. MY FRIEND KEVIN HAD THE BIGGEST YARD ON THE STREET.

SO WE SPENT WHAT EVER TIME WE WERE NOT ALLOWED IN THE PITS AT KEVINS.

ANYWAYS AFTER THE GAME I WAS SUMMONED BACK TO KEVINS BY HIS FATHER SPARKY.

WHEN I GOT THERE … HIS DAD SAID: *"" HEY MIKE! GET OVER HERE! ""*

HE HAD A PAD OF PAPER IN ONE HAND, AND A PEN WITH A CALCULATOR IN THE OTHER.

"" GIVE THIS TO YOUR GRANDFATHER, AND GET BACK TO ME A.S.A.P. WILL YA? ""

I HAD BROKEN A WHOLE SET OF WINDOWS ON HIS PORCH FROM THE SOCCER BALL!

ON THE PIECE OF PAPER THAT KEVINS DAD GAVE TO ME WAS A NUMBER FOR ESTIMATED DAMAGES, AS WELL AS A SMALL NOTE.

THIS NOTE READ: ***"" DON'T COME BACK HERE ANYMORE!   BUT AFTER YOU PAY ME ONE HUNDRED AND FIFTY DOLLARS. ""***

THIS SUCKED! BECAUSE THIS WAS THE FIRST DAY KEVIN AND I WERE ALLOWED TO PLAY SINCE THE OTHER ACCIDENT THAT OCCURRED ALMOST EIGHT MONTHS EARLIER.

THIS IS WHEN WE DECIDED TO PLAY GOLF. KEVIN HAD SAID TO ME: *"" HEY YOU AND YOUR POP PLAY GOLF RIGHT? ""*

I SAID: *"" YES. ""* HE THAN SAID: *"" WELL DO YOU HAVE YOUR OWN CLUBS? ""*

AGAIN MY ANSWER WAS: "" *YES.* "" NEXT THING WE WERE OUTSIDE ON THE SIDE OF MY GARAGE WACKING GOLF BALLS OVER JIM BACA HOUSE.

SO KEVIN ASKS: "" *SO HOW DO YOU HIT THE BALL?* "" SO I SHOWED HIM. THEN HE TRIED IT.

WHEN I TOOK MY SECOND TURN I FIRST LOOKED BEHIND ME TO MAKE SURE HE WAS AT A SAFE DISTANCE.

SO I COULD TAKE MY SWING. HE WAS SO I WANTED TO REALLY BELT IT ONE, AND TOOK A HARD STROKE.

NEXT I HEARD THIS LOUD THUD AND A BIG SIGH! WHEN I LOOKED BEHIND ME …

THERE WAS BLOOD EVERYWHERE! EVEN PIECES OF SKIN ON THE SIDE OF MY HOUSE!

AS FOR KEVIN HE WAS ON THE GROUND ALL MESSED UP. REAL BAD! WELL HE JUST TOOK A NINE IRON TO THE HEAD!

AFTER EIGHTYEIGHT STITCHES, AND SAVING HIS EYESIGHT I WAS GROUNDED FOR WHAT WAS TRULY AN ACCIDENT.

AS WELL AS BEING BANNED FROM MYFRIENDSHIP BY KEVINS PARENTS!

IT WASN'T ENTIRELY MY FAULT. HE WALKED INTO MY SWING. WHEN I CHECKED HE WAS NO WHERE EVEN CLOSE TO ME.

WHAT EVER POSSESSED HIM TO MOVE WE WILL NEVER KNOW?

STICKING TOGETHER

BEING NEXT TO THE SAND PITSWE RAN INTO OLDER KIDS ALL THE TIME. ESPECIALLY ON THE WEEKENDS!

WHY? BECAUSE IT WAS A GREAT PLACE TO PARTY FOR THEM. ALTHOUGH THE WAYS IN AND OUT WERE VERY LIMITED.

MOST OF THE TIME YOU HAD TO WALK IN UNLESS YOU DROVE A PICKUP TRUCK.

ON THIS ONE OCCASION ONE CAR DID MAKE IT IN. WE WERE SURPRIZED! NOT AN EASY DRIVE AT ALL.

WE WERE FOOLING AROUND LIKE USUAL, AND THE OLDER KIDS IN THE CAR DECIDED TO CHASE US. WITH THEIR CAR!

WHEN THEY FINALLY PINNED US IN THE OLDER KIDS JUMPED OUT OF THE CAR.

THEIR WERE FIVE OF THEM, AND ONLY THREE OF US THIS TIME AROUND. JIM BACA, JOHN POWERS, AND I.

THEY PULLED KNIVES ON US AND STUCK THEM IN OUR FACE SCREAMING SHIT TO US... LIKE WE WERE DEAD!

WE NEVER ENCOUNTERED THIS BEFORE! WE WERE ALL SCARED STIFF.

BUT THEN WE JUST FIGURED IT WAS US OR THEM! SO OUT OF FEAR I GUESS? WE KICKED THEM IN THEIR GROINS, AND THEN TRIED TO KNOCK THE KNIFES OUT OF THEIR HANDS!

THEN WE RAN FOR THE WOODS... BECAUSE WE KNEW IF WE MADE IT TO THE WOODS WE WERE SAFE.

WE KNEW ALL THE PATHS INSIDE AND OUT. A FEW OF THEM WE EVEN BLAZED OURSELFS.

THAT WAS GOOD FOR US. WE MADE IT! BUT THE FUNNY THING WAS THE CAR COULDN'T MAKE IT BACK OUT AFTER MAKING IT IN.

WE NEVER SAW THESE KIDS EVER AGAIN. THIS WAS A GOOD THING. ONCE WAS ENOUGH.

WITH ALL OF THIS HERE IS THE REAL FINAL TWIST OF FAIT IN MY PINPOINTS OF WHERE AM TODAY.

INSPIRING WORDS

BACK DURING THE MIDDLE EIGHTIES WHILE TRAINING WITH MY UNCLE HE TOLD ME THAT I SHOULD START TO CONSIDER FORMAL TRAINING IN THE MARTIAL ARTS.

BUT THEIR WASN'T MANY CHOICES AROUND BACK THEN. WHERE WE LIVED THERE WAS ONLY ONE PLACE IN TOWN.

IT WAS CALLED THE WEBSTER INSTITUTE OF KARATE, AND IT IS STILL LOCATED ON THE MAIN STREET IN THE TOWN OF WEBSTER.

I WILL NEVER TALK ILL ABOUT A SCHOOL, BECAUSE IT IS IN BAD FORM IN CHARACTER!

HOWEVER; IF THERE ARE ASPECTS OF THE TRAINING THAT AGAIN ARE ONLY IN MY OPINION ARE NOT GOOD THEN I WILL ADDRESS THEM.

WEATHER THEY ARE LIKED OR DISLIKED, AND I DO NOT THINK OR SEE SOLID MATERIAL COMING OUT OF THIS ESTABLISHMENT.

WHAT OTHERS CALL GREAT… I NOTICE THE LITTLE THINGS. LIKE SLOPPY FOOTWORK, POOR STANCES, AND TECHNIQUES THAT ARE NOT BEING FOLLOWED THREW IN THE MOVEMENT!

IF YOU ARE GOING TO BUILD UP CONFIDENCE THEN PLEASE BUILD IT UP RIGHT!

WITH A STRONG SOLID FOUNDATION OF BASICS. AGAIN THIS IS NOT EVERYONE BUT JUST AN OPINION OF MOST.

SO WHEN I WAS IN MY TEENS I CALLED THIS DOJO, AND ASKED IF I COULD HAVE AN INTERVIEW AND A TOUR.

IMY CALL WAS ANSWERED BY THE OWNER, AND HEAD INSTRUCTOR. DURING THIS INTERVIEW HE HAD TOLD ME THE FOLLOWING …

"" THE MARTIAL ARTS ISN'T FOR YOU. I DO NOT THINK YOU WOULD DO WELL AT IT AT ALL! I AM NOT GOING TO WASTE MY TIME TO TEACH YOU. MAYBE YOU SHOULD FIND ANOTHER SPORT TO TRY? ""

I TO THIS DAY STILL STRONGLY BELIEVE THIS COMMENT SET MY DRIVE IN FULL MODE!

I SOMETIMES WONDER IF THIS MAN REMEMBERS ME TODAY AT ALL? AFTER ALL I STILL WORK IN THIS COMMUNITY, ANDMY FAMILY STILL LIVES IN TOWN.

WELL IF HE DOES OR IF HE DOESN'T ONE THING IS FOR SURE… I MADE A LIAR OUT OF HIS POOR JUDGEMENT CALL AND HIS NEGITIVE REMARKS TOWARDS ME.

BUT THIS TOO IS FINE WITH ME. IT IS HIS ENTITLEMENT TO DO SO. AS IT IS MINE TO REBUTTLE.

BUT THANK YOU. IT MADE THE WORLD OF DIFFERENCE IN MY PATH CHOICES FOR THE BETTER!

BECAUSE THIS IS HOW WE LEARN. FROM OUR MISTAKES, AND I HAVE MADE PLENTY IN MY LIFE TIME.

IT IS IN OUR HUMAN NATURE. WE ALL DO THIS. SO OF US CONSTANTLY!

ONCE YOU CAN STAND UP, AND SAY THIS OUT LOUD YOU WILL HAVE APPROACHED A NEW LEVEL IN YOUR TRAINING!

FOR THE BETTERMENT OF NOT ONLY YOURSELF, BUT TO YOUR STUDENTS TOO.

"" THOU SHALL NOT BE JUDGED UNTIL YOU HAVE WALKED A MILE IN ONES SHOES FROM THEIR OWN LIFE... ""

FAMILY LIFE THREW THE YEARS :

IN THE NEXT SEVERAL CHAPTERS OF THIS BOOK ENTITLED:

CHILDHOOD MEMORIES / YOUTH / YOUNG ADULT / ADULT / MEETING MY WIFE AND MASON.

I WILL BE TALKING ABOUT SOME OF MY PERSONAL EXPERIENCES, AND THOUGHTS ABOUT LIFE.

THAT MAY BE THE GROUND WORK THAT LEADS US INTO WHO WE BECOME AS WE ENTER OUR ADULT LIFE SPANS!

THESE EXPERIENCES START FROM CHILDHOOD, AND THEN EVOLVE THREW THE YEARS UNTIL ADULT HOOD BEGINS.

THEY ARE THE LITTLE THOUGHTS THAT COME BACK TO MY MEMORY THAT I ACCOUNT TO PINPOINTING MY FUTURE AS IT HAS DEVELOPED TODAY IN THE YEAR 2009.

OUR PATHS ARE FOLLOWED BY CHOICES THIS IS MY BASIS FOR THIS SECTION. CHOICE MAKE ALL THE DIFFERENCES IN THE WORLD OF OUR FUTURES!

"" TRYING TO FIND REASON FROM QUESTIONS OF CHOICE MAY LEAD US TO OUR PATH OF DESTINY? M.P.F ""

CHILDHOOD MEMORIES :

AS A CHILD I CAN REMEMBER BITS AND PIECES OF MY EARLY DAYS. STARTING FROM AROUND THE AGE OF FOUR YEARS OF AGE.

THE MEMORIES THAT STICK WITH ME THE MOST ARE LEARNING TO RIDE A BIKE.

MY AUNT JOYCE, AND ADOPTIVE MOM MYRTLE WHO WAS MY GRANDMOTHER TOO TOOK ME OUT EVERYDAY.

UNTIL THE DAY CAME WHEN I HAD LOST THE TRAINING WHEELS, AND TOOK FLIGHT BY MY SELF FOR THE FIRST TIME.

IT WAS A GREAT FEELING! I ACTUALLY CAN STILL REMEMBER IT WELL REFLECTING THE EMOTIONS OF THE DAY AS I WRITE IT DOWN HERE.

EVEN LOSING MY BALANCE, AND SMASHING INTO MY SWINGSET IN THE BACKYARD!

MY SECOND FOND MEMORY WAS LEARNING HOW TO SWIM. MY UNCLE USED TO TAKE ME TO THE LOCAL LAKE IN WEBSTER QUITE OFTEN.

MOST OF THE TIME IT WAS ON AN EARLY SATURDAY MORNING. SOMETIMES AFTER WORK DURING THE WEEK TOO.

NEXT WE WORKED ARE WAY INTO THE KIDS POOL IN OUR YARD. BACK THEM MY POP BOUGHT US AN INGROUND POOL TO SWIM IN.

THE MEMORIES THROUGH THESE YEARS EVEN STILL TODAY WITH MY OWN SON ARE VAST!

MASON LOVES SPENDING TIME IN THE FAMILY POOL WHICH TODAY IS NOW MY UNCLES HOUSE.

WE ARE DIFFENTLY A WATER FAMILY. THE SPAS, POOLS, LAKES, AND OCEANS…

SPEAKING OF THE OCEAN AFTER THE INGROUND POOL, AND BECOMING A GOOD SWIMMER MY UNCLE THEN TOOK ME TO THE OCEAN.

WE PROABLE WENT TWICE A MONTH SOMETIMES MORE TO THE OCEAN STATE PARKS IN CONN.

OUR FAVORITE BACK THEM WAS A PLACE CALLED POINT JUDITH. I LOVED EVERY MINUTE OF IT!

THE FRESH STING OF THE SALTY AIR, THE SMELL OF CRAB FRITTERS IN THE STREETS, AND SWEET COLD HOMEMADE ICE CREAM.

THEN THEIR WAS THE WAVES POUNDING THE BEACH. SEARCHING FOR SHELLS AT THE LIGHTHOUSE ON THE POINT.

IT WAS FUN WAY BACK THEN, AND THIS TOO IS STILL A FAMILY FAVORITE WITH MY FAMILY TAMMY AND MASON!

THE ONLY DIFFERENCE BEING THAT WE TRAVEL ALL OVER THE WORLD TO EXPLORE ITS WONDERFUL BEACHES.

THERE IS ONE THING THAT I NEVER DID LIKE. THIS WAS SUN TAN LOTION, AND I STILL DON'T LIKE IT!

BUT BECAUSE OF ALL THE TIME I DO SPEND OUTDOORS I WEAR IT ALL THE TIME ONCE THE TEMP REACHES A STEADY EIGHTY DEGREES.

MY LAST KEY MEMORY FROM THIS ERA WAS GETTING MY FIRST EVER GAS POWERED GO - KART!

THE FUN WE ALL HAD WITH THIS WAS UNBELIEVABLE.

I THINK THE OLD TRACKS IN THE YARD JUST FINALLY HEALED UP NOT MORE THAN A COUPLE OF YEARS AGO.

I TOOK MY GO - KART OUT EVERYDAY. I JUST LOVED TO RIDE AND RIDE. MY POPS BROTHER UNCLE DOUG WAS THE WORST OF ALL US KIDS.

HE WAS LIKE A RACE CAR DRIVER WHEN EVER HE GOT ON! ALL YOU HEARD ROUND THE BENDS WAS SCREACHING OF TIRES AGAINST THE DIRT FOLLOWED BY SHEER LAUGHTER!

HE WAS A REGULAR DAREDEVIL TO SAY THE LEAST! BEFORE THE GO - KART CAME MY RIDE USED TO BE THE OLD TRACTOR.

THE STORIES I HAD TO MAKE UP FOR ALL THE TIMES I CRASHED IT INTO THE SHED AS WELL AS THE HOUSE WERE SINFUL!

OLD MR GRINCH WOULD HAVE BEEN PROUD OF ME THEN. FOR SURE.

YOUTH :

DURING MY YOUTH I CAN ONLY RECALL THREE MAIN TARGET MEMORIES.

THE FIRST WAS MANY OUTDOOR ADVENTURES IN CAMPING WITH MY UNCLE, COUSIN, AND POP.

THESE WERE THE DAYS WERE THE OLD STORIES OF ROUGHING IT CAME TO BE.

BACK THEN THERE WERE NO MODERN DAY PLEASURES IN CAMPING. NO DIGITAL RADIOS OR DVD PERSONAL PLAYERS.

NO PORTABLE AIR OR HEAT REGULATORS. NOT EVEN BLOW UP BEDS! BUT THEIR WAS AN OUTHOUSE!

AND IF YOU WERE LUCKY A SOME WHAT HOT SHOWER TOO. BUT MOST OF THE TIME IT WAS COLD!

FOOD AND DRINKS ONLY LASTED AS LONG AS THE ICE DID IN THE COOLER.

AGAIN THIS WASN'T LONG EITHER. THEN YOU HAD TO HIKE TO FIND AN OLD COUNTRY STORE FOR NEW SUPPLIES.

THIS COULD TAKE ALL DAY. BUT THE OUTDOOR COOKING OVER THE OPEN FIRE WAS WELL WORTH IT ALL.

I STILL DREAM THAT I HEAR POP ASKING … *"" WHERE DID ALL THE BACON GO? ""*

POP DID ALL OF THE COOKING, AND MY UNCLE, COUSIN AND I DID ALL THE EATING. OH YES AND NIKKI OUR ALASKAN WOLF DOG TOO.

IN THE END THERE WASN'T MUCH LEFT FOR POP TO EAT OR WE USED TO FIND IT FUNNY WHEN HIS HOTDOG STICK BURNT OFF INTO THE FIRE WITH HIS HOTDOG!

THE SECOND WAS PLAYING BASKETBALL. MY FRIEND KEVIN AND I USED TO DO THIS ALL DAY LONG.

I PLAYED IN THE SUMMER PARKS LEAUGE, THE BOYS CLUB, AND I EVEN MADE THE HIGH SCHOOL TEAM ONCE BEFORE I QUIT.

I REALLY DID LOVE TO PLAY BASKETBALL. I EVEN RECEIVED A COUPLE OF AWARDS IN IT AS WELL.

BUT THE MAIN REASON FOR ME STOPPING WAS CLEAR AND SIMPLE.

TO ME IT BECAME A MATTER OF PRINCIPLE! WHICH WAS THIS… EVERY YEAR I MADE THE TEAMS.

I BUSTED MY NUTS AT ALL THE PRACTICES, BUT WHEN I PLAYED HIGH SCHOOL BALL THE ATHLETIC DIRECTOR AT THE TIME MR. DONALD CUSHING AT BARTLETT HIGH SCHOOL THEN MADE ME SIT THE BENCH!

ALL THE TIME FOR EVERY GAME FOR THE WHOLE YEAR!

I NEVER HAD THE CHANCE TO PLAY. EVER! WHY? BECAUSE I HAD A PONY TAIL, AND REFUSED TO CUT IT OFF. THAT'S WHY!

SO I FINALLY TOLD HIM HOW I FELT ABOUT THE WHOLE ORDEAL, AND EXACTLY WHAT I THOUGHT ABOUT HIM AND THE SCHOOL.

AFTER THIS I NEVER PLAYED ANY HIGH SCHOOL SPORTS EVER AGAIN. NOR WAS I ASKED TO.

THE SCHOOL NOW ACTUALLY HAS WHAT THEY REFER TO AS THEIR HALL OF FAME AWARDS FOR SPORTS FROM ALUMNI FROM YEARS PAST.

IT IS TOO BAD THAT I WILL NEVER BE PLACED INTO THIS. MAINLY THAT MY SPORT OF MARTIAL ARTS IS NOT A HIGH SCHOOL EVENT.

ALSO FOR THE FACT OF MY THOUGHTS AND WORDS TO THE SCHOOL WAY BACK THEN.

BUT NOW OVER TWENTY YEARS LATER AND BEING PLACED INTO FOUR HALL OF FAMES…

TWO NATIONAL AND TWO INTERNATIONAL I HAVE GROWN BY LEAPS AND BOUNDS. I HAVE LEARNED FROM MY MISTAKES.

WHO KNOWS PERHAPS ONE DAY MY OLD HOMETOWN WILL REMEMBER ME FOR WHO I HAVE BECOME, AND WHERE IT WAS I CAME FROM?

THE THIRD KEY MEMORY STILL REFLECTS UPON ME TODAY. THAT MEMORY WAS PLAYING MUSIC.

I HAD EXPRESSED AN INTREST IN PLAYING DRUMS SINCE THE AGE OF SIX.

SO MY GRAM AND POP GOT ME SOME PRIVATE LESSONS.

IN DOING SO I HAD TWO GREAT TEACHERS. THE FIRST WAS DURING ME HIGH SCHOOL YEARS WITH ONE OF THE BEST DRUMMERS AROUND.

HIS NAME WAS DAVID PEPKA. THEN LATER ON IN LIFE DURING MY COLLEGE YEARS I HAD HIS TEACHER MR. JIM KELLY.

BOTH HAD SHOWN ME SO MUCH IN THE FIELD OF MUSIC AND ITS STUDIES!

AS A SMALL BOY I PLAYED IN THE SCHOOL MUSIC DEPARTMENT IN MY HOMETOWN OF WEBSTER MA.

I PLAYED FROM THE FOURTH GRADE RIGHT UP THROUGH MY SENIOR YEAR IN HIGH SCHOOL AT BARTLETT HIGH.

TODAY MUSIC IS STILL VERY MUCH A PART OF MY LIFE. I STILL LIKE TO PLAY. ALTHOUGH TIME IS SCARCE I DO OCCASIONALLY FIND THE TIME.

I ALSO ON OCCASION AM ABLE TO SHARE THIS WITH MASON TOO. HE HAS ALSO SHOWN AN INTEREST IN DRUMS FROM TIME TO TIME.

BUT HE HAS MADE NO PERMANENT COMMITMENT TO THE PRACTICE OF DOING SO YET.

WHILE IN THE MUSIC DEPARTMENT IN SCHOOL I PLAYED IN THE CONCERT, MARCHING, AND STAGE JAZZ BAND.

I ALSO WAS PLAYING IN MY OWN BAND THAT WAS STARTED WITH MY FRIEND AT THE TIME JASON ZAPKA.

THE NAME OF THIS BAND WAS LICKETYSPLIT IN HIGHSCHOOL, AND AFTER HIGHSCHOOL WE CHANGED ITS NAME TO FREEBEER.

AS FAR AS THE BAND WENT THIS IS MORE THAN LIKELY HOW I GOT SO USED TO WALKING SO MUCH!

FROM ALL THE PARADES AND FOOTBALL GAME HALFTIME SHOWS. MY FEET AND SHOULDERS WERE ALL MESSED UP!

THIS IS MAINLY BECAUSE I WAS CHOOSE TO PLAY THE TRI - TOMS FOR MARCHING.

THE WEIGHT OF THESE DRUMS WAS INCREDITABLE. THEY WERE REALLY HEAVY.

THEY CUT RIGHT INTO THE BLADES OF MY SHOULDERS BECAUSE THE HARNESS WAS OLD AND LACKING THE PROPER PADDING.

AS FOR MY FEET... WELL THERE WAS MANY A BLOODY SOCK THAT WERE TOSSED AWAY INTO THE TRASH!

OF ALL MY PLAYING MY FAVORITE WAS OF COURSE IN MY OWN BAND. WE HAD A LOT OF FUN!

THE NAME OF LICKETYSPLIT CAME FROM JASON. OUR FRIENDS LOVED OUR LOGO.

FOR THE FIRST THREE YEARS OF ITS BIRTH THE BAND CONSISTED OF JASON ZAPKA, JOE LOOMIS, AND I.

WE PLAYED BACKYARD PARTIES, OUR HIGH SCHOOL FOR VARIOUS ACTIVITES AND EVENTS, ONCE WE EVEN SOLD OUT THE TOWN HALL IN OUR HOMETOWN OF WEBSTER MA!

"" OLD NEWSPAPER CUT OUT FROM THE PATRIOT 1988 ""

BUT BY FAR THE BEST GIG WE EVER HAD WAS PLAYING FOR THE NATIONAL CHEERLEADING CONFERENCE!

THAT WAS AWESOME! AFTER THAT EVENING I NO LONGER HAD A GIRLFRIEND, BUT THAT IS A WHOLE DIFFERENT STORY FOR ANOTHER TIME.

LETS JUST SAY THIS: *" " GIRLS, GIRLS, & MORE GIRLS! " "*

AS THE YEARS WENT BY AND WE BECAME OLDER WE ADDED SOME NEW FACES TO THE BAND.

ALSO WE DECIDED TO CHANGE OUR NAME FROM LICKETYSPLIT TO FREEBEER.

WE HAD AN OVERWHELMING FOLLOWING WHERE EVER WE PLAYED! THIS WAS GREAT!

SO ANYWAYS JOE LOOMIS HAD LEFT THE BAND, AND WAS REPLACED BY MY GOOD FRIEND CORY MALBOUEF.

COREY NEVER REALIZED IS OWN TALENT, BUT HE WAS A GREAT ADDITION TO OUR BAND!

LIKE I SAID HE DIDN'T REALIZE IT FOR SOME TIME, BUT COREY PLAYED A MEAN BASS!

THEN CAME ALONG ERIC KALWARCZYK WHO TOOK OVER JASONS JOB AS LEAD, JOE HALKO WHO COULD DO EVERYTHING, AND DON GAUVIN WHO PLAYED THE KEYS.

WE HAD A GREAT BAND. THE MORE WE PLAYED THE BIGGER OUR FOLLOWING BECAME.

I REALLY MISS THOSE DAYS! WE WERE TOGETHER FOR ABOUT EIGHT YEARS AND JASON AND I FOR AROUND FIFTEEN YRS PLAYING OUR MUSIC.

ACTUALLY ALL OF US WERE PRETTY TALENTED AT WHAT WE DID, AND THE MUSIC WE PERFORMED SHOWED IT!

IT WAS AN EXECELLENT EXPERIENCE IN MY LIFE TO SPREAD THE JOY OF MUSIC FOR ALL TO LISTEN TO AND ENJOY.

WE USED TO PLAY THREE SETS A NIGHT WITH ONLY ONE TEN MINUTE BREAK!

THE FIRST SET WAS OLDIES FOR THE OLDER CROWD, AND THE SECOND SET WAS MOSTLY TOP TWENTY FOR THE INBETWEEN CROWD.

OUR LAST SET WAS SPLIT INTO TWO. THE FIRST WAS COUNTRY FOR THE GOOD ALL BOYS IN TOWNAND THE FINAL WAS REGGAE FOR THE WILDER YOUNGER ADULT WOMEN!

THESE PEOPLE WERE ALWAYS LATE IN THE EVENING TO COME AROUND. THE LIFE OF THE PARTY TYPE.

ALL IN ALL PLAYING MUSIC THEN, AND NOW IS STILL AN EXPERIENCE THAT I HIGHLY RECOMMEND TO ALL.

"" *JASON ZAPKA ~ MICHAEL P. FARADAY ~ DON GAUVIN ~ CORY MALBOUEF ~ DAN POPLAWSKI ~ ERIC KALWARCZYK ~ JOE HALKO ""*

"" *TOP LEFT TO BOTTOM RIGHT ... ERIC'S BACKYARD BASH ~ JAYS GARAGE ~ BAND PHOTO SHOOT ~ THE P.A.C.C. ~ MY MASK ~ T.S.K.K. ~ ? ~ CHEERS BAR ~ STATE LINE CASINO ~ BAND PHOTO SHOOT ""*

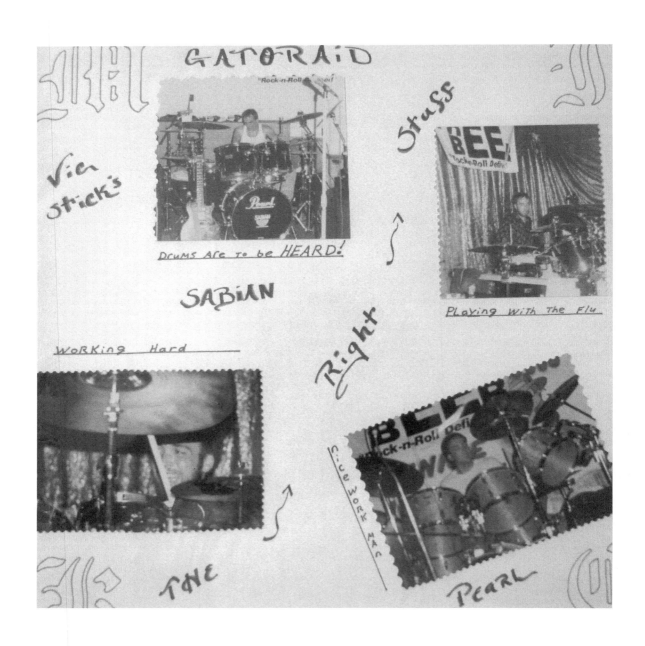

"" ... WORKING MY GROOVE ... ""

"" DRUMS & MORE DRUMS! ""

YOUNG ADULT :

IN MY YOUNG ADULT STAGE OF LIFE I WAS JUST LIKE ANY OTHER HITTING MY TEENS.

SO I THOUGHT ANYWAYS... MY NUMBER ONE GOAL WAS GIRLS! LOTS AND LOTS OF THEM.

I REMEMBER GETTING THAT FAITHFUL SPEECH FROM GRAM AND POP ... ...

"" MICHAEL YOUR JOB RIGHT NOW IS TO FOCUS AND DO WELL IN SCHOOL! YOUR NOT MAJORING IN GIRLFRIENDS! ""

BUT I WAS PLAYING IN A BAND, AND IT JUST SEAMED THAT THERE WERE ALWAYS GIRLS AROUND.

ONES THAT WOULD DO ANYTHING TO BE WITH ME. I LIKED THIS! VERY MUCH SO.

IT SEEMED THAT I WAS ALSO ALWAYS ATTRACTED TO THE BAD GIRL TYPE TOO, OR AT LEAST MOST OF THE TIME!

ALL THE REST OF MY TIME WAS SPENT RUNNING AROUND WITH THE CHEERLEADERS.

THIS TOO WAS AWESOME FOR MANY REASONS... I'LL JUST LET YOU THINK ABOUT WHAT I MEAN?

ALTHOUGH MY PARENTS DID NOT APPROVE OF MY GIRLFRIENDS MOST OF THE TIME I ACTUALLY DID DO RATHER WELL IN MY SCHOOLING.

OUT OF MY FOUR YEARS IN BARTLETT HIGH SCHOOL I MANAGED TO MAKE THE HONOR ROLL EACH QUARTER EVER YEAR EXCEPT FOR TWO TIMES.

SO THAT MAKES FOURTEEN TIMES OUT OF SIXTEEN! BESIDES THIS GREAT ACHIEVEMENT I ALSO MADE AND WAS INDUCTED INTO WHOS WHO AMONG AMERICAN HIGH SCHOOL TWICE!

SO I DID LISTEN TO MY PARENTS, AND I HAD WORKED REALLY HARD!

BUT AS FAR AS WHAT I LIKED TO DO AND WITH WHO... I STILL DID AS I PLEASED!

WHAT I FIND FUNNY ABOUT THIS TODAY IS THAT WOMEN THAT I WENT T SCHOOL WITH BACK IN THE DAY THAT I NEVER THOUGHT I WOULD EVER HAVE A CHANCE WITH …

HAVE TOLD ME: *"" MIKE! REALLY … WHAT WERE YOU THNKING? THE TRAMPS YOU KEPT FOR COMPANY WERE NASTY! YOU COULD HAVE HAD ME. ""*

WELL MY REPLY WAS: *"" WHY DIDN'T YOU SAY SOMETHING WAY BACK THEN? ""*

SO IN THIS LIFE IS FUNNY. ITS ALL ABOUT CHOICES… WHAT IF I DID THIS?

OR WHAT IF I WENT HERE, OR STILL YET WHAT IF? … … … .. ..?

CHOICES IN LIFE ARE NEVER ENDING! IN MARTIAL ARTS WE CALL THIS ASPECT YING AND YANG.

WITH OUT ANY DOUBT! THE CIRCLE OF LIFE AS IT REFLECTS ACROSS THE UNIVERSE. AGAIN … WHAT IF?

NEXT CAME MY DRIVERS LICENSE, AND MY VERY FIRST CAR. I LOVED MY FIRST CAR!

IT WAS A WHITE CAMARO WITH RED INTERIOR, AND IT WAS FAST! TOO FAST IN FACT FOR ME.

MY FRIENDS USED TO CALL ME THE WHITE KNIGHT. DUE TO THE FACT OF ALL THE FAIR MAIDENS I SO CALLED RESCUED?

IT TOOK ME SEVERAL BAD EXPERIENCES BEFORE I LEARNED HOW TO SMARTEN UP.

ONCE I REALIZED THIS, AND TRADED IN MY SPORTS CAR FOR A MORE CONSERVATIVE VEHICAL ALL MY PROBLEMS WENT AWAY.

I TRADE IN MY CAMARO FOR A BRAND NEW BUICK SKYHAWK. THIS CAR WAS A COOL CANDY APPLE RED.

I LOVE THE COLOR RED, BECAUSE IT RELATES TO POWER! IT IS A BOLD STRONG COLOR.

NOW AS FOR ONE OF THOSE BAD EXPERIENCES HERE IS BY FAR THE WORST ONE EVER!

I HOPE THAT EVERYONE WHO READS THIS CAN LEARN FROM MY POOR JUDGEMENT, AND NOT HAVE TO LIVE WHAT I HAVE HAD TO LIVE WITH EVER SINCE THAT DAY!

AFTER SCHOOL WE ALWAYS RAISED HELL! BOTH WITH AND WITHOUT OUR CARS.

THIS ONE DAY FOR WHAT EVER REASON I CAN NOT FIGURE OUT BECAME THE WORST DAY OF MY LIFE!

I HAD MY TWO SISTERS JOSY AND DONNA ALONE WITH MY GIRLFRIEND AT THE TIME SUSAN MANSKI.

WE WERE HEADING HOME AFTER SCHOOL … IT WAS JUST ONE OF THOSE DAYS.

I COULD NOT WAIT TO JUST GET HOME, AND HAVE SOME ALONE TIME WITH MY GIRLFRIEND.

BUT MY FRIENDS HAD OTHER PLANS FOR ME THIS DAY. THEY JUST WANTED TO DO CRAZY STUFF!

SUCH AS ROOF SURFING, AND DRINKING ETC… HOWEVER I WASN'T INTERESTED.

SO WE FOUGHT A BIT, AND I GOT IN THE CAR TURNED UP THE RAIDO TO A FULL BLAST, AND THEN SCREAMED OUT OF THE PARKING LOT!

IT WASN'T UNTIL I HEARD MY FRIEND TROY ARPIN SCREAMING … *""*
MIKE YOU ASSHOLE! STOP!!!! STOP!! DONNIE JUST FELL OFF! … ""

I DIDN'T EVEN REALIZE THEY WERE ON THE BACK OF MY CAR. WHEN THEY WERE FIRST THEIR I TOLD THEM TO GET OFF!

AND WHEN I THOUGHT I HAD SEEN THEM SHUFFLE OF TO THE SIDE I SPED OFF.

THEN BEFORE I SCREAMED OUT OF THERE I HAD BLAIRED THE RADIO. I COULDN'T HEAR ANYTHING.

PLUS THEIR WERE SO MANY PEOPLE IN THE CAR " MY TWO SISTERS, MY GIRLFRIEND, AND MY OTHER FRIEND CHRIS ROGALA. ""

I WAS SO PREOCCUPIED WITH ALL OF THEM THAT I FAILED TO DO THE RIGHT THING AFTER MY FIGHT WITH TROY AND DONNIE.

THAT WAS TO PAY ATTENTION! IF ONLY I HAVE LIKE I SHOULD HAVE …
THINGS WOULD HAVE BEEN DIFFERENT FOR ALL OF US TODAY.

IT WAS REALLY STRANGE. THE FEELING, AND MY STATE OF MIND BOTH
DURING AND AFTER THE ACCIDENT.

IT SEAMED LIKE EVERYTHING WAS A DREAM IN SLOW MOTION. I COULD
SEE, BUT MY PROCESS OF THOUGHT DIDN'T REGISTER.

DONNIE WAS IN VERY BAD SHAPE! THERE WAS NO WAY OF GETTING OUT
OF THIS!

THEREWAS NO ONE AROUND AT FIRST. THEN WE WERE SURROUNDED BY
WHAT SEEMED TO BE ABOUT FIFTY PEOPLE!

ALL AROUND US IN A CIRCLE OF DISBELIEF OF THE EVENT. NEXT I
REMEMBER SEEING THE RED AND BLUE FLASHING LIGHTS!

LOOKING OVER AT MY FRIEND HE LOOKED LIKE A PUDDLE OF BROKEN
FLESH!

HIS WHOLE BODY WAS IN TOTAL CHAOS! HIS EYES WERE TURNED IN SIDE
OUT.

HIS WHOLE BODY WAS SHAKING OUT OF CONTROL. THE BLOOD WAS
EVERYWHERE!

THERE WAS ALSO VARIOUS BODY FLUIDS SPURTING ABOUT. IT WAS NOT
GOOD!

DON LEFT IN AN AMBULANCE, AND I LEFT IN A POLICE CAR! IT WAS A
ROUGH NIGHT IN WITH THE DETECTIVE!

HIS NAME WAS ROGER SMITH. I WILL NEVER FORGET. DURING MY MANY
HOURS OF QUESTIONING AND ANSWERING SESSION WITH HIM!

LATER ON VERY LATE I WAS RELEASED TO MY PARENTS. THIS TOO WAS A
HARD THING TO FACE.

THE NEXT DAY I FOUND OUT THAT DONNIE WAS IN THE INTENSIVE CARE
UNIT AT ST. VINCENTS HOSPITAL IN WORCESTER MA.

HE HAD SUFFERED A BLOOD CLOT IN HIS BRAIN FOR ONE, AND HAD
SEVERAL OTHER SERIOUS ISSUES.

THE FEELING OF REMORSE THAT HAD SET IN WAS UNSPEAKABLE!

WHEN I WENT TO VISIT HIM ALONG WITH TROY AND MANY OTHER FRIENDS I HAD TO FACE HIS PARENTS!

TO MY SURPRISE THEY NEVER BLAMED ME FOR THE ACCIDENT! NOR DID THEY SEEK ANY PUNISHMENT OF DAMAGES.

THEY DIDN'T EVEN SPEAK HARSH TO ME. THIS WAS A HUGH RELIEF. BECAUSE IT WASN'T LIKE THIS BACK IN MY HOUSE WITH MY PARENTS.

IT WAS SEVERAL MONTHS UNTIL DON RECOVERED, AND WAS RELEASHED FROM THE HOSPITAL.

LIKE FOUR MONTHS. THREE OF THOSE UNDER INTENSIVE CARE! NO ONE EVER SAID A WORD TO ME.

THEN BY THE FIFTH MONTH I RECEIVED A DOCUMENT FROM THE COURT SYSTEM.

ATTACHED TO THIS WAS ALSO A TICKET FOR DRIVING TO ENDANGER WITH A FORMAL HEARING DATE.

I WAS SCARED STIFF! SO WERE MY PARENTS. THINGS IN SCHOOL WERE NEVER THE SAME FOR ME AFTER THIS EITHER.

I WASN'T LIKED MUCH BY OTHER PARENTS TO SAY THE LEAST! SO TAKING A NICE GIRL OUT WAS NOT IN MY FUTURE.

THEY WERE NOT ALLOWED! THEN THE COURT DATE ARRIVED…

DONNIE AND I WENT TOGETHER. HE TOLD ME FROM THE DAY HE WAS OUT OF THE I.C.U. RIGHT UP TO THE DRIVE UP TO THE COURT HOUSE THAT …

IT WASN'T MY FAULT, AND HE DIDN'T BLAME ME FOR THE ACCIDENT AT ALL. IT WAS HIS FAULT FOR BEING STUPID.

HOWEVER; IN REALITY IT WAS BOTH OF OUR FAULTS REALLY. WE WERE BOTH STUPID!

DONNIE THE SAID TO ME: "" *IT WAS ME AND TROY WHO DECIDED TO BE FOOLISH. IT WAS A HORRIABLE EXPERIENCE FOR ALL OF US!*

BUT THIS IS WHAT HAPPENS WHEN YOU FOOL AROUND, AND DO STUPID STUFF! ""

WE WALKED INTO THE DUDLEY DISTRICT COURTHOUSE, AND WERE TOLD TO WAIT. BOTH OUR PARENTS WERE THERE AS WELL.

WE WERE CALLED INTO CLOSED CHAMBERS. THE MEETING WENT LIKE THIS:

"" MICHAEL ... DO YOU KNOW HOW MUCH TROUBLE YOU ARE IN? I REPLIED YES. ""

THE JUDGE SAID: *"" NO YOU DO NOT! ""* THEN HE ASKED DONNIES PARENTS IF THEY HAD ANYTHING THEY WANTED TO SAY…

DONNIES DAD SAID: *"" NO YOUR HONOR. THEY ARE GOOD FRIENDS. WHAT HAPPENED WAS AN ACCIDENT THAT COULD HAVE BEEN PROVENTED.*

HOWEVER WE DO NOT WISH TO PRESS ANY CHARGES OR SUE. "" THE JUDGE WAS VERY SURPRIZED!

HE THEN SAID: *"" ARE YOU SURE? ""* DONS DAD SAID: *"" YES WE ARE SURE. THESE BOYS WILL HAVE TO LIVE WITH THE MEMORY.*

HOPEFULLY THEY HAVE LEARNED FROM IT. "" WELL TO SAY THE LEAST MY POP WAS RELIVED AT THIS POINT.

BUT … ! THE JUDGE HADN'T RENDERED HIS DECISION AS OF YET…

NEXT THE JUDGE SLAMMED HIS HANDS DOWN UPON HIS DESK, AND STARTED SCREAMING AT ME!

PRETTY MUCH HE THREW THE BOOK AT ME, AND THEN SAID: *"" YOU ARE THE LUCKIEST PERSON IN THE COURT ROOM THIS MORNING! THAT IN FACT HAD EVER TO THIS POINT WALKED INTO MY CHAMBERS! ""*

THE TICKET WAS DISMISSED, AND THE OTHER CHARGES WERE DROPPED BY THE STATE TOO.

HOWEVER; THE JUDGE HAD TOLD ME VERY SPECIFIC:

"" MICHAEL ... IF YOU EVER APPEAR IN MY COURT AGAIN, IF YOU EVER RECEIVE ANOTHER TICKET FOR ANYTHING AT ALL, OR WHAT EVER ELSE … YOU WILL LOOSE YOUR DRIVERS LICENSE UNTIL YOU REACH THE AGE OF TWENTYONE! TRUST MY WORDS SIR. ""

"" ALSO ON TOP OF THAT YOU WILL RECEIVE ONE HEFTY FINE, AND WILL BE PROVIDED A SHORT SENTENCE OF AT LEAST ONE WEEK IN JAIL. SO YOU CAN REMEMBER THE FIRST CHANCE I GAVE TO YOU! ""

"" DO I MAKE MYSELF CLEAR … ? I THEN REPLIED: "" CRYSTAL. THANK YOU YOUR HONOR. ""

THEN WE ALL WENT BACK HOME, AND BACK TO SCHOOL. AFTER A WHILE ALL WAS FORGOTTEN.

ALL OF US MOVED FORWARD IN OUR LIFES. WE GRADUATED FROM HIGHSCHOOL, AND STARTED OUR NEW LIFES.

SOME OF US WENT TO COLLEGE, AND OTHERS WENT STRAIGHT TO WORK. THEN THEIR WERE THE ONES WHO WE LEFT IN BETWEEN.

THEY DIDN'T QUITE KNOW WHAT TO DO, OR WHERE TO GO IN THEIR ADULT LIFE.

LEAVING HOME WITHOUT MOM AND DAD PROVIDING FOR YOU IS A HARD REALITY TO BEAR FOR SOME PEOPLE.

BUT WHAT STILL MAKES ME FEEL BAD AFTER ALL THESE YEARS IS THIS …

ONCE IN A WHILE ON THE RARE OCCASION THAT I MIGHT SEE DONNIE TODAY I CAN'T HELP BUT NOTICE ONE THING ABOUT HIM FROM THE ACCIDENT.

THIS IS THAT SOMETIMES WHEN WE ARE TALKING IT SEEMS AS IF HE JUST FORGETS WHERE HE WAS IN THE CONVERSATION, AND REPETS HIMSELF LIKE NOTHING WAS EVER SAID.

THIS MAKES ME WONDER? IS THIS BECAUSE OF ME? I FEEL MUCH REGRET ABOUT THIS!

ALTHOUGH NOW THERE IS NOTHING I CAN DO TO FIX WHAT HAD HAPPENED MANY YEARS AGO, I WISH THAT I COULD.

THE ONLY THING THAT I CAN DO IS SHARE THIS STORY OF BEING STUPID FROM MY YOUTH!

TO SHOW YOU HOW FAST YOU CAN CHANGE NOT ONLY YOUR LIFE, BUT OTHERS AS WELL.

PLEASE! ALWAYS THINK OF THE OPTIONS OF CONSEQUENCE BEFORE YOU TAKE ACTION! SAFTEY FIRST.

NEXT CAME THE COLLEGE YEARS FOR ME. I ATTENDED NICHOLS COLLEGE IN DUDLEY MA FOR BUSINESS AND ACCOUNTING.

I ONLY STAYED THERE FOR HALF A YEAR BECAUSE I FOUND OUT I DIDN'T CARE MUCH FOR MY CHOICE.

SO WITH THAT I HAD DECIDED TO TRANSFER TO A TWO YEAR SCHOOL, AND EARN MY ASSOCIATES DEGREE INSTEAD.

THIS DECISION WAS TO HONOR MY PARENTS FOR THEIR WISHES OF ME TO GRADUATE FROM COLLEGE WITH A DEGREE.

AFTER THE FIRST FEW MONTHS I REALIZED THAT THE FOUR YEAR PLAN WAS NOT FOR ME!

THE SCHOOL I TRANSFERRED TO WAS CALLED DUDLEY HALL. IT WAS LOCATED IN WORCESTER MA.

IT WAS HERE THAT I DID WHAT I HAD TO DO SO THAT I COULD FINISH MY TIME WITHIN A ONE YEAR PERIOD.

I ATTENDED EXTRA CLASSES, WENT FOR HOLIDAY BREAK CLASSES, AND TOOK CLASSES IN THE SUMMER TIME AS WELL.

WITH GREAT ACHIEVEMENT, AND LOTS OF TIME SPENT ON TASK I EARNED MY ASSOCIATES DEGREE IN ACCOUNTING AND BUSINESS MANAGEMENT IN ONE YEARS TIME!

THIS ACT TAUGHT ME WHAT DISCPLINE OF MY STUDIES WAS ALL ABOUT.

ONCE OUT OF SCHOOL IT WAS DIFFICULT TO FIND WORK. THERE WERE SEVERAL LOW LEVEL ENTRY JOBS AND TO MANY PEOPLE TO FILL THEM.

BUT I FINALLY LANDED MY FIRST JOB WITH A COMPANY DOING SMALL BUSINESS AND PERSONAL INCOME TAXES.

I ALSO PERFORMED THE FRONT WORK IN THE FINANCIAL PLANNING TOO.

FOR REASONS OF SELF RESPECT TO THE INNOCENT, AND NOT TO PROMOTE BAD PUBLICITY FOR A COMPANY THAT IS VAST IN SIZE I WILL NOT MENTION THE NAME OF THIS BUSINESS.

THIS AGAIN IS MAINLY DUE TO THE CORRUPT ACTIONS THAT I BECAME AWARE OF THAT I HAD NO CONTROL OVER.

I FOUND OUT VERY QUICKLY THAT THESE FEW GUYS WERE PRETTY MUCH MAKING A KILLING STEALING FROM THE ELDERY!

I MAY HAVE BEEN YOUNG, BUT I WASN'T NIEVE. SO UNABLE TO MAKE A DIFFERENCE I LEFT.

REALLY WHO IS GOING TO BELIEVE THE WORD OF A YOUNG KID WHO JUST GRADUATED FROM COLLEGE AGAINST MEN WHO HAD BE WITH THE COMPANY FOR DECADES?

SO INSTEAD OF BEING FIRED FOR ACCUSATIONS I LEFT ON MY OWN TERMS TOSEEK OTHER EMPLOYMENT.

I NEVER EVEN WENT BACK FOR MY LAST CHECK EITHER. ALSO THEY NEVER MAILED IT TO ME.

SOMETIMES PRIDE IS MORE THAN VALUE TO CURRENCY. KNOW WHAT I MEAN?
SO MY NEXT STEP WAS APPLYING TO THE UNITED STATES POSTAL SERVICE.

I WANTED TO BE A LETTER CARRIER. THIS WAS OF INTEREST TO ME. BEING OUTSIDE NOBODY TO BOTHER YOU.

OR SO I HAD THOUGHT … AND GETTING PLENTY OF FREE EXERCISE TOO. THIS I DID GET AND STILL DO.

LITTLE DID I KNOW ABOUT THIS EITHER, BUT I HAVE BEEN WORKING FOR THE GOVERNMENT NOW SINCE DECEMBER THE TWENTY SEVENTH OF 1990.

LATER ON I WILL OUTLINE A FEW OF THE MANY MEMORIES OF WORKING FOR THE POSTAL SERVICE.

THE THINGS I WITNESS EACH DAY IS SO FAR OUT THERE YOU WOULDN'T BELIVE THEM!

HOWEVER YOU JUST CAN'T MAKE THIS STUFF UP! IT IS REALLY GOING ON BOTH INSIDE THE BUILDING AND OUT.

TO WRITE ABOUT ALL THAT I HAVE BEEN THREW WITH THE POSTAL SERVICE COULD BECOME A NOVEL IN ITS SELF!

SO I WILL CHOOSE A FEW THOUGHTS THAT WILL STRONGLY PUT MY POINTS ACROSS.

I HAVE DECIDED TO SAY A BRIEF STATEMENT ABOUT THE COMPANY FOLLOWED BY A SHORT COLLECTION OF PERSONAL STORIES.

THESE ARE EXPERIENCES THAT HAVE TRANSPIRED THREW MY MANY YEARS OF EMPLOYMENT WITH THE SERVICE.

AGAIN THIS WILL BE DISCUSSED LATER ON TOWARDS THE END OF THIS BOOK.

THANK YOU FOR YOUR UNDERSTANDING, AND I HOPE ONCE YOU REACH THE SECTION YOU WILL SEE WHAT IT IS I AM TALKING ABOUT.

MEETING MY WIFE :

DURING MY LIFETIME I HAD MADE PLENTY OF MISTAKES IN RELATIONSHIPS!

BUT THIS IS GOOD, BECAUSE IT HELPS DETERMINE WHAT YOU TRULY ARE SEEKING FOR COMPANIONSHIP IN A MATE.

IT IS DIFFICULT TO FIND WHAT OUR SOCIETY DESCRIBES AS TRUE LOVE, OR THE RIGHT ONE TO DEATH DO US PART.

RELATIONSHIPS HAVE TO BE CONSTANTLY DEFINED! ONCE YOU DO FIND WHAT IT IS YOU THINK YOU WANT THERE IS WORK TO BE DONE.

REALLY IN MY OPINION THE KEY TO A STRONG EVERLASTING WORKING RELATION IS NOT ABOUT LOVE.

IT IS ALL ABOUT THE ACT OF TOLERATION. HOW MUCH CAN YOU TOLERATE?

IF YOU CAN DETERMINE THIS FACTOR IN YOUR LIFE TO YOUR RELATION IN MARRIAGE YOU WILL BE TOGETHER UNTIL DEATH DO YOU PART!

SO WHEN I FIRST MET MY WIFE TAMMY JEAN {BARNES} FARADAY ON THAT LABOR DAY WEEKEND BACK IN 1993 …

I KNEW SHE THIS WOMEN WAS THE ONE! EVEN IF SHE HER SELF DIDN'T KNOW THAT I WAS HERS.

BELIEVE ME AT FIRST SHE WAS NOT CONVINCED, AND IT TOOK ME AWHILE TO DO SO.

I WAS VERY PERSISTENT ON THE COURTSHIP OF HER HAND! IN THE END I WON HER HEART.

I MET HER IN WORCESTER MA AT A PLACE CALLED BACK IN THE DAY PAPA JOES.

IT WAS ONE OF THOSE CLUBS THAT HAD LIMITED FOOD SERVICE AVALIABLE.

WHAT IT LACKED IN ONE TERM IT PROSPERED IN ANOTHER. THIS WAS A PLACE THAT WOMEN WENT TO HAVE A GOOD TIME DANCING THE NIGHT AWAY.

IT ALSO HAD VOLLEYBALL COURTS OUTSIDE FOR US GUYS. THIS WAS AND STILL IS ONE OF MY FAVORITE ACTIVITIES TODAY.

ALL THE ALCOHOLIC DRINKS WERE A PLUS AS WELL. ONCE YOU PUT ALL THESE FACTORS IN PLAY THERE WAS PLENTY TO COOSE FROM.

AS I GLANCED ACROSS THE CROWDED ROOM I SAW HER DANCING WITH HER GIRLFRIEND MARISSA.

THE TWO OF THEM STOOD OUT FROM THE REST OF THE CROWD, BECAUSE THEY WERE THE HOTTEST WOMEN IN THE PLACE!

BY FAR, BUT IT WAS TAMMY I HAD IN INTEREST IN. LIKE I SAID THERE WAS SOMETHING DIFFERENT ABOUT HER?

SO I APPROACHED HER… SHE WAS VERY POLITE AND WE STARTED TALKING.

THEN AFTER A SHORT WHILE WE DANCED TOGETHER A LITTLE BIT. THIS IS ONE THING THAT I AM NOT ONLY BAD AT, BUT HAVE NO INTEREST IN AT ALL.

HOWEVER; IT WAS SOMETHING SHE WAS QUITE FOND OF SO I WENT WITH THE FLOW.

NEXT WE WENT TO A TABLE THEY WERE HOLDING. I WAS WITH MY FRIEND JOE.

LITTLE DID I KNOW THAT TAMMY AND JOE KNEW EACH OTHER. THE TWO OF THEM ACTUALLY WENT TO SCHOOL TOGETHER.

THEY ALSO WORKED TOGETHER AT KMART TOO. BACK WHEN THEY WERE IN HIGHSCHOOL.

THEN SHE TOLD ME SHE REMEMBERED ME FROM SCHOOL AS WELL. I WAS AT A LOSS.

I DIDN'T RECALL HER NOT AT ALL. THEN SHE DESCRIBED ME AS THE STUCKUP JOCK THAT STOOD AGAINST THE WALL LOOKING AT ALL THE CHEERLEADERS.

OK SO SHE HAD MY NUMBER! SHE WASN'T A CHEERLEADER AND SO I GUESS I NEVER TOOK NOTICE.

BUT I NOW WISH THAT I HAD! IF I DID MAYBE I WOULD NOT HAVE WASTED SO MANY YEARS ON WHAT WAS NOTHING MORE THAN BAD MEMORIES.

WELL AT THE END OF THIS NIGHT SHE GAVE HER NUMBER TO JOE. BUT NOT TO ME!

THIS MADE ME ANGRY. SO WHEN JOE AND I LEFT I ASKED HIM FOR HER NUMBER.

HE IGNORED ME. THEN ONCE WE WERE BACK IN MY CAR I ASKED HIM AGAIN…

"" *HEY BUDDY! I BELIEVE THAT NUMBER WAS MENT FOR ME?* "" HIS REPLY: "" *NO IT ISN'T!* ""

I SAID: "" *YES IT IS! MAY I PLEASE HAVE IT?* THEN JOE TOLD ME: "" *NOT IN THIS LIFETIME.* ""

OK I TRIED TO BE NICE ABOUT IT, BUT I SAW THAT I WAS GETTING NOWHERE.

SO I REACHED ACROSS THE CAR, AND CLOCKED HIM ONE! THEN I TOOK THE NUMBER FROM HIM.

AFTER THAT THINGS WENT SURPRISINGLY GOOD. NEXT I WENT LOOKING FOR A SINGLE ROSE.

THIS IS HARD TO FIND AT MIDNIGHT. BUT I FOUND ONE, AND THEN WENT BACK HOPPING THAT HER CAR WAS STILL AT PAPA JOES.

IT WAS AND I PLACED THE ROSE WITH A NOTE ON HER WINDSHIELD.

LATER ON THAT WEEK I DECIDED TO GIVE HER A CALL. SHE WAS SURPRISED TO HEAR FROM ME.

SHE HAD SAID HOW DID YOU GET MY NUMBER? SO I TOLD HER EVERYTHING.

AFTER TALKING TO HER THAT NIGHT WE TALKED AGAIN THE NEXT. THEN ANOTHER…

THEN WE MET UP AGAIN AT THE SAME CLUB THE NEXT WEEKEND. THING WERE MOVING FORWARD NICELY.

FROM THIS POINT ON I SLOWLY BECAME PART OF HER LIFE. OUR FIRST OFFICAL DATE WAS IN OCTOBER OF THAT SAME YEAR.

WE WENT TO SEE A BRUCE WILLIS MOVIE CALLED STRIKING DISTANCE. I EVEN REMEMBER WHAT SHE WAS WEARING THAT NIGHT.

SHE HAD ON A WHITE DRESS SHIRT WITH LOTS OF FLAIR TO IT WITH TIGHT SLEEK BLACK PANTS.

ALSO SHE WAS WEARING A GOLD JACKET WITH BLACK TRIM. OH … MAN! DID SHE LOOK HOT!

I FELT LIKE THE LUCKIEST MAN IN THE WORLD. THE MOVIE WAS GREAT. THEN WE WENT TO CATCH A BITE TO EAT.

WE HAD DECIDED TO GOTO THIS CHINESE PLACE IN WORCESTER CALLED THE HOY TOY.

IT WAS AT THE TIME ONE OF TAMMYS FAVORITE HANGOUTS. THING WERE GETTING EVEN BETTER.

BEFORE I KNEW IT WE WERE SEEING EACH OTHER MORE AND MORE. EVENTUALLY I MOVED IN WITH HER.

TAMMY HAD AN APARTMENT THAT SHE SHARED WITH FRIENDS. ONE OF THOSE FRIENDS WE STILL SEE FROM TIME TO TIME.

HER NAME IS LINDA, AND SHE LIVES IN SOUTH CAROLINA ON MRYTLE BEACH NOW.

EACH NIGHT WE WENT OUT I SHOWED UP WITH ANOTHER BAG OF CLOTHS.

THEN ONE NIGHT AS SHE OPENED UP HER CLOSET, AND A PILE OF BAGS FELL ON HER…

TAMMY SAID: *"" WHERE DID ALL THIS COME FROM? DO YOU THINK YOU LIVE HERE OR SOMETHING? ""*

I SAID: *"" YES? ""* THEN SHE LAUGH … APPERENTLY SO MICHAEL. SHE SAID TO ME.

I LOVE ALMOST EVERY MINUTE WITH HER, BUT AS TIME WENT ON I HATED THE APARTMENT MORE AND MORE!

IT IS DIFFICULT TO HAVE ROOM MATES. ESPECIALLY ONES YOU REALLY DO NOT KNOW WELL.

NOT TO MENTION THAT I NEVER HAD LEFT HOME BEFORE FOR MORE THAN A COUPLE OF NIGHT HERE AND THERE.

SO THE DAY FINALLY CAME THAT I SAT TAMMY DOWN AND SAID: *" " LETS LOOK FOR OUR OWN PLACE. " "*

SHE SAID: *" " OK BUT IT NEEDS TO BE CLOSE FOR ME TO WHERE I AM NOW. IF AT ALL POSSIABLE THANK YOU. " "*

LIKE WHERE I ASKED HER? SHE THEN SAID WELL I AM FROM WORCESTER, AND YOU ARE FROM WEBSTER.

SO HOW ABOUT SOME WHERE IN BETWEEN THE TWO? WELL IT CAME TO BE AUBURN.

WE HAVE LIVED HER EVER SINCE. THE SELLING POINT OF OUR HOME WAS THE FIREPLACES. OF ALL THINGS TO BASE YOUR WHOLE LIFE TOGETHER ON.

ON THE REALISTIC SIDE OF THINGS THE LOCATION WAS VERY CLOSE TO ALL MAJOR ROUTES, AND PERSONAL NECESSITIES.

THIS WAS A BIG STEP FOR US BOTH, AND OUR FIRST HOME TOGETHER. NO MORE APARTMENTS!

WE PURCHASED THIS HOME IN APRIL OF 1994. THIS WASN'T EVEN A YEAR SINCE WE HAD STARTED DATING.

TALK ABOUT WHAT IF'S… BUT I HAD THE FEELING THAT IT WAS MENT TO BE. ALL THESE YEARS LATER… … … I WAS RIGHT!

LIKE EVERYONE ELSE THERE IS SO MUCH TO DO, AND LITTLE TIME TO ACCOMPLISH YOUR TASKS.

BUT WE ARE HAPPY FOR THE PROJECTS THAT WE HAVE FINISHED THAT MAKE OUR LIFE AND OUR HOME TOGETHER.

AFTER WE MOVED INTO OUR NEW HOME IT WAS ABOUT FIVE OR SIX MONTHS LATER THAT I ASKED TAMMY TO MARRY ME.

SHE SAID YES! THEN ON JULY 23RD OF 1995 OUT BY MY FAMILIES POOL ON THE GAZABO WE WERE MARRIED.

WHAT A BEAUTIFUL DAY IT WAS! THE WALKWAY WAS THREW LILAC HEDGES, AND DOWN ALONG SIDE THE POOL.

WE HAD A SMALL GROUP OF ABOUT TENTY FIVE OR THIRTY OF FAMILY AND CLOSE FRIENDS IN ATTENDANCE.

THEN AFTER WE HAD A LARGE RECEPTION OF AROUND ONE HUNDRED AND SEVENTYFIVE GUESTS.

OUR RECEPTION WAS HELD IN WEBSTER MA AT THE P.A.V. CLUB. IT WAS ONE NIGHT I WILL REMEMBER FOR THE REST OF MY LIFE!

BEING ONE OF THE MOST MEMORABLE EVENTS OF MY LIFE IF I COULD GO BACK IN TIME AND CHANGE THINGS IT WOULD HAVE BEEN TO HAVE MY MOM NANCY THERE.

AT THE TIME I WAS VERY UNHAPPY WITH HER AND DIDN'T INVITE HER TO OUR WEDDING.

FOR THIS I AM TRULY SAD, AND WISH I HAD BEEN A BETTER PERSON. TODAY WE ARE VERY CLOSE.

SO I GUESS THAT THING IN OUR LIFE DO HAPPEN FOR STRANGE AND UN - EXPLAINABLE REASONS.

OTHER THAN THIS I WOULDN'T HAVE CHANGED A THING.

THERE WERE SOME REAL FUNNY EVENTS THAT HAPPENED DURING THE PARTY.

LIKE FOR ONE MY NEPHEW ANDY FELL INTO A DRINK BUCKET! WE NOTICED IT AFTER THE FACT WHILE WATCHING OUR WEDDING VIDEO.

IT WAS REALLY FUNNY! WE SHOULD HAVE SENT IT IN TO THAT SHOW. AMERICAS FUNNIEST HOME VIDEOS.

THEN THERE WAS THE WEDDING GAMES. FOR THE BRIDE AND GROOM GARDER DANCE FOR ONE.

TAMMY AND I GAVE OUR FAMILIES AS WELL AS OUR FRIENDS A REAL SHOCK!

WHEN I WENT HEAD FIRST UP HER DRESS, AND CAME OUT WITH HER FANCEY UNDERWEAR IN MY TEETH.

YOU CAN BET ALL THE SINGLE MEN LINED UP FOR THAT CATCH! BUT I
USED HER GARDER FOR THAT, AND I KEPT THE GOOD STUFF!

THE NEXT MORNING WE WERE OFF TO DISNEYWORLD. IT WAS AWESOME!
LIFE HAD NOW BEGAN A NEW PURPOSE FOR ME.

SPENDING THE REST OF MY LIFE … WITH THE WOMAN OF MY DREAMS!

MS. TAMMY JEAN BARNES NOW AS MRS TAMMY JEAN FARADAY SOUNDS
GREAT.

*"" MY WIFE TAMMY HAD THIS PORTRAIT PAINTED FOR ME FOR CHRISTMAS
1994""*

"" JULY 23RD 1995 ""

MASON :

IT WAS AROUND THE EARLY SPRING OF 1999 WHEN TAMMY AND I WERE WONDERING WHEN WE MIGHT BE BLESSED WITH CHILDREN.

WE TRIED HARD ENOUGH THAT'S FOR SURE!   BUT NOTHING WAS HAPPENING.

SO WE SET UP AN APPOINTMENT WITH OUR DOCTORS TO SEE WHAT MIGHT BE GOING ON?

WHEN TAMMYS RESULTS CAME BACK SHE WAS FINE. IT WAS ME WHO HAD THE PROBLEM.

MY RESULTS CAME BACK IN AT A NINTYNINE . NINE AS A SOLID NO! WHAT A BLOW.

I WAS REALLY DOWN AND OUT AFTER THIS NEWS! SO WE JUST DID WHAT EVER WE WANTED.

WHEN EVER WE WANTED OR WISHED TO DO SO. IT WAS DURING THIS PERIOD OF TIME THAT MY MARTIAL ARTS TRANING WAS COMING TO ITS PEAK.

I WAS TRAVELING QUITE A BIT ALL AROUND THE STATES FOR TOURNAMENTS.

THEN THAT SPECIAL DAY CAME. I WAS APPROACHED BY TEAM AMERICA!

I HAD JUST WON THE STATE CHAMPIONSHIPS AT THE REGGIE LEWIS TRACK AND FIELD CENTER IN DOWNTOWN BOSTON.

THIS HAPPENED IN SEPTEMBER OF 1999. I WAS ASKED IF I HAD A MOMENT BY THE REPRESENTATIVE?

I SAID: "" *SURE.* "" THEN I WAS OFFERED A SPOT ON THE TEAM. RIGHT THERE NO QUESTIONS ASKED.

I DIDN'T SAY YES A FIRST. I HAD TOLD THEM I NEEDED TO CHECKOUT SOME OF THE INFORMATION THAT THEY HAVE GIVING TO ME FIRST.

I WASN'T SURE WHAT THEY WERE FEEDING ME? IT WAS ALL TO GOOD TO BE TRUE.

THEN I WOULD GET BACK TO THEM AND LET THEM KNOW ABOUT MY COMMITMENT.

SO I MADE SOME CALLS AND TALKED TO SOME OTHER PEOPLE I TRUSTED IN THE MARTIAL ARTS.

IT TURNOUT IT WAS THE REAL DEAL! SO I CALLED THE HEAD COACH MR. BRUCE SMITH RIGHT AWAY.

AND THAT WAS THAT. THE NEXT THING I KNEW I WAS TRAINING TO GOTO AUSTRILIA FOR THE WORLD GAMES IN THE YEAR 2000.

THIS WAS THE FIRST TIME IN MY LIFE THAT TAMMY AND I WERE SEPERATED FOR A PERIOD OF TIME.

SHE WASN'T ABLE TO GET LEAVE FROM HER WORK AT THE SHREWSBURY CHILDREN'S CENTER TO COME WITH ME.

THIS WAS EXTREMELY DIFFICULT FOR US BOTH! SO THE NIGHT BEFORE I LEFT ON THIS HUGH ADVENTURE TAMMY PLANNED A SPECIAL NIGHT FOR ME.

FIRST WE WENT OUT TO EAT AT CHUCK'S STEAKHOUSE. THEN WE WENT TO SEE THE MOVIE FINAL DESTINATION OF ALL MOVIES TO GO SEE!

MIND YOU I WAS LOOKING AT OVER TWENTYNINE HOURS FLIGHT FROM PROVIDENCE RI, TO ATLANTA, TO LOS ANGELES CA, TO SYDNEY AUSTRILIA.

IF YOU HAVE SEEN THIS MOVIE THEN YOU KNOW WHAT I MEAN. THEN WE WENT HOME AND SPENT OUR FINAL NIGHT TOGETHER.

THE NEXT MORNING I WAS PICKED UP TO GOTO T.F. GREEN IN PROVIDENCE. IT WAS 5:OO A.M..

AS THE LIMO DROVE OFF I LOOKED BACK TO GIVE TAMMY THAT LAST GLANCE…

IT BROKE MY HEART TO SEE HER IN TEARS! I WILL NEVER FORGET THE FEELING EVER.

IT DOWN RIGHT SUCKED. I LOVE HER SO MUCH, AND SHE KNEW IT. THIS IS WHAT ONLY MATTERED IN THE END!

BECAUSE THIS MADE ME FEEL SO HORRIABLE I WANTED NOW MORE THAN EVER TO MAKE HER PROUD OF ME.

THIS WAS THE FIRST OF MANY TIMES I HAD SAID TO MYSELF… "" *I AM NOT TRAVELING ALL ACROSS THE WORLD TO COME HOME EMPTY HANDED!* ""

WHEN I CAME BACK HOME A LITTLE OVER TWO WEEKS LATER WE HAD A LOT OF CELEBRATING TO DO!

AND WE DID JUST THAT. FIRST TO BE RE CONNECTED AFTER OUR FIRST TIME APART,   AND SECOND I HAD JUST WON MY FIRST EVER WORLDGAMES!

I BROUGHT HOME TWO GOLD AND THREE SILVER MEDALS FROM AUSTRILIA.

THEN ABOUT TWO MONTHS LATER .. TAMMY BECAME SICK. SHE STARTED BEING SICK A LOT.

NEXT BECAUSE OF THIS SHE MADE AN APPOINTMENT WITH HER DOCTOR.

WHEN SHE CALLED ME AT WORK LATER ON THAT LATE DAY IN JUNE SHE TOLD ME SHE HAD SOMETHING TO TELL ME ABOUT.

IT DROVE ME CRAZY ALL DAY. THAT NIGHT I WAS SUPPOSED TO LEAVE STRAIGHT FROM WORK WITH MY FRIEND MICHAEL AND GOTO A KISS CONCERT.

I ASKED HER IF SHE WANTED ME TO CANCLE AND COME STRAIGHT HOME? SHE SAID: "" *NO. GO HAVE A GOOD TIME I'LL SEE YOU TONIGHT.* ""

THE NIGHT DRAGGED ON LIKE WHAT SEEMED TO BE FOREVER! ALL KINDS OF THOUGHT WERE RUNNING THROUGH MY MIND.

BUT NOT THE THOUGHT THAT I WAS GOING TO BE TOLD LATER ON THAT EVENING.

TAMMY WAS FINALLY PREGNANT! SHE WAS TOLD THAT SEE WAS FIVE WEEKS ALONG.

WE WERE BOTH SO EXCITED! THEN IT HIT ME. MY DOCTOR TOLD ME NEVER. SO LIKE WHAT WAS GOING ON?

SO I CALLED HIM. HIS RESPONSE TO ME WAS … ITS YOUR LUCKEY DAY!

THE POINT ONE PERCENTAGE CHANCE CAME TO BE.

PLUS THE TEST WAS TAKEN SEVERAL YEARS AGO. HE THEN EXPLAINED TO ME THAT OUR BODIES GO THROUGH CHANGES OVER A PERIOD OF TIME.

THAT THIS COULD AND WOULD MAKE A DIFFERENCE. SO I SAID: *" WHY DIDN'T YOU TELL THIS TO ME YEARS AGO? "'*

TAMMY AND I LAUGH ABOUT THIS NOW, AND PAY TRIBUTE TO THE WEIRD SEAFOOD THAT I ATE IN AUSTRILIA.

IT WAS CALLED A SEABUG. IT WAS ABOUT THE SIZE AND SHAPE OF A FRISBEE.

PERSONALLY I BELIEVE IT WAS A MUTATION OF A LOBSTER TYPE FROM HIROSHIMA RADIATION AFTERMATH FROM BACK IN THE DAY.

THERE ARE SOME REAL STRANGE SPECIES AROUND THIS AREA AFTER THE FIRST ATOMIC BOMB.

WE THINK THAT BY EATING THIS IT CHANGED MY BODY CHEMICAL COMPOUNDS. YOU NEVER KNOW?

NOW WE HAD NEVER THE LESS ANOTHER PURPOSE IN LIFE TO PREPARE FOR.

THE BIRTH OF OUR FIRST CHILD! LET THE NESTING BEGIN. SO WE MADE HIS ROOM, AND FILLED IT UP WITH CUTE CHILD DÉCOR.

THIS WAS LOTS OF FUN. PICKING OUT CLOTHS, AND TOY, AND JUST ABOUT EVERYTHING ELSE TOO.

TO THIS DAY I STILL HAVE HIS FIRST ULTRASOUND IMAGE ON MY DESK AT WORK.

WE WERE GOING TO HAVE A BOY. WHEN WE STARTED THIS NEW VENTURE WE NEVER WANTED TO KNOW THE SEX OF OUR CHILD.

WE WANTED IT TO BE A SURPRIZE. HOWEVER THE ULTRA SOUND CLEARLY SHOWED US WE WERE HAVING A BOY!

SO WE NAMED HIM MASON DOUGLAS FARADAY. IF HE WAS GOING TO BE A GIRL THE NAME WAS GOING TO BE ALEXANDRIA ANAITA FARADAY.

THE NAME MASON DOUGLAS HAS FAMILY HISTORY BEHIND IT. SO WHEN WE PUT ONE THING TOGETHER WITH ANOTHER IT WORKED FOR US.

BUT I DO HAVE TO ACKNOWLEDGE THE FACT THAT AT FIRST WE HAD KNOW IDEA.

IT WASN'T UNTIL GRAM AND POP HAD INFORMED US ABOUT FAMILY HISTORY.

I ORIGINALLY WANTED TO NAME HIM MASON STORM FARADAY. HOWEVER MY WIFE SAID NO WAY!

REMEMBER THIS IF YOU REMEMBER NOTHING ELSE… "" *A HAPPY LIFE IS A HAPPY WIFE!* ""

ALSO IF WE DID HAVE TO GO THE OTHER WAY IN THE PICKING OF THE NAME FOR A GIRL THAT NAME HAD FAMILY HISTORY TO MY WIFES SIDE OF THE FAMILY.

THEN ON ONE OF THE WORST SNOWSTORMS THAT WE HAVE HAD PROABLE SINCE THE BIG BLIZZARD OF SEVENTYEIGHT OUR SON MASON DOUGLAS FARADAY WAS BORN!

THIS TOOK PLACE ON MARCH SECOND OF 2001. HE WAS BORN AT MEDCITY WORCESTER MA.

I WAS WITH MY WIFE THROUGH THE WHOLE ORDEAL FROM BEGGING TO END.

I HELPED DELIVER MY BOY AND I ALSO CUT THE CORD MYSELF. VERY UNIQUE EXPERIENCE!

I MUST SAY THOUGH IT WAS TOUGH. IT TOOK TWO TRIES TOCUT THAT CORD!

AGAIN IT WAS AWESOME! THE MOST ENLIGHTENED EXPERIENCE I HAVE EVER WITNESSED.

THE VERY FIRST TIME I EVER HELD HIM IT FELT SO STRANGE. I CALLED HIM MY LITTLE ALIEN.

HE WAS OUR MIRACLE BABY! OUR FIRST AND ONLY. MASON IS MY BEST BUDDY.

TAMMY, MASON AND I ARE VERY CLOSE! WE DO EVERYTHING TOGETHER.

TOGETHER WE HAVE TRAVELED AROUND THE WORLD AND BACK AGAIN WITH HIM.

HIS VERY FIRST TRIP WAS AT SIX MONTHS OLD. WHEN I FOUGHT IN IRELAND AT THE WORLDGAMES.

HE CAME WITH US TO THE EMERALD ISL. HOW MANY PARENTS CAN SAY THEY DID THIS?

WE HAVE BEEN VERY FORTUNATE. THIS IS FOR SURE! TO BE ABLE TO DO SO MUCH WHERE OTHERS CAN NOT.

WHEN EVER WE CAN MAKE A SMALL DIFFERENCE IN SOMEBODYS LIFE NO MATTER WHAT THAT MIGHT BE… WE DO IT!

BUT MY WIFE DOES THE MOST OF ALL. SHE IS LIKE A MODERN DAY MOTHER THERSA!

THOSE OF YOU WHO KNOW HER WILL AGREE. SHE IS ONE THOUGHTFUL PERSON, AND ONE HELL OF A WOMEN!

MASON MAKES US VERY PROUD! HE IS A GREAT SON. HE ALSO HAS COME SUCH A LONG WAY SINCE HE WAS BORN.

WE HAD RUN INTO SEVERAL PROBLEMS WITH HIM AFTER HIS BIRTH.

ON THE NIGHT HE WAS BORN DURING THE NIGHT HE WAS TAKEN AWAY, AND PUT INTO THE I.C.U.!

HE HAD SPIT UP AN UNUSUAL AMOUNT OF A GREEN FLUID! HE BECAME VERY SICK.

HE ALSO HAD OTHER PROBLEMS SUCH AS A LOW SALT LEVEL, AND SOMETHING WITH HIS BLOOD TOO.

MASON WAS IN THE INTENSIVE CARE UNIT FOR ABOUT A MONTH BEFORE HE WAS RELEASED INTO A REGULAR ROOM.

TAMMY AND I NEVER LEFT HIS SIDE! NOT EVEN ONCE. WE LIVED IN THAT HOSPITAL FOR ALMOST SEVEN WEEKS!

THE STRESS WAS OR SHOULD I SAY BECAME UNBAREABLE! ALTHOUGH THE HOSPITAL PROVIDED US WITH A FAMILY ROOM.
SO THIS ALLOWED US TO STAY TOGETHER FOR THE ENTIRE LENGTH OF TIME.

AS TIME WENT ON … HE WAS PROGRESSING WELL, AND THE DAY CAME WHEN WE COULD FINALLY TAKE HIM HOME!

I STAYED HOME WITH THE BOTH OF THEM FOR TWELVE WEEKS STRAIGHT. BEFORE I RETURNED TO WORK.

GOING BACK WAS ROUGH. ESPECIALLY DOING WHAT I DO FOR A LIVING.

THEN AFTER ALL THIS WE HAD OTHER PROBLEMS WITH MASONS HEALTH, BUT NOTHNG OUT OF THE ORDINARY.

ITS JUST HARD TO BE FIRST TIME PARENTS AND HAVE ALL THIS HAPPEN TO YOU. IT BREAKS THE HEART!

IF YOU CAN GO THREW ALL THAT TAMMY AND I HAVE GONE THROUGH IN OUR LIFE AND MARRIAGE TOGETHER THEN YOUR BOND IS QUITE STRONG!

SO EVERYTHING WAS NEW TO US AND THIS WAS UNTIL MASON HAD HIS FIRST IMMUNE SHOTS!

WE CAN NOT PROVE THE FACT, BUT IT SEEMS THAT MOST CHILDREN WHO RECEIVED THIS SHOT DURING THIS PERIOD OF TIME HAS DEVELOPED SOME TYPE OF HARDSHIP!

THESE HARDSHIPS ARE ALL RELATED TO ONE OF TWO TOPICS. THE FIRST BEING LEARNING DISABLITIES, AND THE SECOND BEING MEDICAL IN ORIGIN.

WHERE THESE DRUGS TAINTED? WAS OUR SON ONE OF THE BABIES WHO RECEIVED A BAD BATCH?

OR MAYBE … JUST MAYBE DID THIS SHOT CAUSE AN ALLERGIC REACTION TO SOME OF THE CHILDREN WHICH RESULTED IN AUTISM?

WE WILL NEVER KNOW THE ANSWERS TO THESE QUESTIONS FOR SURE!

BUT WHAT WE DO KNOW IS THIS… AFTER OUR SON RECEIVED THIS SHOT AT THE AGE OF TWO WITHIN THE NEXT THREE MONTHS WE NOTICED A HUGH CHANGE IN HIM.

MASONS BEHAVIOR AS WELL AS HIS OVERALL HEALTH STARTED TO CHANGE FOR THE WORST!

MASON HAD STARTED TO BECOME DISTANT FROM US! HE STOPPED TALKING ALL TOGETHER, AND ALL AT ONCE.

NEXT HE DIDN'T EAT THE WAY HE USED TO! BEFORE HE ATE ANYTHING AND EVERYTHING PUT IN FRONT OF HIM.

NOW HE WOULD ONLY EAT CERTAIN FOODS. AGAIN NOTHING LIKE HE USED TO.

THEN THERE WAS THE ISSUE OF SLEEPING… MASON WOULD BE UP FOR A PERIOD OF LIKE TWENTY HOURS STRAIGHT!

HE DIDN'T TAKE ANY NAPS DURING THIS TIME EITHER. THEN HE WOULD SLEEP FOR FOUR HOURS.

EXACTLY AFTER FOUR HOURS ALMOST EVERYDAY HE WOULD START HIS DAY.

FOR ANOTHER TWENTY HOURS! TALK ABOUT A STRAIN ON YOUR RELATIONSHIP!

NEVER MIND THE FATIGUE OR MENTAL STRESS MY MARRIAGE WAS SUFFERING FROM THE CONSTANT PRESSURE FROM THIS ORDEAL!

SO TAMMY AND I TOOK MASON TO THE DOCTORS. THE DOCTOR THEN TOLD US THIS:

"" *MASON IS HEALTHY AND HAPPY. LEAVE IT ALONE.* ""

WELL TAMMY AND I DIDN'T EXCEPT THIS FOR AN ANSWER! WE SOUGHT ANOTHER MEDICAL OPINION FROM THE STAFF AT UMASS HOSPITAL.

IT WAS HERE WE WERE TOLD THAT OUR SON HAD A FORM OF AUTISM. ITS LABEL WAS TERMED: { A. S. D. }.

THEY THEN INFORMED US OF WHAT WE HAD TO DO NEXT, AND HOW TO GO ABOUT IT.

UMASS TOOK US STEP BY STEP AND HELPED US CONFRONT MASONS MEDICAL PROBLEM.

NEXT THE TEAM OF DOCTORS WE HAD PUT MASON IN A PROGRAM FOR KIDS WHO ALSO SUFFERED FROM SIMILAR CONDITIONS.

THIS PROGRAM LEAD BY THE HOSPITAL WAS LOCATED AT THE GALVIN CENTER IN SHREWSBURY MA.

THIS PROGRAM WORKED AWESOME! THE STAFF WORKED WITH MASON TWO TO THREE TIMES A WEEK.

ON TOP OF THIS ONE OF THE STAFF ALSO VISITED OUR HOME ONCE A WEEK TO WORK WITH MASON TOO.

HER NAME WAS RUTH. SO BETWEEN HER, UMASS, MY WIFE TAMMY, AND I MASON WAS ON THE PATH TO RECOVERY.

TAMMY GAVE UP HER CAREER AS A TEACHER FOR ALMOST FIVE YEARS.

JUST SO SHE COULD BE THERE AND HELP MASON AS MUCH AS POSSIABLE. I WISH I WAS ABLE TO GET MORE TIME OFF FROM WORK SO THAT I COULD HAVE HELPED MORE TOO.

HOWEVER THAT WASN'T AN OPTION AT OUR DISPOSAL.

THE PROGRAM THROUGH UMASS LASTED FOR TWO YEARS. THEN UMASS SETUP THE NEXT STEP IN MASONS THERPY PROGRAM.

THEY CONTACTED THE AUBURN SCHOOL SYSTEM, AND HELPED US ENROLL MASON INTO A SPECIAL PROGRAM THERE.

THIS PROGRAM WAS LOCATED AT THE MARY D. STONE SCHOOL BEHIND THE AUBURN TOWN OFFICES.

WE COULDN'T BE MORE HAPPIER WITH UMASS OR OUR TOWN FOR ALL THE SERVICES THAT THEY PROVIDED TO OUR FAMILY!

THE ATTENTION AND THE CARE TO DETAIL THROUGH THE AUBURN SCHOOL SYSTEM WAS UNSURPASSED!

THE ENTIRE STAFF IS WELL TRAINED AS WELL AS EXTREMELY CARING.

WITH THEIR HELP OUR SON NOW LIVES A NORMAL LIFE. BOTH AT HOME AND WITH HIS FRIENDS.

MASON IS NOW IN THE FORTH GRADE AND HIS AUTISM IS GETTING TO THE POINT FOR WHICH YOU WOULD NEVER KNOW IT EXISTED IN THE FIRST PLACE.

HIS GRADES ARE EXECELLENT, AND HIS BEHAVIOR IS FAIRLY GOOD MOST OF THE TIME.

THE ONLY PROBLEM WE STILL REALLY FACE IS HIS EATING HABITS. THIS STILL NEEDS A LOT OF WORK.

BUT IT TOO IS GETTING BETTER. MASON HAS MADE REMARKABLE IMPROVEMENTS!

HE MAKES TAMMY AND I AS WELL AS OUR ENTIRE FAMILY VERY PROUD OF ALL HIS ACCOMPLISHMENTS!

SO TO ALL OF YOU WHO WERE THERE FOR US IN THE SCHOOL SYSTEM, AND THROUGH THE UMASS MEDICAL CENTER … THANK YOU VERY MUCH FOR ALL YOUR HARD WORK AND EFFORTS.

THIS PATH WAS EXTREMELY LONG AND VERY DIFFICULT TO PROGRESS THROUGH.

SO MANY FAMILIES OUT THERE NEGLECT THE TRUTH OF THE MEDICAL PROBLEMS OF THEIR CHILDREN.

WHEN THEY FINALLY REALIZE AND ACCEPT THE PROBLEM IT IS USUALLY TO LATE TO OVERCOME THE DISABILITY!

THE SOONER YOU ACT THE BETTER CHANCE YOU HAVE TO DEFEAT IT.

TAMMY AND I DID WHAT WE HAD TO, AND PUT IN THE TIME THAT WAS REQUIRED SO OUR SON WOULD HAVE A GOOD LIFE!

WE DIDN'T EXPECT OTHERS TO DO THE JOB FOR US! WE TOOK MATTERS INTO OUR OWN HANDS.

WE SOUGHT OUT THE MEDICAL HELP AND SERVICES PAIRED WITH OUR LOVE AND CONSTANT WORK TOO THAT WAS NEEDED TO CORRECT MASONS DISABILITY.

THIS AGAIN WAS NOT EASY BY ANY MEANS! BEYOND POPULAR BELIEFE OF OTHER FAMILY MEMBERS!

IT TOOK LOVE … CARING … TIME … TEACHING … AND ABOVE ALL A COMBINED TOTAL EFFORT!

MASON IS GOING TO BE TURNING TEN PRETTY SOON, AND HE IS BACK TO NORMAL.

EVEN THOUGH WE HAVE FOR THE MOST PART PULLED THROUGH MASON STILL REQUIRES CONSTANT STRUCTURE IN HIS LIFE.

WE DO OUR BEST AT ALL COSTS TO KEEP IT THERE FOR HIS WELL BEING!

NOW IF WE COULD ONLY GET HIM TO EAT A VEGGIE. THIS WOULD BE NICE.

MASON IS A HAPPY BOY WITH MUCH INTELLECT AND COMPASSION! HE IS ALSO EXCEPTIONALLY POLITE.

HE ASLO DOES VERY WELL AS I MENTIONED EARLIER IN SCHOOL WITH HIS STUDIES.

WE ARE VERY PROUD PARENTS INDEED!

MASON IS A REAL FUNNY CHARACTER AT TIMES, AND WE LOVE HIM MORE THAN ANYTHING IN THE WHOLE WORLD!

HE ENJOYS TRAVELING VERY MUCH. A VACATION TO HIM DOESEN'T BEGIN UNTIL WE GET ONTO A PLANE.

HE LOVES TO FLY, AND TRAVEL THE WORLD WITH HIS MOTHER AND I.

MASON ALSO ENJOYS MAKING PROJECTS AT HOME WITH HIS LEGOS, AND LEARNING ABOUT GHOSTS!

ANYTHING WITH UNEXPLAINED MYSTERIES, GHOST HUNTERS, THE PARANORMAL, AND ENCRYPTED MYTHICAL MONSTER FOLKLORE IS HIS CUP OF TEA!

MASON IS MY BEST BUDDY! WE SHARE MANY ADVENTURES IN LIFE TOGETHER ALONG SIDE MY WIFE TAMMY WHO IS THE LOVE OF MY LIFE.

" " MY SON THE WORLD TRAVELER ... ... 2010 FLORIDA " "

AILMENTS IN LIFE THAT CAUSED SET BACKS :

OBESITY

AS A YOUNG CHILD …   AROUND THE AGE OF FIVE TILL AROUND THE TIME I TURNED TWELVE OR SO …

I SUFFERED AND HAD A HUGH PROBLEM WITH OBESITY. I RECALL BEING NINE YEARS OF AGE, AND WEIGHING IN AT ONE HUNDRED AND EIGHTY THREE POUNDS?

WHEN I REACHED THE FIFTH GRADE I REMEMBER GOING DOWN TO THE NURSES STATION FOR OUR IN SCHOOL FISCAL.

I WAS ASKED TO STEP ONTO THE SCALE …   THEN THE COVERING DOCTOR SAID TO ME:

"" ARE YOU KIDDING ME? … ! YOU MY BOY ARE TWO HUNDRED AND FIFTEEN POUNDS! AND YOU ARE ONLY FIVE FEET TALL. ARE YOU PROUD OF YOURSELF? ""

MY ANSWER TO HIM WAS: *"" YES I AM. ""* ONE MIGHT THINK THIS SHOULD HAVE BEEN ENOUGH TO CONVINCE ME TO LOSE SOME WEIGHT.

A LOT OF WEIGHT AT THAT! HOWEVER; IT WASN'T UNTIL THE NEXT YEAR WHEN I HIT THE SIXTH GRADE.

I THEN REALIZED I NEEDED A CHANGE. KIDS ARE CRUEL YES THEY ARE …

THERE WAS THIS GIRL. HER NAME WAS LYNN SHAYS, AND I WAS MADLY IN LOVE WITH HER!

ONE DAY WHILE WE WERE AT THE TOWN LIBRARY I GOT UP THE NERVE TO ASK LYNN TO THE MOVIES.

WHAT SHE THEN TOLD ME CHANGED MY LIFE FOREVER! FROM THE END OF THE SIXTH GRADE UNTIL PRESENT TIME.

LYNN HAD SAID THIS: *"" I DO NOT HAVE SEX WITH FAT BOYS! ""*

WELL THAT'S ALL IT TOOK! BECAUSE THEN I WAS ON A MISSION. SCHOOL LET OUT FOR THE SUMMER ABOUT TWO WEEKS LATER …

IT WAS AT THIS TIME I STARTED TO DIET AND EXERCISE! BY THE END OF THE SUMMER I HAD CHANGED.

I HAD ACTUALLY CHANGED A LOT. I WENT FROM TWO HUNDRED AND FIFTEEN LBS TO ONE HUNDRED AND THIRTY POUNDS!

YES THIS NUMBER IS DRASTIC! BUT IF YOU KNOW ANYTHING ABOUT ME … I AM DETERMINED AND I AM NOT KIDDING EITHER.

NOW I COULDN'T WAIT TO SHOW MY FRIENDS AT SCHOOL THE NEW ME! NOT TO MENTION TO SEE LYNN, AND SEE HER REACTION?

WHEN I WENT BACK TO SCHOOL THAT NEXT FALL ONLY A FEW OF MY FRIENDS KNEW WHO I WAS.

I HAD LOST EIGHTYFIVE POUNDS FROM JUNE TO LABOR DAY. JUST THREE SHORT MONTHS OF HARD WORK HAD PAID OFF.

I FELT GREAT!   BUT LYNN I FOUND OUT MOVED AWAY OVER THE SUMMER.

NEVER THE LESS THIS WAS A HUGH ACHIEVEMENT AND TURNING POINT IN MY LIFE!

ASTHMA

I HAVE LIVED WITH THIS DIAGNOSIS PRETTY MUCH MY WHOLE LIFE. SINCE THE AGE OF THREE YEARS OLD.

OVER THE YEARS AS MY HEALTH IMPROVED FROM LOSING ALL THAT WEIGHT, AND ENGAGING IN REGULAR EXERCISE I HAVE LEARNED HOW TO CONTROL IT.

ALTHOUGH I STILL LIVE WITH THIS TODAY IT HARDLY EVER KICKS IN THESE DAYS.

HOWEVER THERE WAS A BRIEF INSTANCE WHERE I HAD BECOME SO ILL FROM THIS SICKNESS THAT I HAD ALMOST DIED!

I HAD MISSED FIVE MONTHS OF SCHOOL, BEFORE I MADE A FULL RECOVERY.

BACK WHEN I WAS A SMALL CHILD THE MEDICINE THAT WAS AVAILABLE WAS NOTHING LIKE WHAT WE HAVE TODAY!

EVEN THOUGH I AM NOT ONE THAT IS MUCH FOR TRADITIONAL RELIGON I HAD WHAT MAY BE CONSIDERED A VISION? … … …

THIS I WILL ALWAYS REMEMBER UNTIL THE DAY I MEET THIS VISION AGAIN!

AS I WAS DRIFTING AWAY FROM MORE AND MORE SICKNESS … I REMEMBER LIKE ALL OF A SUDDEN! …

SEEING A VERY BRIGHT LIGHT! AS IT SLOWLY APPROACHED ME CLOSER AND CLOSER …

I FELT A WARM LOVING KIND OF FEELING. COZY. WHOLESOME …

THEN I SAY A MAN! HE WAS TALL AND SLENDER IN BUILD STANDING OVER MY BED!

AS HE LEANED DOWN OVER ME … I SAY HIS EYES. THEY WERE A BRIGHT CLEAR BLUE.

VERY MUCH LIKE THE OCEAN ON A CRYSTAL CLEAR DAY! THEN HE PUT HIS HAND ON MY FACE …

BUT I WASN'T SCARED. IT DID FEEL STRANGE THOUGH … BUT AT THE SAME TIME IT ALSO FELT COOLING!

EVERYTHING BECAME PEACEFUL … WHEN I AWOKE MY FEVER HAD FINALLY BROKEN AFTER WEEKS OF SUFFERING!

THEN EACH DAY FOR IF I REMEMBER CORRECTLY WAS ABOUT TWO WEEKS …

I BECAME BETTER AND BETTER! I FELT MUCH STRONGER THAN USUAL AS WELL.

I HAD SPOKEN TO MY PARENTS ABOUT THIS … MY POP SAID I WAS JUST DREAMING.

BUT MY GRANDMOTHER TOLD ME THAT I WAS BLESSED!

WHAT EVER DID REALLY HAPPEN … I MAY NEVER KNOW. BUT I DO KNOW THIS: …

I NEVER EVER WAS THAT SICK EVER AGAIN IN MY LIFE!

ACID REFLUX

WHEN I WAS ONLY THIRTY - TWO YEARS OLD, I WAS CONFIRMED BY MY DOCTOR, AFTER MUCH TESTING TO BE SUFFERING FROM THIS MEDICAL PROBLEM.

THE NIGHT BEFORE I WAS HEADING TO KILLARNEY IRELAND WE WERE RUSHING TO FINISH GETTING PACKED FOR OUR TRIP.

IT WAS A STRESSFULL DAY! OUR SON AT THE TIME WAS ONLY SIX MONTHS OLD.

I DECIDED TO TAKE HIM AND MY WIFE TAMMY OVER SEAS WITH ME WHILE COMPETING IN THE WORLD GAMES!

IT WAS EARLY AROUND 6:00 P.M. WE HAD JUST FINISHED OUR DINNER …

ALL OF A SUDDEN I BEGAN TO GET SOME REAL BAD CHEST PAINS! I THOUGHT AT FIRST I WAS HAVING A HEART ATTCK.

IT FELT THAT INTENSE! NEVER HAD I EXPERIENCED SUCH A PAIN BEFORE.

MY RIGHT ARM WENT NUMB! … MY HEAD WAS POUNDING LIKE AN EXPLOSION WENT OFF INSIDE MY HEAD! …

THEN I FELT WEAK TO THE KNEES! NEXT I BROKE OUT INTO A SWEAT! …

THEN I STARTED HAVING PROBLEMS BREATHING FROM ALL THE PAIN IN MY CHEST!

TAMMY RUSHED ME TO UMASS MEMORIAL HOSPITAL. IT IS LOCATED IN WORCESTER MA.

THEY TOOK ME RIGHT IN! ALL I KEPT TELLING MYSELF WAS … I AM WAY TO YOUNG FOR THIS!

I SAID THIS OVER … AND OVER … AGAIN!!! TRYING TO BELIEVE MY OWN WORDS.

AFTER SEVERAL TESTS THEY TOLD ME THAT MY HEART WAS FINE. THAT WAS A GREAT NEWS!

SO I THEN ASKED: THEN WHAT IS THE PROBLEM THEN? … … …

THE DOCTORS THEN SAID: "" *WE FOUND AN UNUSUAL AMOUNT OF ACID IN YOUR DIGSTIVE SYSTEM.* ""

"" THIS ACID IS EATING AWAY AT YOUR THROAT AS WELL AS YOUR STOMACH. ""

O.K. ... SO HOW DO YOU PLAN TO FIX ME UP? ... I AM LEAVING TO COMPETE IN THE WORLD MARTIAL ARTS GAMES TOMORROW!

THE DOCTOR ASKED ME WHERE? I REPLIED: *"" IRELAND. KILLARNEY IRELAND. ""*

HE SIAD GOOD LUCK, AND TAKE THESE PILLS. THEY SHOULD HELP YOU UNTIL YOU GET BACK TO THE STATES.

SO I ASKED WHAT THEN? ... WE NEED TO FIND OUT HOW BAD THE INTERNAL DAMAGE FROM THE ACID IS.

I TOLD THE DOC O.K. SEE YOU WHEN I RETURN FOR MORE TESTING. THEN I WAS OFF.

AT THIS POINT I STRONGLY BELIEVE MY WIFE THOUGHT I WAS ABSOLUTELY CRAZY!
FIRST OF ALL FOR STILL GOING ON THIS TRIP. SECOND FOR STILL THINKING THAT I WAS GOING TO COMPETE TOO!

WHEN YOU ARE REPRESENTING YOUR COUNTRY ALL YOU CAN THINK ABOUT IS PERFECTION.

NOTHING ELSE MATTERS! I WAS GOING TO MAKE THE UNITED STATES KNOWN AS A WORTHY GUEST!

SO WE WENT. ALL THREE OF US PLUS MY SISTER JAY.

THROUGH ALL THIS ADVERISTY OF HEALTH I STILL MANAGED TO TAKE HOME THREE SILVER MEDALS FOR THE UNITED STATES!

THE COUNTRY THAT I LOVE.

NEXT WHEN WE ARRIVED BACK HOME I DID GO BACK TO THE DOCTORS FOR MORE TESTING.

NOW I HAVE TO TAKE A PILL FOR THE REST OF MY LIFE! I DID ASK THE DOCTOR IF THIS WAS CAUSED BY MY DIET PERHAPS?

I THOUGHT I ATE PRETTY GOOD MOST OF THE TIME? BUT I WAS SHOCKED WHEN HE TOLD ME NO!

ACCORDING TO THE DOCTOR MORE THAN LIKELY IT WAS CAUSED BY LIVING A STRESSFULL LIFESTYLE!

SO TO THIS I SAY THANK YOU TO THE UNITED STATES POSTAL SERVICE.

PLANTERS FACIATIAS

SPEAKING OF THE GOOD OLD POSTAL SERVICE HERE IS ANOTHER TRIBUTE TO THEIR NAME.

WHEN I CAME DOWN WITH THIS I ASKED MY DOCTOR WHAT IS NEXT NOW?!

I DIDN'T KNOW WHAT WAS WRONG WITH ME THIS TIME EITHER. MY DOCTOR BEING HUMOROUS SAID: *"" YOUR OVER THIRTY NOW ... ITS ONLY GOING TO GET WORST YOU KNOW? ""*

SO I SAID THANK YOU DOC AGAIN! BUT THEN HE EXPLAINED TO ME THAT ALL THE POUNDING OF MY BODY BETWEEN WORK AND TRAINING IN THE MARTIAL ARTS WAS STARTING TO TAKE ITS TOLL!

HE ACTUALLY AT ONE POINT AND TIME TOLD ME IT WOULD BE IN MY BEST INTEREST TO STOP MY TRAINING.

WELL ... WE ALL KNOW WHAT THE ANSWER TO THAT ORDER WAS. NO!

SO HE FIXED MY FEET OVER A PERIOD OF ABOUT FIVE MONTHS. THROUGH THERPY AND MEDICAL EXERCISES.

BUT EVERYDAY I HAVE THIS PAIN IN MY FEET. SOME DAYS IT IS WORST THAN OTHERS!

SOMETIMES IT IS SO HARD TO WALK NEVER MIND TRYING TO CARRY THE MAIL FOR SIX HOURS A DAY, FOR FIVE DAYS A WEEK!

BUT I KEEP MOVING FORWARD. YOU NEED TO FOCUS HARD AND BLOCK THE PIN OUT.

WHAT AN AWESOME FEELING IT IS FOR THE FIRST STEP IN THE MORNING OUT OF BED!

A SINGLE TEAR USUALLY RUNS DOWN MY CHEEK FROM THE PAIN, AND THEN I GO GET READY FOR WORK.

THE MORAL OF THIS CHAPTER IS THIS … NO MATTER WHAT HARDSHIPS LIFE MAY THROW AT YOU …

JUST KEEP ON FOLLOWING YOUR DREAMS, AND DON'T LOOK BACK!

THE ONLY ONE THAT IS GOING TO PREVENT YOU FROM BEING WHO YOU WISH TO BE OR BECOME, AND TRULY ACCOMPLISHING WHAT YOU WANT … IS YOU! SO FOLLOW YOUR HEART! MAKE YOUR DREAMS BECOME REALITY!

AND LIFE WILL BE REWARDING. I PROMISE YOU THIS! BELIEVE ME …

WHAT IF? … I NEVER LOST MY WEIGHT AND CONQUERED THE PROBLEM.

WHAT IF? … I NEVER MET TAMMY OR HAD MY SON MASON.

WHAT IF? … I NEVER HAD THE ASTHMA.

WHAT IF? … I NEVER DEVELOPED ACID REFLUX.

WHAT IF? … I NEVER HAD FOOT PROBLEMS.

WHAT IF? … I DID STOP ALL MY TRAINING.

WHAT IF? … I JUST THREW IN THE TOWEL AND QUIT EVERYTHING I DO.

WHAT IF? …*""YOU KNOW WHAT… IT JUST ISN'T WORTH IT ANYMORE! ""*

THE ANSWER TO WHAT IF IS THIS … IF I NEVER LOOKED PAST ALL THE BAD …

THEN I NEVER WOULD HAVE BECOME THE MAN THAT I AM TODAY! THAT'S WHAT IF!

THE CAUSE AND THE EFFECT OF TRIBULATIONS IN LIFE CAN TEACH YOU A WHOLE LOT ABOUT YOURSELF.

THAT IS IF YOU LEARNED FROM THE MISTAKES THAT YOU MADE IN THE PAST, AND MOVE FORWARD WITH A POSITIVE ATTITUDE TO THE FUTURE!

THIS IS VERY EASY TO SAY … BUT EXTREMELY HARD TO DO!

THE DECISION HAS TO BE MADE FROM YOUR HEART. THIS WILL MAKE ALL THE DIFFERENCE IN THE WORLD.

"" SYDNEY GEORGE ~ MASTER HILDA & GRANDMASTER GLENN WILSON ~ GRANDMASTER RON " THE BLACK DRAGON " VAN CLIEF ~ MASTER KYOSHI MICHAEL P. FARADAY ~ MASON & TAMMY FARADAY ""

"" MAY 30TH 2010 ORLANDO FLORIDA ... W.H.F.S.C. ""

FAMILY MEMBERS :

THIS IS MY TREE

{ THIS IS FOR THE MAIN PURPOSE OF REFRENCE TO MY ROOTS }

MY SIDE OF THE TREE :

MYRTLE GERTRUDE (BASINS) FARADAY:

ALSO KNOWN AS MY GRANDMOTHER, BUT THOUGHT OF ME AS MY SECOND MOM! SO MANY OF MY CHILDHOOD MEMORIES ARE WITH HER.

WE DID SO MUCH TOGETHER IN LIFE, AND ALL WILL NEVER BE FORGOTTEN!

I AM SO GLAD THAT MY SON MASON HAS HAD MANY GREAT YEARS WITH HER, AND HOPEFULLY THERE WILL BE MANY, MANY MORE …

HOW SHE MANAGED TO DO SO MUCH BACK WHEN I WAS JUST A LITTLE GUY IS AMAZING TO ME.

IT WOULD BE AN AWESOME CHANGE IF OTHERS IN MY FAMILY WOULD STOP TAKING ADVANTAGE OF HER, AND START HELPING HER OUT ONCE IN A WHILE!

BECAUSE IT IS THE RIGHT THING TO DO! SHE IS THE MAIN FOUNDATION IN ALL OUR LIVES! SHE DESERVES THE MOST RESPECT OF ALL!

BECAUSE IF IT WAS NOT FOR HER NONE OF US WOULD BE HERE, OR WHERE WE ARE TODAY EITHER … THANK YOU MA!

SINCE I WROTE THIS PASSAGE A FEW YEARS AGO, SADLY MY MOM HAS PASSED RECENTLY THIS PAST YEAR.

DONALD HENRY FARADAY :

DONALD IS MY GRANDFATHER BY BIRTH, BUT MY DAD BY CHOICE! I HONORED HIM ANS MY GRANDMOTHER BY TAKING THEIR LAST NAME IN THE YEAR 1994.

FOR ALL OF THE UPBRINGING THEY PROVIDED TO ME. BESIDES I HATED MY PREVIOUS LAST NAME BY MY MOTHERS MARRIAGE!   WITH A PASSION!!

MY POP WAS A GREAT MAN. HE WAS WELL RESPECTED BY MANY. ESPECIALLY IN THE BUSINESS WORLD OF THE WIRE AND CABLE INDUSTRY!

HE WAS THE OWNER AND FORE FOUNDER OF ASTRO WIRE AND CABLE CORP. IT WAS LOCATED IN WORCESTER MA.

HE ALSO HAD ANOTHER BUSINESS IN WEBSTER. DURING HIS RETIREMENT YEARS. IT WAS CALLED WEBSTER MACHINE PRODUCTS.

HERE HE BUILD FROM THE GROUND UP MACHINES THAT WERE IN NEED FOR OTHER BUSINESS IN THE PRODUCTION OF WIRE MAKING.

BESIDES THESE TWO BUSINESSES HE HAD HIS HANDS IN ONE MORE. IT WAS A SMALL ENTITY CALLED STAR TEK, AND INVOLVED COMPUTERS.

MY GRANDFATHER ALSO SERVED DURING THE SECOND WORLD WAR, WHERE HE WAS ONE OF ONLY TEN PEOPLE WHO CAME BACK HOME FROM THE THIRD DIVISION OF THE ARMY!

HE HELD THE RANK OF MASTER SARGENT IN AN OUTFIT LABELED DARBY'S RANGERS.

HE WAS A MAN TO BE EXTREMELY PROUD OF! HE TOOK CARE OF HIS FAMILY AND THEN SOME.

TOO BAD OTHERS TOOK HIM FOR GRANTED! HE MEANT THE WORLD TO ME. HE HAD TAUGHT ME MOST OF WHAT I KNOW.

HIS PASSING IN 2005 WAS TOO EARLY FOR ME! I MISS HIM GREATLY.

POP WAS ALSO AN AWESOME ATHLETE. SETTING MANY A RECORD IN HIGH SCHOOL SPORTS, AND THE ARMY AS WELL.

THEN HE USED TO BOX A LOT. HE EVEN WAS A SPARRING PARTNER TO THE LATE GREAT WILLY PEP. BACK IN THE DAY.

I COULD WRITE A WHOLE BOOK JUST ON MY GRANDFATHER, BUT TO ME HE WILL ALWAYS BE REMEMBERED AS MY FATHER.   NOT MY GRANDFATHER!

PANSY CORRINNE STRANGE :

THIS WOMAN WAS MY GREAT, GREAT GRANDMOTHER. SHE AS A YOUNG GIRL WAS SENT FROM IRELAND OVER TO AMERICA.

PANSY WAS WHAT WAS CALLED AN INDENTURED SERVANT TO A WEALTH FAMILY IN NEW YORK.

SHE WAS ALSO A MEMBER OF THE Mc' DOUGLAS CLAN.   APPARENTLY PANSY SPENT A PERIOD OF TIME IN SCOTLAND AS WELL.

WHAT I CAN'T FIND OUT THOUGH IS IF SHE WAS IN IRELAND FIRST OR SCOTLAND FIRST, OR THE OTHER WAY AROUND.

BUT THIS IS WHERE THE Mc' DOUGLAS CLAN AFFILIATION CAME FROM.

I WISH I COULD FIND OUT MORE INFORMATION ABOUT HER, BUT IT IS DIFFICULT TO DO SO.

I AM GOING ONLY BY WHAT MY MOTHER NANCY CAN REMEMBER OF HER FROM HER CHILDHOOD.

ANYWAYS THE FAMILY FROM NEW YORK LIKED PANSY SO MUCH THAT THEY DECIDED NOT ONLY TO FREE HER FROM HER SERVICES …

BUT THEY ALSO DECIDED TO ADOPT HER INTO THEIR FAMILY. THEY CHANGED HER WHOLE NAME FOR A WHOLE NEW LIFE FOR HER!

HER NEW NAME WAS GLADYS IRENE, AND HER NEW LST NAME THEIR LAST NAME WAS MASON.

HARRY FARADAY

THIS WAS MY GREAT, GREAT GRANDFATHER. HE HAD TWO SONS DOUGLAS AND DONALD.

I ALSO KNOW HE HAD RE - MARRIED AND HAD A DAUGHTER. HOWEVER I HAVE NO INFORMATION ABOUT THIS SADLY.

NOW HARRY MET GLADYS AND HERE BEGINS THE FARADAY LEGACY!

MY GREAT, GREAT GRANDFATHER HAD MANY INTERESTS IN LIFE FROM WHAT I HAVE GATHERED.

I REMEMBER SMALL AMOUNTS OF CONVERSATION WITH MY POP ABOUT HIM NOW AND THEN.

HARRY HAD SOMETHING TO DO WITH A LINE OF PHARMACY STORES DOWN SOUTH, ALONG WITH SEVERAL OTHER WHAT MAY BE CONSIDERED GET RICH QUICK BUSINESS?

DOUGLAS MASON FARADAY

MY UNCLE DOUG WAS A REAL FUNNY MAN. HE WAS WELL RESPECTED IN THE FIELD OF EDUCATION IN THE STATE OF CONNECTICUT.

HE WORKED WITH CHILDREN WHO HAD DISABILITIES. I ALSO KNOW HE WAS HONORED FOR THIS ON MORE THAN ONE OCCASION!

HE MARRIED A WOMAN NAMED MARION, AND TOGETHER THEY HAD ONE CHILD NAMED WENDY FARADAY.

I ALSO KNOW THAT SHE HAS SINCE MARRIED, BUT HAVE KNOW IDEA WHO OR WHERE THEY RESIDE FOR THAT MATTER.

SHE IS VERY DISTANT TO OUR FAMILY AND THIS IS BY HER CHOICE.

NANCY ANN (STELMACH / WILLARD / MORGAN) FARADAY :

NANCY IS MY BIRTH MOTHER. ALTHOUGH WE HAD OUR MANY DIFFERENCES THROUGHOUT LIFE …

SHE HAS BEEN VERY CLOSE TO ME THIS PAST DECADE. IT HAS BEEN GREAT TO FINALLY BE ABLE TO SHARE LIFE WITH HER AND EXPERIENCE MANY FUN TIMES WITH HER, AND MY FAMILY.

THANK YOU AS WELL, FOR ALL THAT YOU DO WHEN YOU CAN DO IT. SHE IS A GOOD GRANDMOTHER TO MASON!

I NOW REALIZE THAT HER LIFE WAS VERY HARD, AND THE CHOICES SHE HAD TO MAKE WERE MORE THAN LIKELY EXTREMELY DIFFICULT FOR HER!

BUT MY SIBLINGS NEED TO GROW UP, AND PUT THEIR EGOS BEHIND THEM!

I BELIEVE THAT IF THEY HAD TO WALK ONE MILE IN THE LIFE OF OUR MOTHER … BACK IN THE PAST THEY WOULDN'T HAVE MADE IT!

SHE HAS COME A LONG WAY SINCE THEN, AND I AM FOR ONE VERY PROUD OF HER FOR THIS!

SOMEDAY PERHAPS WHEN IT ISN'T TOO LATE MAYBE THEN MY SISTER'S AND MY BROTHER WOULD HAVE THOUGHT ABOUT THIS?

THE PAST IS THE PAST, BUT THE FUTURE IS MADE NOW! PLUS IT IS SHORT. HER CURRENT HUSBAND BRUCE OF MANY YEARS NOW IS A GREAT STEP DAD, AND A GOOD GRANDFATHER TO MASON AS WELL!

I ENJOY HIS COMPANYALL THE TIME, AND TOGETHER WE SHARE A BOND FOR THE BEATLES AND THEIR MUSIC.

THE MAN CALLED UNCLE FARADAY :

MY UNCLE IS UNCLE AND THIS IS THE ONLY NAME HE WISHES TO BE KNOWN BY.

HE HAS A HEART OF GOLD! IF ASKED THIS MAN WOULD GIVE YOU THE SHIRT OFF HIS BACK.

EVEN IF IT WERE THE LAST OBJECT OF HIS BELONGINGS. RESPECT FOR HIM REACHES A WHOLE NEW LEVEL FOR ME.

NO MATTER WHAT … HE HAS ALWAYS BEEN THERE FOR NT ONLY HIS FAMILY AND FRIENDS, BUT EVEN A STRANGER IN NEED OF HELP!

I SERIOUSLY DO NOT KNOW WHAT THE HELL IS WRONG WITH EVERYONE IN MY FAMILY.

OUR UNCLE IS ALSO GREATLY UNDER APPRECIATED! FOR ALL HE HAS DONE, AND ALL THAT HE DOES FOR EVERYONE.

WE HAVE TOGETHER ALSO SPENT A GREAT DEAL OF TIME. MY MEMORIES ARE FULL OF GREAT TIMES SPENT WITH HIM.

PAST ~ AND ~ PRESENT!

THANK YOU FOR EVERYTHING THAT YOU DO UNCLE. ALTHOUGH AS I STATED EARLIER HE WISHES TO BE UN - NAMED.

THIS IS HIS CHOICE AND I FULLY RESPECT THAT. EVEN THOUGH I CAN'T UNDERSTAND IT.

HIS NAME IS UNCLE … AND THOSE WHO DO KNOW HIM ARE BETTER FOR IT!

TAMMY JEAN (BARNES) FARADAY :

MY BELOVED WIFE. HER AND MY GRANDMOTHER SHOULD BE NOMINATED FOR HUMANITY AWARD OF THE YEAR.

FOR ALL THAT THEY DO TO HELP OTHERS WHO ARE IN NEED OF THE HELPING HAND!

ESPECIALLY WHEN THEIR HELP IS OFTEN ALL TO WELL FORGOTTEN BY MOST! AND UNDER APPRECIATED BY MANY …

TAMMY IS WELL ADMIRED IN HER WORK WITH CHILDREN. SHE WORKS IN THE AREA OF EARLY CHILDHOOD EDUCATION UP TO THE KINDERGARDEN LEVEL.

CURRENTLY SHE IS EMPLOYED BY THE GODDARD SCHOOL SYSTEM WHERE SHE HAS BEEN NOW FOR SEVERAL YEARS.

TAMMY IS ALL YOU COULD EVER ASK FOR IN A WIFE. SHE IS VERY UNDERSTANDING.

SHE ALSO PUTS UP WITH ME AND ALL MY ADVENTURES AFTER ALL! BUT BY FAR SHE IS THE BEST MOTHER IN THE WORLD FOR OUR SON!

NOT ONLY DO I LOVE HER MADLY, BUT I ADMIRE HER TOO. IF I ONLY HAD THE HEART THAT SHE HAS.

MASON DOUGLAS FARADAY :

MY ONE AND ONLY SON. HE IS MY LIFE, AND MEANS THE WORLD TO ME!

WE ENJOY MANY THINGS TOGETHER IN LIFE.   HE IS QUITE THE CHARACTER.

{ CARTOONS, MARVEL COMIC'S, WATER PLAY, TRAVELING, PICTURE TAKING, NATURE IN ALL ITS WONDERS, HORSE PLAY, AND MUCH, MUCH MORE! }

I CAN NOT IMAGINE MY LIFE OR WORLD WITHOUT HIM BY MY SIDE! HE MEANS EVERYTHING TO ME.

IF I HAD TO DIE SO HE COULD LIVE … THEN SO BE IT! I WOULD ONLY DO THIS FOR HIM, AND HIM ALONE!

JOSEPHINE WILLARD & EMILY ~ KATE ~ ANDREW MITCHELL :

IS MY SISTER, AND SHE IS ALSO THE NEXT ELDEST OF MY SIBLINGS. SHE HAS THREE CHILDREN …

MY NEPHEW ANDREW, AND MY TWO NICE'S EMILY AND KAITI.   HER CURRENT HUSBANDS NAME IS RALPH.

SADLY WE ARE NOT CLOSE TO ONE ANOTHER. I REMEMBER A LOT OF OUR CHILDHOOD TOGETHER THOUGH.

ONE THING I AM GRATEFUL FOR IS THAT WE WERE ABLE TO HAVE ONE NICE TRIP TOGETHER.

THIS IS WHEN I TRAVELED TO IRELAND FOR THE WORLD GAMES IN 2001. SHE CAME ALONG WITH MASON, TAMMY, AND I.

JOHN & DONNA (WILLARD) & PENNY HOGAN :

DONNA IS MY OTHER SISTER. WHEN I FIRST WROTE THE PRIVATE VERSION OF THIS BOOK BACK IN 2009 SHE WAS EXPECTING HER FIRST CHILD WITH HER LONG TIME HUSBAND JOHN.

SINCE THEN SHE HAS GIVING BIRTH TO MY NEW NICE … PENNY. WHO IS A CUTIE.

AT ONE TIME IN OUR LIVE WE WERE VERY CLOSE TO ON ANOTHER. BUT BECAUSE OF UNDERLINING CIRCUMSTANCES OF LIFE WE ARE NO LONGER.

HOWEVER; I DO SEE HER MORE THAN JAY.

BRIAN WILLARD :

IS MY BROTHER. WE WERE ALSO VERY CLOSE DURING A PERIOD OF TIME.

BUT WE ARE SOME WHAT DISTANT EVEN THOUGH HE IS ONE OF MY STUDENTS CURRENTLY.

FOR A BRIEF TIME BRIAN LEFT MY TEACHINGS TO GO BACK TO COLLEGE.

NOW HE HAS BEEN BACK AND DOING WELL THESE PAST TWO YEARS.

EVEN THOUGH HE DOESN'T WANT TO HER THIS … HE STILL HAS A GREAT DEAL OF GROWING UP TO DO.

THIS DOESN'T MEAN I AM NOT PROUD OF HIM. IT ONLY MEANS HE NEEDS TO HEAR IT FORM SOMEBODY WHO CARES.

HIS MAIN ISSUE IS THE TRUE MEAING OF RESPONSIBILITY. ONCE HE HAS GRASPED THIS HE WILL MORE TO THE NEXT LEVEL.

HOWEVER; I MUST GIVE HIM LOTS OF CREDIT AND SAY … HE PAYS ATTENTION TO ALL HIS NEICES AND NEPHEWS AND MAKES TIME FOR THEM.

UNCLE BERNIE & AUNT MURIAL STELMACH :

THESE TWO FINE PEOPLE ARE MY AUNT AND UNCLE ON MY BIRTH FATHERS SIDE OF THE FAMILY.

THEY ARE VERY NICE AND IT IS A PLEASURE TO SEE THEM WHEN EVER I MAY.

ALTHOUGH I DO SEE THEM MUCH MORE THAN MY FATHER HENRY AND THE REST OF THE STELMACH FAMILY.

HENRY STELMACH & SHERRY STELMACH :

IS MY FATHER BY BIRTH. HE ALSO HAS TWO OTHERSONS WHO ARE MUCH YOUNGER THAN I WIFE HIS THIRD WIFE SHERRY.

IN FACT AS FAR AS ALL MY SIBLINGS BETWEEN MY BIRTH MOM AND DAD I AM THE OLDEST.

HE IS A GOOD MAN. TO BAD THINGS IN LIFE SEPERATED US. ALTHOUGH IT DOESN'T HAVE TO NOW …

I JUST HAVE MIXED EMOTIONS FOR WHICH I JUST CAN'T SEEM TO LET GO OF!

BOTH HIM AND MY STEPMOTHER SHERRY ARE VERY FRIENDLY WITH MASON AND TAMMY.

THIS IS A GOOD THING FOR MASON. IT MAKES ME HAPPY.

MY FARTHER AND I HAD SPENT SOME TIME TOGETHER HERE AND THERE, BUT NOT NEARLY ENOUGH.

THIS IS JUST AS MUCH MY FAULT AS IT IS HIS. BUT I THINK OF HIM ON OCCASION. HE IS MY FATHER.

MOE AND SILINA STELMACH :

THESE ARE MY GRANDPARENTS, MY SONS GREAT GRAND PARENTS, AND MY FATHERS PARENTS.

THEY HOWEVER HAVE BOTH PASSED THROUGHT THE YEARS.

HENRY JR & SETH STELMACH :

THESE TWO MEN ARE MY STEPBROTHERS. WE SEE THEM EVERY NOW AND AGAIN.

EMMA BASINS :

EMMA WAS MY GREAT GRANDMOTHER. SHE WAS THE MOTHER OF MY ADOPTEDMOM AND GRANDMOTHER MYRTLE.

SHE HAD FIVE CHILDREN: HAROLD ~ DORIS ~ ESTER ~ JOYCE ~ AND MYRTLE.

HER HUSBAND MY GREAT GRANDFATHER WAS REFERED TO AS POPPY.

I HAVE SOME VERY FOND MEMORIES WITH EMMA, BUT I WISH I COULD REMEMBER MORE!

I DO REMEMBER WE PLAYED A LOT OF CARDS AND BOARDGAMES TOGETHER.
SOMETIMES WE WENT FOR WALKS AROUND THE OLD NEIGHBORHOOD TOO.

WHAT MAKES ME FEEL BAD ABOUT REMEMBERING HER WAS WHEN SHE HAD TO GOTO THE NURSING HOME!

IT WAS DOWN RIGHT FRIGHTFUL AND NOT SO NICE THERE. I DIDN'T VISIT HER AS MUCH AS I SHOULD HAVE.

ALTHOUGH I WAS AROUND MASONS AGE NOW … BEFORE I KNEW IT … SHE WAS GONE!

JOYCE BASINS :

AUNT JOYCE IS ALSO MY GODMOTHER. SHE AND HAROLD ARE THE ONLY ONES LEFT FROM MY GREAT GRANDMOTHER.

AUNT JOYCE IS A STUBBORN WOMEN, AND WE HAVE HAD OUR DISAGREEMENTS!

BUT WHEN IT COMES TO THE YOUNGER CHILDREN OF THE FAMILY … PENNY, MASON, EMILY, KAITI, AND ANDREW …

SHE WILL DO ANYTHING AND EVERYTHING FOR THEM. SHE HAS THE HEART OF AN ANGEL.

GODBLESS YOU AUNTIE JOYCE FOR ALL THE PEOPLE YOU HAVE SAVED!

BILL & ESTER KOKOCINSKI :

BILL AND ESTER ARE MY UNCLE AND AUNT. THEY WERE GOOD PEOPLE.

THEY WERE ALSO MY COUSIN BOBS MOM AND DAD.

ROBERT KOKOCINSKI :

WAS ONE OF MY CLOSEST COUSINS. HIM MY UNCLE AND I JUST ABOUT WENT THROUGH LIFE TOGETHER AS ONE.

I HAVE A LIFETIME OF GREAT MEMORIES WITH KOKO. HE TOO HAD JUST RECENTLY PASTED.

KOKO WAS ALSO THE GODFATHER TO MY SON MASON.

HAROLD & DORIS BASINS :

MY UNCLE AND AUNT. I SEE HAROLD ONCE IN A GREAT WHILE. FOR THE MOST PART HE HAD ALWAYS KEPT A QUIET LIFE.

HE ALSO HAD THREE SONS. DONALD, DENNIS, AND DAVID. THEY ARE ALL HARD TO FIND.

JERRY & DORIS LANGER :

WERE MY OTHER UNCLE AND AUNT. BEFORE THEY HAD PASTED …

MY WIFE AND SON HAD THE CHANCE TO SPEND SOME QUALITY TIME WITH THEM.

WE SPENT TIME AT THE FAMILY POOL TOGETHER AND PLAYED LOTS OF CARDS WITH THEM.

MY AUNT DORIS WAS THE BEST PASTRY MAKER I EVER KNEW! THEY TOO WERE ALSO WORLD TRAVELERS.

JERRY JR. & JANE LANGER :

JERRY WAS THE OLDEST SON OF JERRY AND DORIS. JERRY JUNIOR HAS SOME GREAT STORIES ABOUT LIFE THAT HE CAN SHARE WITH YOU.

ON ANY OCASSION FOR THAT MATTER. HE RECENTLY WENT THROUGH A ROUGH PATCH OF HEALTH.

MY UNCLE WHO I DECLARE AS THE MAN WITH THE HEART OF GOLD AND AFTER HE DONATED A KIDNEY TO JERRY WHO IS HIS UNCLE I NOW DECLARE HIM A SAINT!

IT IS NICE TO SEE SUCH SINCERITY OF PASSION FOR THE HUMANITY OF THE UN - SELFISH!

BECAUSE OF MY UNCLE HIS UNCLE AND MY FELLOW RELATIVE IS DOING GREAT AND SHOULD HAVE MANY MORE WONDERFUL YEARS OF LIFE.

BOB & ELAINE LANGER :

BOB IS THE YOUNGER BROTHER OF JERRY JR. HE TOO IS A FUNNY MAN TO TALK TO.

BOTH HIM AND HIS WIFE ARE VERY KIND, AND IT IS ALWAYS A PLEASURE TO SPEAK TO ANY OF THE LANGERS.

MICHAEL LANGER :

IS THE GHOST OF THE FAMILY. ONLY HIS SISTER MY COUSIN CHERYL SEES HIM EVERY NOW AND THEN. CURRENTLY LIVING IN TEXAS.

VINCENT & CHERYL (LANGER) CORDOVA :

AS MY SON CALLS HIM MR MINCE. ALTHOUGH HIS REAL NAME IS VINCE, BOTH HIM AND MY COUSIN CHERYL ARE AWESOME PEOPLE.

I WISH EITHER THEY OR WE LIVED CLOSER. WHEN EVER IT IS POSSIABLE WE LOVE TO SPEND TIME WITH THEM.

THEY TOO ALSO LVE IN TEXAS. A FEW YEARS AGO WE WERE ABLE TO SPEND A WEEK WITH THEM.

ONE OF THE BEST WEEKS WE EVER HAD. THEY KNOW HOW TO THROW A GET TOGETHER!

MATT & BLAKE CORDVA :

MATT IS THE OLDER SON AND BLAKE IS THE YOUNGER SON OF MY COUSIN CHERYL AND MR. VINCE.

BOTH OF THESE BOYS ARE NOT ONLY FUN TO HANG AROUND WITH, BUT WELL MANNERED!

MY WIFES SIDE OF THE TREE

ROGER & NANCY (SWENSON / BARNES) TRABUCCO :

NANCY IS MY MOTHER - IN - LAW. SHE IS MARRIED TO ROGER TRABUCCO WHO IS MY WIFE'S STEPFATHER.

NANCY IS REFERED TO AS NANA BY MY SON, AND IS A WONDERFUL WOMAN.
SHE HAS A BIG HEART AS WELL. SHE WOULD HELP ANYBODY THAT ASKS SOUND FAMILIAR?

SHE DRIVES ME CRAZY THOUGH WHEN IT COMES TO TIMELY ADVENTS!

ALL IN ALL WE HAVE SEVERAL ACTIVITIES TOGETHER. I SHALLLIST A FEW OF THE MEMORABLE ONES…

{ YANKEE CANDLE TRIPS, THE LOCAL FAIRS, GOING TO NEWPORT BEACH, ALONG WITH WEEKEND TRIPS TO MA, VT, RI, NH, AND MAINE. OH YES AND THAT ONE TRIP TO FLORIDA. }

BRANDY BARNES :

BRANDY IS MY SISTER - IN -LAW. SHE IS FINISHING UP HER STUDIES CURRENTLY AT THE UNIVERSITY OF MICHIGAN.

WE ARE VERY PROUD OF HER. SHE DECIDED AFTER A BAD MARRIAGE TO GO BACK TO COLLEGE TO BE A VETERINARIAN.

THIS MAY 2011 SHE WILL HAVE GRADUATED, AND HAS ALREADY PASSED HER BOARDS.

SHE IS A GREAT SISTER AND AN AWESOME AUNT TO BOTH MASON AND AUTUMN!

SHE DOES A LOT FOR BOTH OF THEM, AND WHEN SHE COMES HOME FOR VISITS SHE ALWAYS HAS TIME FOR THEM TOO.

HER AND I HAVE SPENT A GREAT DEAL OF TIME TOGETHER THROUGHT THE YEARS.

BRANDY IS ACTUALLY MORE LIKE A SISTER TO ME THAN MY OWN. ALL THE MEMORIES THAT I DO HAVE WITH HER ARE GREAT ONES!

ONE OF MY FAVORITE IS AT NEWPORT BEACH. IT INVOLVES MY SON AND HER RADIO!

STRIKE THAT THERE WAS ONE BAD EVENT.

WHEN WE ALL WENT TO SEE THE LAST SHOW AT THE BOSTON GARDEN BEFORE THEY LEVELED IT TO BUILD THE NEW ONE.

THAT WAS THE LED ZEPPLIN CONCERT!

WHEN IT COMES DOWN TO THE BEST AS I SAID BEFORE HER GOING BACK TO COLLEGE TO BE A VET AT HER AGE, AND NOT ONLY FOLLOWING THROUGH WITH IT ….

BUT BECOMING A DOCTOR OF VETERINARIAN MEDICINE. EXCELLENT JOB SIS A JOB WELL DONE!

ALSO BRANDY IS THE GODMOTHER OF MY SON MASON.
SHE HAS BEEN DATING A VERY NICE MAN WHO WHENEVER WE ARE ABLE TO ENJOY HIS COMPANY TOO.

HIS NAME IS DR. GANGA PATIL.

ANDREW & NICOLE (TRABUCCO) & AUTUMN ROKES :

NICOLE IS MY OTHER SISTER - IN - LAW. SHE IS THE YOUNGEST OF MY WIFES FAMILY.

SHE IS MARRIED TO MY BROTHER IN LAW ANDREW ROKES, AND TOGETHER THEY ARE THE PARENTS OF MY NIECE AUTUMN.

ANDREW IS A FINE YOUNG MAN. HE SERVED OUR COUNTRY WITH THREE TOURS IN THE DESERT WARS!

DURING NICOLES LIFE I HAD THE PLEASURE OF TWO GREAT HONORS WITH HER.

THE FIRST WAS WATCHING HER GROW UP FOR MOST OF HER LIFE! I HAVE KNOWN HER SINCE HER FOURTH BIRTHDAY WHICH WAS THE FIRST ONE I ATTENDED.

THE SECOND WAS HAVING HER STUDY MARTIAL ARTS WITH ME FOR SEVERAL YEARS.

NICOLE LEFT ME ONCE SHE ATTAINED HER BLUEBELT OR 5TH KYU. NICE JOB.

IT WAS A ROUGH FOUR YEARS THAT SHE WILL NEVER FORGET I AM SURE!

TOGETHER WE ALSO HAVE MANY MEMORIES TOGETHER. BOTH GOOD ONES AND BAD ONES.

DENNIS & CINDY (SWENSON) BLAIR :

AUNT CINDY HAD THE MOST INTELLECT OF ANY PERSON I EVER KNEW! I LOVED THIS WOMAN VERY MUCH.

I MISS HER GREATLY AND IN MY LAST BOOK " LIMELIGHT TO THE DEVIL'S PARADISE " I MADE IT PRETTY MUCH A TRIBUTE TO HER LIFE!

SHE WAS SUCH A HOOT. WE BY FAR HAD THE MOST TIME SPENT TOGETHER ALONG WITH UNCLE DENNY THEN ANY OTHER FAMILY MEMBER ON TAMMIES SIDE.
WE TRAVELED ALL OVER TOGETHER AND HAD MANY EXECELLENT TIMES!

SHE WAS SO PROPER, AND THOUGHTFUL. SHE TOOK HER TIME IN EVERY ASPECT SO WHAT EVER IT WAS SHE DECIDED TO DO …

IT WAS PERFECT! THANK YOU FOR EVERYTHING YOU HAVE DONE FOR ME…

YOU WILL NEVER BE FORGOTTEN MY FRIEND! YOUR MEMORY WILL FOREVER BE WITH US.

SHE TRIED TO TEACH ME ONLY ONE THING IN LIFE. AND THAT WAS LEARNING HOW TO MAINTAIN PATIENCE!

THIS IS ALSO THE BIG LESSON THAT MY SENSEI MR. VAN CLIEF IS ALSO TRYING TO INSTILL UPON ME TOO!

BACK THEN IT WAS A LOSING BATTLE! HOWEVER; TODAY I THINK SHE WOULD BE PROUD OF MY ACHIEVEMENT IN THIS FIELD.

ALTHOUGH IT IS STILL NOT PERFECT, IT HAS BECOME MUCH BETTER.

UNCLE DENNY IS VERY MUCH LIKE MY UNCLE IN MANY WAYS… HE IS CARING, GIVING, JUST OUTSTANDING IN EVERYWAY!

HE IS ANOTHER GUY WHO DESERVES MUCH MORE RESPECT THAN HE RECEIVES BY OTHERS!

NOT ONLY BY HIS FELLOW WORKERS, BUT CERTAIN FAMILY MEMBERS AS WELL.

AS I HAD MEMTIONED WITHIN THIS BOOK, HE IS MORE LIKE A BROTHER TO ME THAN AN UNCLE.

TOGETHER HIM, MY WIFE AND SON HAVE TRAVELED ALL OVER THE STATES.

WE HAVE EVEN VISITED CANADA TOO. THE MEMORIES OF OUR ADVENTURES IN LIFE ARE AWESOME!

ALSO THEY ARE VAST… THE ONE THAT WILL ALWAYS BE REMEMBERED BY ME IS OUR TRIP TO UTAH.

THIS IS FULLY OF CRAZY ADVENTURES … ESPECIALLY WITH THE WILD BUFFALO ALONG SIDE THE ROAD!!!

UNCLE DENNY IS ALSO THE BEST COOK IN THE WHOLE FAMILY. YUM - YUM!!

WHEN EVER I NEED HIM, FOR WHAT EVER THE RASON MAY BE … HE IS THERE. NO MATTER WHAT!

THANK YOU FOR BEING YOU UNCLE DENNY. IN FRIENDSHIP AND FAMILY.

RAY & SUE BARNES :

RAY IS MY FATHER - IN - LAW HE IS MARRIED TO TAMMY'S STEPMOTHER SUE.

SUE HAS THREE DAUGHTERS …

{ THE OLDEST IS JEN (BLEVINS) WHITE. AND SHE HAS THREE CHILDREN. BECKY, PAT, DEE - DEE. BECKY IS ALSO A MOTHER. }

{ SHARON (BLEVINS) ? AND HER CHILD. SHARON LIVES THE FURTHEST AWAY IN VIRGINA. IT IS HARD TO CATCH UP WITH HER. }

{ THE YOUNGEST IS SARA. SHE TOO HAS THREE CHILDREN. LEANNA ROSE, JOE, AND ASHLEY. WHEN WE VISIT DOWN SOUTH SARA IS THE SISTER WE SEE THE MOST. }

RAY IS A UNIQUE AND A GREAT GUY! HE HAS STUDIED THE ART OF KUNG - FU FOR MOST OF HIS LIFE.

HE IS A WHITE DRAGON AND A DESCENDENT PUPIL OF DR. PI. HE EARNED HIS BLACKBELT BACK IN THE SEVENTIES.

WHEN WE VISIT HIM RAY LOVES TO PLAY ROUGH. SOMETIMES EXTREMELY ROUGH AT THAT.

RAY IS A FAMILY MAN. A GOOD FRIEND TO HAVE, AND ONE GREAT FATHER - IN - LAW.

AUNT ANITA :

THIS WAS MY WIFES GREAT AUNT. I ONLY GOT TO KNOW HER FOR A SHORT PERIOD OF TIME.

HOWEVER; THE TIME WAS GOOD. SHE WAS VERY OUT GOING, AND NEVER FORGOT HER KID'S.

EACH AND EVERY ONE OF THEM! BOTH YOUNG AND OLD AS WELL.

SHE WAS A STRONG WOMEN THAT WAS LOOKED UPON FOR GUIDANCE.

GARY SWENSEN :

THIS IS THE BROTHER OF NANCY AND CINDY. HE IS ALSO MY WIFES UNCLE THAT IS NEVER SEEN OR HEARD FROM.

SANDY CHAMBERLAN :

SANDY WAS GARY'S SECOND WIFE, AND AN AUNT TO TAMMY. SHE HAS TWO DAUGHTERS.

ONE IS LEANDRA AND HE SON ANTHONY. THE OTHER IS SHELL. SANDY IS A VERY NICE LADY.

WE SEE HER A FEW TIMES A YEAR AND IT IS ALWAYS A PLEASURE TO SEE HER THE GIRLS AND HER BOYFRIEND OF MANY YEARS TODD.

* THE MAIN REASON I DECIDED TO DO THIS SECTION OF THE FAMILY TREE WAS TO GET AN OUTLINE OF OUR FAMILIES FOR OUR SON MASON TO HAVE.

IF NEEDED HE CAN TRACE HIS ROOTS BACK TO ANSWER ANY QUESTIONS THAT MAY PRESENT THEMSELVES, IN THE YEARS TO COME.

MASON LOVES INFORMATION ON HIS FAMILY HISTORY SO HERE YOU HAVE IT.

THIS AS OF DECEMBER 29TH IN THE YEAR 2010 IS THE COMPLETE AND TOTAL INFORMATION THAT IS AVAILABLE TO MY KNOWLEDGE.

THIS HOLIDAY SEASON MASON HAD A HERITAGE PROJECT DUE FOR CHRISTMAS.

UPON RESEARCHING THIS INFORMATION TAMMY AND I DID A FAMILY TREE WITH THE PROGRAM CALLED MY HERITAGE.COM.

WE ALSO FOUND TWO EXTREMELY STRONG POINTS OF INTEREST BETWEEN THE TWO FAMILES.
ONE THAT EACH HEAD MALE FROM BOTH SIDES WAS IRISH, AND EACH HEAD FEMALE FROM BOTH SIDES WAS GERMANY.

NOW THIS WAS PETTY COOL TO FIND OUT. NEITHER OF US EVER REALIZED THIS FACT.

THE IRISH IN OUR FAMILY

&

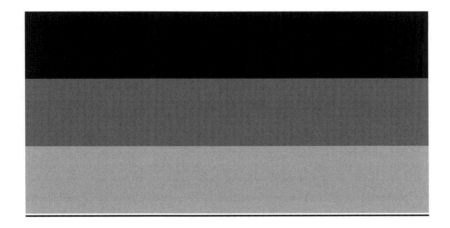

THE GERMAN IN OUR FAMILY

MY INTERESTS IN MARTIAL ARTS TODAY :

WELL BESIDES WORKING ON MY OWN MATERIAL OF TRIALS AND TRIBULATIONS …

I ALSO BELIEVE IN SETTING GOALS. BOTH IN MY PERSONAL LIFE AND MY TRAINING TOO.

WHEN YOU SET GOALS IT IS ALWAYS BETTER TO SET TWO TO FOCUS ON. ONE SHORT AND ANOTHER LONG TERM.

MY NEW FAVORITE THING TO DO IS TEACH SEMINARS FROM WHAT I LABEL AS MY MATERIAL COLLECTION.

THIS COLLECTION IS DIVIDED INTO SEVERAL TOPICS. WHICH ARE THE FOLLOWING:

BOXING CONCEPTS

CONVERTING BOXING INTO THE MIXED MARTIAL ARTS

KARATE

KENPO

JUDO

JUJITSU

KUNG - FU

DEFENSE AGAINST { CLUBS ~ KNIFES ~ GUN }

PRINCIPLES OF DEFENSE { STAFF ~ NUNCHAKU ~ SAI ~ KAMA }

CORE WORKOUTS

TEAM PARTNER WORKOUTS

WHO EVER MAY WISH ME TO PROVIDE A SEMINAR TO THEIR DOJO MAY PICK FROM THIS LIST OR MAY COMBINE UP TO TWO TOPICS.

PLEASE TAKE NOTE HOWEVER THAT EACH TOPIC COMES WITH A WORKOUT, EVEN THE WORKOUTS!
WHAT I MEAN BY THIS IS THAT A DOUBLE WORKOUT BECOMES A HELL NIGHT!

ALSO EACH CLASS IS FOR TWO TO THREE HOURS PENDING THE NUMBER OF STUDENTS THAT ATTEND. YOU MAY CONTACT ME AT:

FARADAYPOWER@MSN.COM

FOR PRICING AND ADDITIONAL INFORMATION OR ANY OTHER QUESTIONS THAT MAY CONCERN YOUR INTERESTS.

IN ALL CORRESPONDANCE PLEASE REFER SUBJECT MATTER TO MARTIAL SEMINAR.

SO I KNOW THAT I NEED TO ADDRESS THE SUBJCT. OTHERWISE I ERASE ALL EMAILS FROM ORGINS I AM NOT FAMILIAR WITH. THANK YOU.

ANOTHER THING I LIKE TO DO … IS TO RESEARCH ALL OF THE MARTIAL ARTISTS THAT I HAVE AN INTEREST IN.

IT IS REALLY FUN TO FIND OUT ALL THAT I CAN ABOUT THEIR LIVES AND THEIR TRAINING EXPERIENCES.

THIS IS A GREAT TOOL FOR ALL TO LEARN BY. IT ALLOWS YOU TO COMPARE YOUR TRAINING TO THEIRS, AND SEE HOW INCORPORATING NEW IDEAS WILL BENEFIT YOU.

MY ABOVE ALL TIME FAVORITE AND A MAN WHOM I HAVE HAD THE RARE OPPORTUNITY TO MEET A FEW TIMES IS MR. CHUCK NORRIS.

HE IS A GREAT MAN. WHO TAKES THE TIME TO LISTEN TO YOUR QUESTIONS, AND THEN ANSWER THEM WITH CONVICTION!

HE ALSO ON OCCASION WILL ASK YOU A FEW QUESTIONS OF HIS OWN. JUST TO SEE WHERE IT IS YOU STAND.

NEXT WITHOUT ANY DOUBT; I AM A HUGH FAN OF THE U.F.C. OR CALLED BY ITS OTHER NAME …

THE MIXED MARTIAL ARTS. MY SENSEI RON VAN CLIEF FOUGHT IN U.F.C. # 51. AGAINST ANOTHER LEGEND ROYCE GRACIE.

THE SPORT OF THE MIXED MARTIAL ARTS HAS BY FAR GROWN INTO THE MOST POPULAR SPORTING EVENT OF ALL TIMES!

JUST ABOUT EVERY GYM YOU GOTO CHECK OUT HAS AT LEAST ONE IF NOT MORE CLASSES AVALIABLE FOR THIS TYPE OF TRAINING.

BUT BE AWARE …. NOT ALL ARE THE SAME, AND NOT ALL ARE ON THE UP AND UP!

WHAT EVER YOU DECIDE TO DO, REMEMBER THIS: IF IT DOESN'T LOOK OR SOUND RIGHT THEN IT PROABLE ISN'T!

BEING A RESIDENT OF MASSACHUSETS, AND DOWNTOWN BOSTON BEING ONLY FOURTY - FIVE MINUTES FROM MY HOUSE …

THE OLD STOMPING GROUNDS OF THE U.F.C. PRESIDENT DANA WHITE FROM SOUTH BOSTON ISN'T FAR AT ALL.

HE HAS BUILD AN INCREDITABLE EMPIRE! GOOD FOR HIM. IT HAS BEEN AWESOME ENTERTAINMENT FOR ALL OF US TO ENJOY!

AND WITH THE SPIKE NETWORK SHOWING THE TRAINING HOUSES SOMETIMES YOU CAN PICK UP SOME REALLY COOL IDEAS TO USE.

MY FAVORITE FIVE U.F.C. FIGHTERS TO WATCH AS WELL AS TO LEARN FROM ARE:

{ "G.S.P." GORGE RUSH ST. PIERE ~ RANDY "THE NATURAL" COUTURE ~ CHUCK "THE ICE MAN" LIDDEL ~ DAN HENDERSON, AND KEN FLORIAN }

ALL MY FRIENDS AND I LOOK FORWARD TO ALL THE FIGHT NIGHTS ON PAY - PER - VIEW.

WE ALL POOL TOGETHER AND DESIGNATE WHO IS TO BRING WHAT FOR THE PARTY.

WE NEED TO ORDER THE SHOW … THEN GET THE BEER … NEXT IS THE PIZZA AND THE HOT WINGS … AND FINISH UP WITH THE CHIPS AND DIP.

NOW THIS IS WHAT A GREAT TIME IS ALL ABOUT. GOOD FRIENDS, GREAT SHOW, AND LOTS OF AWESOME SNACKS.

OH YES ALSO FOR ME TO MAKE IT TO THE MAIN EVENT I NEED TO STASH AWAY A TRIPLE SIZED MONSTER ENERGY DRINK.

MY INTEREST IN LIFE TODAY :

BESIDES CONSTANTLY LIVING AND THINKING IN THE MARTIAL WAY …

I ENJOY MY TIME WITH MY FAMILY. MOST OF ALL MASON AND TMMY.

SOME OF THE THINGS WE LIKE TO DO ARE TO WATCH MOVIES, PLAY INDOOR MONSTER MINI GOLF, PLAY GAMES ON THE WII, AND GO ON CRAZY DAY TRIPS IN THE CAR.

ALSO MY WIFE AND I HAVE PICTURE TAKING CONTESTS WITH ONE ANOTHER.

WE LIKE TO SCRAP BOOK OUT OUR FAMILY ALBUMS TO PASS ALONG TO MASON, AND FOR ALL THE FAMILY TO ENJOY.

DURING THE SUMMER TIME WEDO A FAR AMOUNT OF TRAVELING. WE ARE CURRENTLY WORKING ON SEEING ALL OUR FIFTY - TWO STATES.

WE ARE CURRENTLY UP TO TWENTY - FIVE ALONG WITH FIVE OTHER COUNTRIES UNDER OUR BELT.

EACH YEAR WE TRY TO VISIT ONE STATE THAT WE HAVE NEVER VISITED BEFORE.

THIS UP COMING YEAR 2011 WE PLAN TO VISIT NEW MEXICO FOR OUR NEW ONE.

ANOTHER SUMMERTIME FAVORITE OF OURS ISSPENDING LOTS OF TIME AT THE OCEAN!

MASON AND I LOVE TO HIT THE WAVES! EITHER WITH OR WITHOUT OUR BOARDS.

WHILE WE ENJOY THIS TAMMY ENJOYS STROLLING THE BEACH IN SEARCH OF SHELLS.

WHEN MASON AND I NEED A BREAK FROM THE POUNDING WE USUALLY JOIN TAMMY IN HER SHELL PICKING JOURNEY.

OUR FAVORITE BEACHES TO VIST THAT ARE WITHIN DRIVING DISTANCE TO US ARE:

{ BEACH THREE IN NEWPORT RI., AND YORK BEACH IN MAINE. }

MY WIFES UNCLE OWNS A NICE BEACH HOUSE ON LONGSANDS BEACH IN YORK MAINE.

WE HAVE MANY A FOND MEMORY WITH OUR FAMILIES THERE! GREAT PLACE TO GET AWAY.

ESPECIALLY WITH HER LATE AUNT CINDY AND UNCLE DENNY!

MY WIFES UNCLE IS MORE LIKE A BROTHER TO ME, THAN MY REAL ONES.

WE HAVE DONE SO MANY ACTIVITIES TOGETHER THAT IT IS HARD TO TRY AND LIST THEM ALL.

BUT TO LIST THE BEST IS NO PROBLEM AT ALL. THE BEST BY FAR IS ALL THE ADVENTURES WE HAVE HAD TRAVELLING AROUND THE UNITED STATES.

THE STORIES … THE MEMORIES … ARE AWESOME AS WELL AS THEY ARE VAST!

SPEAKING OF THE OCEAN AND FAMILY TIME, TAMMY AND I HAD THE CHANCE TO BUY TWO NEW PROPERTIES THIS PAST YEAR IN 2010.

TAMMY BOUGHT US A OCEAN FRONT CONDO ON COCO BEACH FLORIDA, AND I BOUGHT US AN OCEAN FRONT CONDO ON PALM BEACH IN ARUBA.

WE ARE LOOKING FORWARD TO MAKING MANY MORE FOND MEMORIES AT THESE PROPERTIES.

LIKE OUR SON ALWAYS SAYS TO US … IT ISN'T A VACATION UNLESS WE TAKE A PLANE.

NOW IN THE AUTUMN SEASON WE ARE TERRIABLE BUSY! WE MAKE TRIPS TO THE YANKEE CANDLE VILLAGE IN DEERFIELD MA FOR ONE.

ALSO WHILE IN THAT AREA WE HAVE OUR FAVORITE PUMPKIN PATCH TO VISIT! THIS PATCH IS IN HATSFIELD MA.

THE HARVEST OF PUMPKINS, GORDS, AND CORN STOCKS ARE AWESOME HERE. THE BEST AROUND!

THEN WE LOVE TO PICK OUR APPLES OUT IN THE BROOKFIELDS, WHICH IS ALSO IN MA.

WHILE AT THIS ORCHARD ... WE GET SOME GREAT TREATS ALONG WITH A NICE FARLY LONG TRACTOR RIDE AROUND THE ORCHARDS.

NEXT HALLOWEEN IS MY WIFE AND SONS FAVORITE HOLIDAY OF ALL!

WE ALWAYS HAVE A HALLOWEEN COSTUME PARTY FOR ALL OUR FAMILY AND FRIENDS TO ATTEND.

OH YES ... THIS IS ALSO THE TIME WE TAKE LONG RIDES OFF THE BEATEN PATH TO HUNT FOR THE FALL FOLIAGE.

NOW IT WOULDN'T BE AUTUMN WITHOUT AT LEAST ONE TRIP INTO BOSTON IF NOT MORE TO WALK AROUND AND CHECKOUT THE CITY SIGHTS.

THEN IN WINTER TIME WE HAVE SNOWBALL FIGHTS IN THE YARD, AND WE GO SLEDDING AT ROCKET LAND PARK.

THIS PARK IS ONE OF THE OLD ICONS OF OUR TOWN OF AUBURN LOCATED IN MA.

THEN MASON LIKES US TO BUILD SNOWMEN AND MAKE SNOW ANGLES TOO.

MY WIFE TAMMY MAKES AN AWESOME HOT COCO. WITH ALL THE FIINGS TOO!

THIS IS MY FAVORITE TIME OF YEAR. EXCEPT FOR THE COLD. I LOVE ALL THE FAMILY TIME AND ACTIVITIES ASSOCIATED WITH THE SPIRIT OF CHRISTMAS.

HOWEVER; I WOULD RATHER BE ON THE ISLANDS WITH THOSE WARM TROPICAL BREEZES!

EVERYNIGHT STARTING FROM DECEMBER FIRST UNTIL CHRISTMAS DAY ... WE WATCH A HOLIDAY MOVIE EVERY NIGHT BEFORE BED TIME.

MY FAVORITE HOLIDAY MOVIES TO WATCH WITHOUT LOSS EACH YEAR IS:

THE CHRISTMAS STORY AND IT'S A WONDERFUL LIFE. THESE ARE THE CLASSICS!

ANOTHER IS GOING FOR OUR HOLIDAY TREE. THE BEST PLACE AROUND IS ACTUALLY IN OUR TOWN ALSO.

IT IS THE FARMERS DAUGHTER, AND EACH YEAR WE VISIT IT SEEMS LIKE THE FIRST TIME WE EVER SET FOOT ON THIS FARM.

TAMMY WILL NOT ACCEPT ANYTHING ELSE! WE HAVE TO HAVE THE REAL THING OR NOTHING AT ALL.

MOST OF THE TIME OUR TREE IS COMPLETELY DONE UP IN A DISNEY THEME.

BUT THIS YEAR FOR THE FIRST TIME WE MADE A NEW CHANGE TO REPRESENT OUR HERTIAGE OF IRISH AND GERMAN, ALONG WITH OUR TRAVELS AROUND THE WORLD.

WITH ALL THE CRAZYNESS OF THIS HOLIDAY TIME AT CHRISTMAS … WE CELEBRATE THE TWELVE DAYS OF CHRISTMAS WITH MASON.

DECEMBER 12TH THROUGH THE 24TH. WE FOLLOW THIS RITUAL TO THE LETTER.

THIS WORKS OUT REAL GOOD FOR US AND IT IS BETTER FOR MASON TO EXPERIENCE ALL ITS WONDER.

IT'S THE MOST BEAUTIFUL TIME OF THE YEAR!

BY DOING THIS MASON HAS TIME TO ENJOY EACH GIFT RATHER THAN OPENING SEVERAL AT A TIME.

THEN THERE IS NO PRESENTS GETTING PUSHED ASIDE AND OVERLOOKED. NO LOST OR BROKEN PIECES.

THEN ON CHRISTMAS MORNING WE ALL CAN'T WAIT TO SEE WHAT SANATA HAS LEFT IN OUR STOCKINGS AND UNDER THE TREE!

AFTER WE CHECK EVERYTHING OUT AND IT IS SAFE TO DO SO, WE START OUR FIREPLACE AND ENJOY THE FESTIVITIES FOR THE DAY.

NOW WE DO CELEBRATE TIME WITH FAMILY AND FRIENDS ON BOTH CHRISTMAS EVE AND DAY.

THE EVE IS USUALLY ALL FRIENDS, AND THE DAY IS MOSTLY FAMILY.

LAST UP IS THE SPRING TIME. I LOVE THE SMELL OF THE FRIST CUT GRASS.

ITS ALSO A FAMILY TRADITION TO VISIT THE MYSTIC AQUARIUM IN OLD MYSTIC CONN.

THEIR AQUARIUM IS FAR BETTER THAN THE ONE IN BOSTON!   NO COMPARSIAN AT ALL.

THIS IS ALSO THE TIME I LIKE TO START THE OUTDOOR FIREPLACE EVENINGS.

WHY DURING THE SPRING AND SUMMER RATHER THAN THE FALL AND WINTER?

BECAUSE I LIKE IT BETTER DURING THIS TIME OF YEAR. ITS MUCH MORE COMFORTABLE FOR ALL TO ENJOY.

NEXT OUR VOLLEYBALL NET GOES UP, AND I OPEN UP OUR HOT TUB TOO.

THESE ARE JUST A FEW OF THE MANY THINGS MY FAMILY AND I ENJOY THROUGHT THE SEASONS.

THE BEST PART OF IT ALL …   IS THAT WE DO ALL THESE ACTIVITIES TOGETHR AS A FAMILY!

AH …   THE MOST POPULAR ATTRACTION FOR US I ALMOST FORGOT. TO VISIT ALL THE ZOOS WE CAN FIND DURING OUR TRAVELS!

“” WITHOUT THIS … LIFE WOULD BE MEANINGLESS! M.P.F. “”

FUTURE GOALS :

THE SOCIETY IN WHICH WE LIVE TODAY LIFE IS SO SHORT THAT MOST PEOPLE DO NOT EVEN REALIZE THE TRUTH OF THE MATTER!

IF THEY ARE NOT PROCRASTINATING OVER WHAT IS REALLY UN - IMPORTANT ISSUES …

THEN THEY ARE SECOND GUESSING THEIR LIFESTYLE AS A WHOLE!

I STRONGLY BELIEVE YOU NEED TO LIVE FOR TODAY EACH AND EVERY MINUTE.

IF YOU MAKE THE MOST OF YOU LIFES EXPERIENCES ALL THE TIME, THEN YOU WILL HAVE NONE OF THE ABOVE DETAILS IN MENTION.

DON'T WORRY ABOUT WHETHER THE DAY IS GOOD OR BAD. JUST MAKE YOUR LIFE MEANINGFUL!

IF THERE IS JUST ONE THING IN LIFE THAT YOU WANT THEN WORK AS HARD AS YOU CAN TO OBTAIN THAT DREAM.

AS FOR I … ALL THAT I WISH FOR IS HEALTH AND HAPPINESS FOR ALL MY FAMILY AND FRIENDS.

THIS IS NUMBER ONE ON MY LIST. AS FAR AS WHAT MY EXPECTATIONS ARE FROM A MARTIAL ARTS POINT OF VIEW …

IS TO ONE DAY BE REMEMBERED AS ONE OF THE LEGENDS OF OUR TIME, AND STAND WITH ALL THE OTHER GREAT LEGENDS OF THE ARTS.

FROM GREAT ACHIEVEMENTS AND DEDICATION TO HELPING WHO EVER I MAY …

PARED WITH THE DISCIPLINE OF MY SYSTEM OF TAIKYOKUKEN KEN SHO RYU.

TO BE CONSIDERED A LEADER IN INSPIRATION AND MODERN IDEAS OF TRADITIONAL THOUGHTS.

SINCE I FIRST HAD WRITTEN THIS A FEW YEARS AGO … I HAVE BEEN WORKING WITH ONE OF THE LEGENDS OF OUR TIME!

GRANDMASTER RON VAN CLIEF HAS TAUGHT ME SO MUCH ABOUT MYSELF IN WHAT REALLY HASN'T BEEN LONG AT ALL.

FROM THE TIME I WAS TAKEN IN UNDER HIS WING OF GUIDANCE BACK IN 2009 TILL PRESENT THE JOURNEY HAS BEEN EXCEPTIONAL!

HE KEEPS ME QUITE BUSY AND AT TIMES I FEEL AS THOUGH IT IS VERY DIFFICULT TO KEEP UP WITH HIM.

BUT THIS IS WHAT THE TRUE MEANING OF DISCIPLINE IS FORMED BY!

MAKING THE ADAPTION OF ONES SPIRIT MEET THE NEEDS TO CONQUER KNOWLEDGE!

EACH TIME I MEET ONE OF MY GOAL IN LIFE AND FINISH IT TO MY LIKING I ALREADY HAVE THE NEXT ONE FIGURED OUT.

I DO NOT ACCEPT THE FOLLOWING: "" *IT WILL NEVER HAPPEN FOR YOU! OR YOU ARE CRAZY TO EVEN TRY. FACE THE FACT YOUR JUST A MAILMAN WHO LIVES IN AUBURN!* ""

THIS IS SIMPLY JUST NOT GOOD ENOUGH FOR ME. EVERYTHING THAT I DO I STRIVE TO BE THE BEST THAT I CAN!

THIS APPLIES TO MY FAMILY, MY WORK, AND MY MARTIAL ARTS.

CONSTANTLY I RECEIVE NEGITIVE COMMENTS ABOUT MY CHOICE OF LIVING THE MARTIAL WAY …

HOWEVER; IN LIVING THIS WAY THE STUDY OF MARTIAL ARTS ALONG WITH ALL ITS TRAINING HAS GIVEN ME A GREAT LIFE!

NEXT WITHIN THE UP COMING FEW YEARS MY HUGH GOAL IS TO BE RECONIZED AS A SOKE.

I WANT MY SYSTEM OF TAIKYOKUKEN KEN SHO RYU, AND ALL MY TRAINING TO BE ACCEPTED INTO THE ARTS BY MY SUPERIORS.

THIS WILL BE A HUGH ACCOMPLISHMENT FOR ME AND FOR MY PUPILS IN MY SYSTEM!

BEING THE GRANDMASTER OF TAIKYOKUKEN KEN SHO RYU. THE STYLE I PERFECTED OVER TIME.

THE TRIALS AND TRIBULATIONS FROM THE ONSLAUGHT OF DESIGN TO FIELD TESTING THIS SYSTEM OF MINE THROUGHT THE WORLD DURING MY TRAVELS HAS BEEN REMARKABLE.

THE LAST GOAL WOULD BE MY MOST ULTIMATE DREAM!

THIS WOULD BE TO HAVE TWO STUDENTS WHO EVENTUALLY ACCOMPLISH THE DAN LEVEL OF MY SYSTEM.

THEN FOR THEM TO TAKE WHAT I HAVE TAUGHT THEM AND FUTHER THE IDEALS!

THESE TWO SPECIAL STUDENTS WOULD BECOME MY TOTAL SPHERE WHICH WOULD CONSIST OF THE CORE OF MY TRAINING'S.

AT ONE POINT OF TIME DURING THIS ACCELERATION I WOULD TEACH EACH OF THEM SOMETHING I HAVEN'T TAUGHT TO THE OTHER!

IN DOING THIS I WILL HAVE ACCOMPLISHED MY ULTIMATE GOAL. THE SPHERE OF TAIKYOKUKEN KEN SHO RYU.

BECAUSE BY DOING THIS ONE CAN NOT BE COMPLETE WITHOUT THE OTHER IF I AM GONE.

IF THEY WANT TO FINISH THE PUZZLE OF MY TOTAL CREATION! THEY WILL NEED TO COME TOGETHER TO COMPLETE THE SPHERE.

I HOPE IN MANY WAYS THE TWO STUDENTS THAT I WILL BE - ABLE TO GRANT THIS WISDOM TO ARE MY CURRENT STUDENT OF SEVERL YEARS NOW …

MS. KAITI FLYNN, AND MY SON MASON DOUGLAS FARADAY. THIS WILL ALSO PROVIDE SPACE BETWEEN THE YEARS IN THEIR TRAINING'S.

SO THAT PERHAPS ONE DAY THEY WILL CONTINUE MY TRADITIONS! AND SO ON … AND SO ON … !

THE MYSTRY OF IT WILL ALWAYS BE: WHAT DIDN'T I SHARE WITH THE OPPOSITE?

WHO KNOWS EXACTLY WHAT AND TO WHAT DEGREE?

WITH ALL OF THIS KEEP IN MIND REMEMBER THE FOLLOWING STATEMENT:

"" A TRUE MASTER KEEPS ONE SECERT OF HIS PERSONAL TRAINING TO HIMSELF.

BECAUSE IF YOU PUT ALL YOUR CARDS ON THE TABLE THE STRENGTH OF HAVING THE UPPER HAND WILL NOT EXIST!

TO STAND ABOVE ALL THE REST ... YOU NEED TO HAVE AT LEAST ONE SECRET KEPT IN THE DARK!

THIS IS THE WAY OF THE MASTER.

BY: PROFESSOR KYOSHI MICHAEL P. FARADAY ""

"" THE STRAND AT GALVASTON ISL. TEXAS 2008 ""

THE PROPOSAL :

THE DAWN OF THE INTERNET IS TRULY AMAZING! IT IS THE FOREMOST INFORMATION SYSTEM IN THE WORLD TODAY.

YOU CAN FIND ALL THE INFORMATION YOU EVER WANTED AND THEN SOME.

IT IS ALSO A GREAT TOOL TO KEEP OR GET IN TOUCH WITH ONE ANOTHER.

USING THE COMPUTER IS QUICK AND EASY TO DO. PERSONALLY I LIKE THE FACEBOOK WEB PAGE THE BEST.

ON THIS SITE YOU CAN RESEARCH TREMENDOUS AMOUNTS OF INFORMATION!

THEN YOU CAN SHARE YOUR THOUGHTS AND OPINIONS WITH A VAST COMMUNITY OF PEOPLE.

THIS IS HOW THE PROPOSAL TOOK SHAPE. ONE EVENING I WAS AT MY LIMIT AS FAR AS HOW THE TRAINING OF OUR BELOVED MARTIAL ARTS HAS TURNED INTO!

THIS SO CALLED STANDARDIZED WATERED DOWN VERSION OF THE ONCE TRUE ANCIENT FORM OF CULTURE HAD TURNED MY STOMACH.

SO I PUT FORTH ON FACEBOOK A BOLG OF HOW AND WHAT MY FEELINGS IN REGAURDS TO OUR TRAINING IN TRADATION HAS BEEN ALL BUT FORGOTTEN!

EVERYTHING ABOUT THIS WAY OF LIFE FROM THE ACIENT TEMPLES HAS TURNED INTO GREED. THIS IS NOT THE WAY!

THE QUALITY OF THE STUDENTS THAT ARE COMING OUT OF THE MANY UN - QUALIFIED DOJOS TODAY IS WAY BELOW PAR.

BY FAR IT IS A DISCREDIT TO ALL THE MASTERS WHO LIVE THE MARTIAL WAY!

THEN I RECEIVED THREE EMAILS FROM THE FOLLOWING PEOPLE:

{   GRANDMASTER SIFU ALAN DACASCOS FROM HAWAII,   SENSEI BRITTANY VICTORIA S. BAKER FROM LOS ANGELES, AND GRANDMASTER RON VAN CLIEF! }

ALL THREE HAD MUCH TO SAY ABOUT MY BOLG THAT I POSTED ON FACEBOOK THE NEXT DAY.

THEN WE STARTED TO TALK MORE IN DEPTH OF THE CONCERNS OF MY TOPIC OF POST. TRADITION AND THE MARTIAL ARTS!

SO HERE AS THEY WERE WRITTEN ARE THOSE THOUGHTS.   THE FOLLOWING STATEMENTS ARE EXACTLY AS THEY WERE WRITTEN FROM ME TO THEM.

THEN THE ANSWERS THAT EACH ONE PROVIDED AS FEEDBACK TO ME…

SIFU AL DACASCOS / HAWAII

THE QUESTION'S?

MR. DACASCOS;

THANK YOU FOR BEING A FRIEND.   I HAVE A QUESTION FOR YOU REGAURDING MY TRAINING …

AFTER 25+ YEARS I FEEL AS IF I HAVE HIT A WALL! I FEEL THAT OUR SPORT HAS BECOME TOO MUCH ABOUT MAKING MONEY, AND FASE FEEDBACK FROM ALL THESE SO CALLED INSTRUCTOR'S.

WHAT HAPPENED TO HONOR AND HARD WORK? IF I HAVE A STUDENT THAT WORKS VERY HARD I APPLAUDE THEM.

HOWEVER; IF ON THE SAME TOKEN THEY ARE NOT READY TO TEST THEN THEY ARE NOT READY!

I DON'T CARE IF IT TAKES YEARS TO OBTAIN NEW RANK. AS LONG AS I FEEL THEY GIVE THEIR BEST, AND THE SKILL LEVEL IS ACCEPTABLE TO MY STANDARDS.

MY STANDARDS ARE QUITE HIGH! I FULLY BELIEVE IN THE OLD SCHOOL STYLE. ALL OUTDOORS TRAINING.

FULL HANDS ON AND LOTS OF BASICS.

I WISH MORE INSTRUCTORS WOULD GO BACK TO THIS. I CAME TO BELIEVE IN THESE THEORIES SINCE MY TRIP TO THE WORLD GAMES IN 2000.

THESE GAMES TOOK PLACE IN SYDNEY AUSTRILIA. THE IDEAS I SPEAK ABOUT CAME AFTER I WAS INVITED BY THE TEAM CAPTAINS OF AUSTRILIA TO JOIN THEIR WORKOUT.

IT TOOK PLACE DOWN BY DARLING HARBOR IN THE PARK. WHAT AN EYE OPENER! IT WAS GREAT.

NOW I CAN NOT FIND ANY INSTRUCTOR IN MY AREA SO FAR TO FUTHER MY TRAINING.

DO YOU KNOW OF ANY ONE CLOSE TO ME? WHO WOULD BE SUITABLE PERHAPS TO ME?

THANK YOU FOR YOUR TIME; RESPECTFULLY MIKE.

THE ANSWERS!

"" MIKE THANKS FOR THOSE KIND WORDS. AS FOR TRAINING; WE ALL HIT BRICK WALLS.

YOUR FEELINGS ARE VALID, BUT LOOK AT IT THIS WAY … THAT IS WHAT MAKES YOU DIFFERENT.

AS LONG AS YOU STICK TO YOUR OWN PRINCIPLES, CONCEPTS AND GROW ON YOUR OWN ATTRIBUTES, YOU ARE UNIQUE.

FIGHT AND THINK OUT OF THE BOX. REALITY COMBAT IS CHAOS AND IF YOU TRAIN WITH THAT IN MIND, YOU WON'T BE WORRIED ABOUT WHAT OTHERS DO.

ONLY WORRY ON HOW THEY DO IT. WRITE ME ANYTIME AND IF I CAN HELP, THAN THAT'S GREAT!

ALOHA; SIFUAL ""

MY REPLY BACK ...

"" GOOD AFTERNOON AL;

THANK YOU FOR YOUR REPLY. I DIDN'T EXPECT YOU TO GET BACK TO ME SO FAST. AS FOR THE KIND WORDS ... YOU ARE VERY WELCOME.

I ONLY SPEAK THE TRUTH AND YOU HAVE EARNED THE RESPECT ON MANY LEVELS.

I LIKE HOW YOU DESCRIBE THE CHAOS IN COMBAT. IN RELATION TO THE WAY WE TRAIN.

IT HAS BEEN MANY A YEAR THAT HAS PASSED BY THAT SOMEBODY AGREES WITH MY THOUGHTS.

HOWEVER; AS FOR MY PERSONAL TRAINING ... I WOULD REALLY LIKE TO FIND A MASTER TO TRAIN WITH AGAIN.

ONE THAT IS TRADITIONAL AND CAN FUTHER MY EXPERIENCE! MY NEW GOAL WITHIN THE NEXT THREE TO FOUR YEARS IS TO BE CONSIDERED FOR MY 7TH DEGREE.

ITS EXTREMELY HARD FINDING THIS IN MASSACHUSETS OR EVEN RI.

WOULD YOU HAVE ANY LEADS TO POINT ME INTO? OR I HAVE DEVELOPED MY OWN SYSTEM WHICH IS A BLEND OF AMERICAN KENPO AND OLD SCHOOL SHOTOKAN.

WHAT WOULD I HAVE TO DO TO GET IT RECONIZED AS AN ART, AND BE DECLARED THE MASTER IN MY OWN PERSONNEL STYLE?

I HAVE TALKED TO AN OLD INSTRUCTOR OF MINE SHIHAN ALAN D' ALLESSANDRO WHO AT ONE TIME WAS AN UNDERSTUDY OF THE LATE PROFESSOR NICK CERIO.

ALAN IS NOW TRAINING UNDER MASTER DON RODRIGUES IN RI. BUT WHEN I STUDIED WITH HIM YEARS AGO, AND EXPRESSED MY FEELINGS OF BRANCHING OUT WITH MY OWN STYLE ...

I WAS BLACK BALLED OUT OF HIS DOJO, AND LABELED A DISCREDIT TO THE ARTS!

HE DIDN'T LIKE THE IDEA AT ALL, AND I WAS THEN PASSED UP ON MANY OCCASIONS AS FAR AS PROGRESS. SO I LEFT HIS TEACHINGS ...

WHEN I STARTED THE SHOTOKAN WITH SHIHAN WAYNE MELLO WHO TRAINS UNDER HANCHI JOHN ALMEDIEA ...

I FOUND OUT THE HARD WAY THAT HIM AND ALAN WERE GOOD FRIENDS! HELPING ONE ANOTHER PROMOTE EACH OTHERS ENDEAVORS.

SO NOW YOU KNOW WHY I NO LONGER TRAIN THERE AS WELL ... SO FOR THE PAST FEW YEARS NOW I HAVE BEEN DOING ALL MY OWN MATERIAL.

HOWEVER; I ALSO HAVE BEEN FEELING LOST WITHOUT THE GUIDANCE OF A TRUE MASTER!

MANY THANKS MIKE. " "

BRITTANY - VICTORIA S. BAKER / LOS ANGELES CALIFORNIA

THE QUESTION'S?

BRITTANY;

WHAT IS YOUR BACKGROUND FOR TRAINING? I AM CURRENTLY SEEKING A NEW EXPERIENCE IN MINE!

THERE IS KNOWBODY IN MY AREA THAT CAN FUTHER MY PATH ...

I HAVE BECOME SO DISGUSTED WITH THE WAY OUR SPORT HAS BECOME ALL ABOUT $$.$$!

WHAT HAPPENED TO TRADITION, HONOR, AND RESPECT?!

I ONLY TRAIN FOR MESELF THESE DAYS. HOWEVER; I AM LOOKING FOR A FEW UNIQUE PEOPLE TO TRAIN PRIVATELY, OR TO TRAIN PRIVATELY WITH.

MY NEXT GOAL IS TO BE RECONIZED AND CONSIDERED FOR MY 7TH DEGREE.

WITHIN THE NEXT THREE MAYBE FOUR YEARS …I HAVE GOT TO FIND SOMEONE WHO FITS MY NEEDS.

THANK YOU FOR LISTENING WHILE I BLOW OFF STEAM!

GOOD LUCK IN ALL YOUR DREAMS … MIKE

THE ANSWER'S!

"" IT'S ALWAYS GREAT TO BE ABLE TO SHARE WITH OTHER MARTIAL ARTISTS! LIKE YOU I AM VERY BOTHERED BY MARTIAL ARTS BEING MISREPRESENTED AND MISUNDERSTOOD WHEN PEOPLE TRY TO CASH IN ON WHAT THEY BELIEVE TO BE , OR TREAT LIKE THE NEXT PASSING TREND!

{ ESPECIALLY WHEN IT COMES TO BELT TESTING. }

I HAVE ACTUALLY WITNESSED " BLACKBELTS " BEING OUTRANKED OR OUTSKILLED BY YELLOW BELTS.

ONLY BECAUSE THEY WERE EAGER TO FORK OUT CASH AND BUY INTO THE FLASHY … { BUT UNREALISTIC AND THEREFORE DANGEROUS } HYPE OF SOME MONEY HUNGRY CREEPS WHO ARE TREATING THIS MORE LIKE A BUSINESS INSTEAD OF A DOJO.

THAT IS WHY I AM ABLE TO TRAIN WITH SOME OF THE BEST TEACHERS IN THE WORLD FOR FREE!

WE ARE LIKE FAMILY, AND I AM TRULY BLESSED TO BE ABLE TO TRAIN WITH LIVING LEGENDS WITHOUT SHELLING OUT A DIME!

I JUST BUILT A DOJO AND AM TEACHING { WHICH REALLY MEANS LEARNING } MIXED MARTIAL ARTS TO KIDS.

I AM ALSO WATING TO GO PRO AGAIN. EXCEPT THIS TIME TRY SOMETHING LIKE THE XMA OR WORLD COMBAT LEAGUE.

I PROABLY DIDN'T ANSWER YOUR QUESTION AND I APPOLOGIZE …

I HAVEN'T BEEN ABLE TO SLEEP MUCH FOR THE LAST 3 DAYS! SO SIMPLE TASKS ARE GETTING TO BE A BIT OF A CHALLENGE.

HOPE YOU KEEP IN TOUCH. YOU SEEM TO HAVE THE GIFT OR ABILITY TO KEEP MORE CLEAR HEADED THAN MOST, AND ACTUALLY MAKE PLANS.

WHICH USUALLY LEADS TO HEALTHY DECISION MAKING. SO THANKS FOR REACHING OUT AS A FELLOW ARTIST AND MAKING ME SMILE. =^>

<u>MY REPLY BACK ...</u>

"" YOUR WELCOME BRITTANY. I AM VERY PLEASED TO HEAR YOU AGREE WITH ME AND MY BELIEFS.

I HAVE IN DEPTH TALKS LIKE THIS WITH SIFU AL DACASCOS TOO. I WOULD LOVE TO KEEP IN TOUCH WITH YOU AS WELL.

I STRONGLY BELIEVE IN TRADITION AND HARDCORE TRADITIONAL TRAINING!

{ OUTDOORS NO MATTER WHAT THE DAY HOLDS. } IF MY STUDENTS DON'T LIKE IT ... THEN THEY DO NOT HAVE TO TRAIN WITH ME.

MAYBE THIS IS A BIT HARSH! BUT AT LEAST I WILL NOT HAVE TO WORRY ABOUT THEM.
I KNOW YOU KNOW WHAT I MEAN BE THIS ... IF I EVER GET OUT TO OR CLOSE TO LA AGAIN ...

I WOULD LIKE TO MEET YOU AND TAKE IN A DAY OF TRAINING. WHAT DO YOU THINK?

I WISH I COULD GET SOME OF THE GREATS TO MEET UP WITH ME AND DO SOME TRAINING TOO.

LIKE SOMEWHERE OUT IN THE MIDDLE OF NO WHERE. JUST US AND A NICE PRIVATE PLACE.

WHEN THEY ARE OUT MY WAY ... IN THE BOSTON AREA. THEN I WOULD TAKE THEM OUT FOR THE NIGHT WITH MY FAMILY.

SAME GOES TO YOU AND YOUR FAMILY. IF YOU ARE IN THE AREA ... LET ME KNOW, AND WE WILL TAKE CARE OF YOU AND DO SOME AWESOME TRAINING.

YOUR FRIEND MIKE ""

RON " THE BLACK DRAGON " VAN CLIEF / ST THOMAS U.S.V.I.

MY BLOG TO MR. VAN CLIEF ...

RONDO;

NICE TO SEE YOU AGAIN. THE LAST TIME WE SAW EACH OTHER WAS WHEN YOUR FAMILY AND MINE MET AT THE OLIVE GARDEN DOWN IN DELAWARE.

WISH YOU WERE CLOSER. I WOULD LOVE TO TRAIN WITH YOU!

CURRENTLY I AM HAVING EXTREME DIFFICULTY FINDING WHAT I AM LOOKING FOR IN MY AREA.

MY GOAL IS WITHIN THE NEXT FOUR YEARS TO BE CONSIDERED FOR A 7TH DEGREE.

WOULD YOU HAVE ANY POSSIABLE LEADS FOR ME? OR IDEAS?

P.S. THE NEXT TIME YOU ARE IN MY AREA ... { BOSTON - CT - OR RI } PLEASE ACCEPT MY OFFER TO MEET AGAIN FOR DINNER.

WE ALSO HAVE PLENTY OF ROOM IF YOU NEED A PLACE TO GET SOME DOWN TIME.
HOTELS ARE FOR STRANGERS. HOSIPITALITY IS FOR FRIENDS. ENJOY YOUR TIME ON THE ISLAND.

I WILL LEAVE YOU WITH THIS RIDDLE ... WHAT DO YOU HOLD AS YOUR MOST VALUABLE IN TRADITION ... ?

KATA - BASICS - OR ... THE BASICS IN YOUR KATA?

MIKE, TAMMY AND MASON FARDAY

TO MY SURPRISE!

"" MIKE, I BELIEVE YOU ARE UNDER A DECEPTION RONDO IS NOT MY BROTHER, OR A VAN CLIEF! HE HAS BEEN PREPETUATING THAT LIE FOR DECADES ..

I HAD ONE BROTHER, LARRY VAN CLIEF. HE WAS KILLED IN ACTION IN VIETNAM IN 1966 ..

MANY BELIEVE HE IS MY BROTHER ... THAT IS A TOTAL LIE ... RONDO IS A LIAR ...

HE HAS SOME SEVERE MENTAL PROBLEMS .. BECAUSE WHO SAYS THEY ARE SOMEONES BROTHER JUST TO GET ATTENTION ...

FOR THE RECORD MY NAME IS RON VAN CLIEF ... THERE IS NO RONDO ... HAVE A GREAT AY ... RON VAN CLIEF THE BLACK DRAGON.

MIKE, SEND ME A VIDEO OF YOU AND I WILL CONSIDER YOU PROMOTION ... VIDEO / PHOTOGRAPHY AND BIO .. THAT IS THE BEST I CAN DO.

RON VAN CLIEF RONVANCLIEF@YAHOO.COM OR MY CELL 1 - XXX - XXX - XXXX.

T RONDO VAN CLIEFS REAL NAME IS TOM ERVIN .. I DON'T KNOW WHY HE LIES TO EVERYONE ABOUT BEING MY BROTHER. IT IS SAD THAT SO MANY PEOPLE BELIEVE HIM ...

AGAIN ... RONVANCLIEF@YAHOO.COM OR CALL MY CELL AT 1 - XXX - XXX - XXXX.

MIKE, I WOULD LIKE YOU TO REPLY SO THAT I KNOW YOU RECEIVED MY MESSAGE RON. ""

MY REPLY ...

"" THANK YOU MR. VAN CLIEF. I AM SO SORRY THAT I HAVE BEEN MIS - LEAD SINCE 2000.

I AM DEEPLY SORRY TO HEAR ABOUT YOUR BROTHER. MY UNCLE WAS A RANGER IN NAM.

I HAVE HEARD SOME OF THE STORIES. SO I FEEL YOUR PAIN. THAT IS JUST NOT RIGHT.

OUR TROOPS DO NOT RECEIVE THE RESPECT THAT THEY DESERVE.

THAT IS NOT HOW A REAL MARTIAL ARTIST SHOULD REPRESENT HIMSELF! WHAT HAPPENED TO HONOR AND TRADITION?!

WELL AGAIN THANK YOU FOR TAKING THE TIME TO ANSWER ME. THAT WAS VERY NICE.

HOPE YOU ARE ENJOYING YOUR VACATION. I AM JUST TOTALLY BESIDE MYSELF WITH THE INFORMATION YOU HAVE PROVIDED TO ME.

HOWEVER; THANK YOU FOR THE OFFER OF CONSIDERATION. I WOULD LOVE THE CHANCE TO TAKE THIS OPP. OF YOUR OFFER.

WHAT EXACTLY WOULD YOU LIKE TO SEE AS FAR AS THE VIDEO? I BELIEVE IN TRADITIONAL KATA & STRONG BASICS!

I ALSO LIKE TO PRATICE MY OWN MATERIAL. ALSO I LIKE SOME WEAPONS:

{ SIA ~ NUNCHAKU ~ & KAMA. } BUT I DO NOT CONSIDER THIS TO BE A HIGH VALUE IN THE TRAINING OF MARTIAL ARTS FOR ME.

I WILL PUT TOGETHER A RESUME & BIO. HOPE TO TALK TO YOU SOON. WHEN THE TIME COMES ... WHERE SHOULD I BE SENDING THE PACKET TO YOU? "

THE TOTAL PROPOSAL !!!!

"" THE DEMO SHOULD INCLUDE ONE FORM TRADITIONAL OR ECCLECTIC .. THEN ONE WEAPON TRADITIONAL OR CONTEMPORY.

PHOTO SHOULD INCLUDE ONE HEADSHOT AND ONE FULL BODY SHOT. (WITH OR WITHOUT A GI.)

YOU CAN GET MY MAILING ADDRESS FROM MY WEBSITE: WWW.RONVANCLIEF.COM .

REGAURDING THE RONDO ISSUE ... WHEN HE NEXT CONTACTS YOU COULD YOU LET HIM KNOW YOU KNOW THE TRUTH ..

HAVE A GREAT DAY! RON CELL 1 - XXX - XXX - XXXX OR EMAIL RONVANCLIEF@YAHOO.COM ""

LEARNING THE TRUTH :

WHEN I WAS INFORMED BY MR. RON VAN CLIEF { THE BLACK DRAGON } THAT THE MAN I KNEW FOR A DECADE ...

WHO WAS CALLING HIMSELF RONDO VAN CLIEF WAS FALSIFYING HIS CREDITABILITY ... I FEL BETRAYED!

AND WHEN I FOUND OUT THAT I HAD BEEN GOING ON FOR DECADES ... EVEN BEFORE I WAS MADE AWARE OF THE ISSUE I FELT VERY ASHAMED!

ASHAMED THAT A MAN COULD LOOK ME RIGHT INTO THE EYES, AND TELL ME HE WAS WHO HE SAID HE WAS.

JUST TO GAIN PROFIT OF REPUTATION BY ASSOCIATION OF NAME.

BUT WHAT WAS DECENT IS THAT RON VAN CLIEF DIDN'T HOLD THIS AGAINST ME.

THEN TO MY SURPRISE HE GRANTED ME THE OFFER OF PROPOSAL TO FUTHER MY OWN TRAINING!

BY PROVIDING ME WITH THIS PROJECT THAT BECAME A SPIRITUAL JOURNEY!

THIS WAS AN INVITATION THAT I COULD NOT PASS UP! BECAUSE IF I HAD IT WOULD NEVER COME AGAIN!

SO I EMBRACED THIS AWESOME OPPORTUNITY WITH AN OPEN MIND.

<u>*ACCEPTANCE :*</u>

"" MR VAN CLIEF; I WILL BE WORKING ON THIS THROUGHT THE MONTH OF OCTOBER.

I ALREADY STARTED UPDATING MY RESUME LAST NIGHT. LOOKING FORWARD TO SENDING YOU A NICE PACKET ... FOR YOUR CONSIDERATIONS.

AGAIN MANY THANKS.

I SHALL KEEP YOU UPDATED UPON EACH OF MY TASKS UNTIL FINISHED. THEN WHEN THE COMPLETE FINISHED PROJECT IS READY ...

IT WILL BE MAILED OUT TO YOU. ENJOY THE WEEKEND! YOUR FRIEND MIKE. ""

<u>*THE UPDATE :*</u>

"" AS OF 10 - 2 - 09 MY RESUME IS NOW UPDATED AND FINISHED. I HAVE BEGAN BIO PAPER.

WHEN I HAVE SOME TIME POSSIBLY THIS THURSDAY 10 - 08 - 09 MY DAY OFF FROM WORK ...

I MAYITH YOUR PERMISSION GIVE YOU A CALL ON YOUR CELL THAT YOU PROVIDED TO ME.

WHAT IS GOOD FOR YOU? SO I CAN PROPERLY SAY HI AND HAVE A CHAT WITH YOU?

THANK YOU MIKE. ""

RON VAN CLIEF " THE BLACK DRAGON " :

RON VAN CLIEF IS WELL RESPECTED IN THE MARTIAL ARTS COMMUNITY. EVERYONE WHO IS ANYONE SEEKS HIS CONSULT.

IN THE STUDING OF THE MARTIAL WAY! HE IS A MAN OF MANY ACCOMPLISHMENTS!

HE IS A FIVE TIME WORLD CHAMPION. A FIFTEEN TIME ALL AMERICAN CHAMPION.

RON AT THE AGE OF FIFTYONE FOUGHT MR. GRACIE IN UFC NUMBER FOUR!!!!

HE HAS CREDITS TO HIS MANE FOR ACTING, BEING AN AUTHOR, AN ACTION DIRECTOR, AND MANY AN INSTRUCTIONAL VIDEO AND DVD'S!

HE IS THE SOKE OF CHINESE GOJU! WHEN HE FINALLY DECIDE TO RETIRE FROM THE TOURNAMENT WORLD AT THE AGE OF SIXTY.

ALTHOUGH HE STILL ENTERS OCCASIONALLY. YES AGAIN THAT WAS SIXTY YEARS OF AGE!

HE MANAGED TO WIN ALL AMERICAN CHAMPIONSHIPS IN FIGHTING AS WELL AS KATA.

IN 2002 HE WAS INDUCTED INTO THE BLACKBELT MAGAZINES HALL OF FAME. THIS IS AN AWESOME FEAT!

MR . VAN CLIEF ATTENDED THE UNIVERSITY OF MARYLAND COLLEGE PARK IN 1961.

THEN MR VAN CLIEF ATTENDED THE UNIVERSITY OF MARTIAL ARS AND SCIENCES, AND GRADUATED IN 1965.

HE GRADUATED WITH A PHD IN ZEN PSYCHOTHERAPIST. { MARTIAL ARTS EDUCATION AND PHYSICAL FITNESS, ZENSHU, AND ZENPSYCHOTHERPY!

TODAY HE RETAINS HIS OWN BUSINESS. IT IS CALLED VAN CLIEF ENTERPRISES.

WHERE HE IS A CREATIVE CONSULTANT. HIS BIO IS EXTREMELY IMPRESSIVE!

AND IT IS A HIGH HONOR FOR ME TO EVEN BE GRANTED THE CHANCE FOR HIM TO REVIEW MY WORK. IN ALL ITS PARTS!

IF MR VAN CLIEF FINDS THIS PROJECT TO HIS STANDARDS IT IS POSSIABLE HE MAY REWARD ME THE TITLE OF 7TH DAN!

IF I NEVER HAD RECEIVED HIS PROPOSAL FOR THIS PROJECT I DO NOT BELIEVE I WOULD EVER HAVE WRITTEN THIS SHORT BOOK.

IN THE WRITING OF THIS MY FIRST BOOK: " THE FIVE RULES ….. A PATH TO BECOMING A MASTER " IT WAS TRULY ENJOYABLE TO ME!

I HAVE PIECED TOGETHER ALL MY KNOWLEDGE, PRINCIPLES, AND THEORIES FROM THE PAST TWENTYFIVE YEARS OF TRAINING IN THE MARTIAL WAY!

TO DATE THIS IS MY 1ST MASTERPIECE!

NOW THAT I HAVE BEGUN MY TWENTYSIXTH YEAR THIS JUNE OF 2009 …

I CAN'T WAIT TO SEE HOW MY TRAINING SHALL PROGRESS WHEN I HIT THE SILVER ANNIVERSARY OF MY TRAINING!

MASTER { QUICKSILVER } MICHAEL P. FARADAY 10 - 28 - 09 *

"" 30TH ANNIVERSARY 2013 ""

"" BLAST FROM THE PAST ... 2003 MEXICO AT THE BARCELLO RESORT.

{ MEMBERS OF TEAM IRELAND ~ TEAM AMERICA ~ TEAM GERMANY }

(LEFT TO RIGHT)

" JOHN COLLINS ~ SOPHIE LEE COLLINS ~ THRESA COLLINS ~ SUSANNE BRKIC ~ MICHAEL FARADAY ~ MASON FARADAY ~ RAY ? ~ FREDDY ~ DEREK COLLINS ~ JOHN COLLINS ~ TAMMY FARADAY

THE FLAG IS FROM GERMANY.

BEHIND THE MAKING OF THE DVDS :

FOR MY FIRST PROJECT I DIDN'T KNOW IT YET, BUT I WAS ABOUT TO LEARN A WHOLE LOT ABOUT THE FILMING INDUSTRY.

I KNEW WHAT I HAD TO DO, BUT HADN'T THE VAGUEST IDEAS WHERE TO START.

AS FAR AS WHAT I WAS ASKED TO DO … THAT I KNEW WHAT I WANTED, AND WAS GOING TO PERFORM.

HOWEVER; WHERE AND WHO WAS GOING TO PRODUCE THIS PROJECT WAS THE PROBLEM.

THEN ON MY DAILY ROUTINE AT WORK I CAME TO ONE OF MY FRIENDS HOUSE.

THE POPLAWSKI FAMILY. IT WAS ON THIS DAY MY FRIEND GARY HAD ASKED ME IF I WAS ALRIGHT?

I REPLIED YES, BUT WHY DO YOU ASK? GARY WAS WORRIED BECAUSE I LOOKED LIKE A ZOMBIE WANDERING AROUND FOR MONTHS.

WHENEVER HE SAW ME WHILE WORKING IT SEEMED AS IF I WAS WORN DOWN, AND WITHDRAWN FROM MY USUAL SELF.

SO I EXPLAINED TO HIM WHAT I WAS INVOLVED WORKING ON, AND SOME OF THE FRUSTRATIONS THAT CAME ALONG WITH IT.

THIS IS WHEN GARY TOLD ME THAT HIS WIFE LIZ WAS INVOLVED IN THE FILM BUSINESS.

I NEVER KNEW. LIZ HAD BEEN WORKING FOR THE LOCAL NEWS MEDIA CENTER IN SHREWSBURY FOR A LONG TIME.

NOT ONLY HAS SHE DONE EXTENSIVE DOCUMENTARIES ALONG WITH OTHER VARIOUS PRODUCTIONS FOR THIS COMPANY, BUT SHE ALSO COMPLETED THEM FROM BOTTOM TO TOP.

SO FILIMING AND PRODUCTION WERE OLD HAT TO HER … THIS WAS GREAT NEWS!

THEN GARY SAID TO ME: *"" I WILL TALK TO HER TONIGHT AND SEE IF SEE WOULD BE INTERESTED IN HELPING YOU? ""*

AFTER THAT DAY ALL THE REST JUST FELL INTO PLACE. WE HAVE BEEN WORKING TOGETHER EVER SINCE.

LIZ DOES EXCELLENT WORK, AND IT IS ALWAYS A PLEASURE COLLABORATING ON MY PROJECTS WITH HER.

HER BUSINESS IS CALLED THRU THE YEARS. I HIGHLY RECOMMEND HER TALENTS FOR THOSE WHO MAY HAVE AN INTEREST.

SHE DOES ALL KINDS OF PROJECTS.   TO NAME A COUPLE BESIDES DOCUMENTARIES AND LIVE ACTION DVDS …

SHE ALSO WORKS PUTTING MEMORIES TOGETHER FROM OLD PHOTOS, AND TURNING THEM INTO PRECIOUS DVDS TOO.

NOW FOR MY FIRST DVD PROJECT "" *KATAS* "" I WAS ASKED TO PICK TWO KATAS TO PERFORM.

ONE HAD TO BE OPEN HAND, AND THE OTHER HAD TO INCLUDE A WEAPON OF MY CHOICE.

OF THESE TWO KATAS ONE ALSO HAD TO BE TRADITIONAL, AND THE OTHER COULD BE OF ANY STYLE.

SO I DECIDED TO PERFORM BASSAI DAI WHICH IS TRADITIONAL JAPANESE EMPTY HAND KATA, AND GENTLE BREEZE FOR MY WEAPON KATA.

GENTLE BREEZE IS FROM MY OWN SYSTEM. IT IS A KATA USING THE NUNCHAKU, AND THIS IS OF MY TRADITION.

NEXT PUTTING MUCH THOUGHT INTO WHAT WAS ASKED OF ME …. IF IT WAS I WHO ASKED FOR THIS I WOULD BE EXPECTING MORE!

SO WITH THIS I DECIDED TO SHOW EACH KATA IN THREE DIFFERENT WAYS.

THE FIRST WAY WAS WHAT WAS ASKED OF ME. THE SECOND WAY I SHOWED THE KATAS AS A BUNKI.

WHAT BUNKI MEANS IS TO SHOW THE APPLICATION OF DEFENSE FROM YOUR VIEWS OF WHAT IS HAPPENING AGAINST ATTACKERS.

SO FOR THIS I ENLISTED MY GOOD FRIENDS AND OLD TRAINING PARTNERS.

MASTER CHUCK TARR, AND SENSEI JOHN GIAQUAINTO TO HELP DEMONSTRATE THE APPLICATIONS.

THE LAST PHASE I DECIDED TO PUT THE SECOND STEP INTO SLOW MOTION.

THIS WOULD ALLOW THE VIEWER TO SEE EACH PART OF THE APPLICATION CLEAR AND PERCISELY.

BETWEEN THESE THREE PHASES OR STEPS YOU COULD SEE THE TRUE BEAUTY OF EACH KATA ALONG WITH ALL THE TECHNIQUES INVOLVED.

SO ENDS MY FIRST EVER PROJECT MAKING A DVD FILM OF LIVE ACTION IN THE MARTIAL ARTS.

DURING THE WHOLE PROCESS I LEARNED SO MUCH. IT WAS AN AWESOME EXPERIENCE!

FORM THIS POINT ON I COULD NOW MOVE FORWARD WITH A BETTER KNOWLEDGE OF THE PROCESS INVOLVED.

SUCH AS THE DIRECTION OF ANGLES THAT PROVIDE THE BEST VIEWS, THE SHADES OF LIGHTING AND HOW IT AFFECTS THE VISUAL OUT COME, AND HOW THE TEMP OF THE ROOM FIGURES INTO THE FILMING TOO.

FOR MY SECOND DVD PROJECT I WANTED TO SHOW SOMETHING QUITE DIFFERENT THEN THE LAST.

FOR THIS ONE "" *A TRIBUTE TO THE ORIENT* "" I WANTED TO SHOW ALL MY REQUIRED KATAS FOR THE DAN LEVELS.

FROM SHODAN TO KYOSHI. { 1ST DEGREE BLACKBELT TO 7TH DEGREE BLACKBELT }.

EACH LEVEL HAS TWO REQUIRED KATAS. ONE EMPTY HAND, AND ONE EXTENSION OF ARM. { WEAPON }

ALSO EACH WEAPON IS A DIFFERENT FOR EACH LEVEL. STARTING FROM THE VERY BASIC TO THE EXTREMELY DIFFICULT.

THIS PROJECT ONLY INVOLVED LIZ AND I. BETWEEN THE FIRST ONE WE HAD MADE TO THIS ONE …

THERE WAS NO COMPARISON AT ALL! THE QUALITY OF THE SECOND PROJECT WAS INCREDITABLE!

IN WATCHING THE DIFFERENCES BETWEEN THE TWO IT WAS CLEAR THAT I HAD LEARNED HOW TO FORMAT MY ABILITIES OF MARTIAL ARTS INTO FILM.

FOR THE THIRD INSTALLMENT OF MY DVD COLLECTION I WANTED TO SHOW ALL THE TECHNIQUES FROM MY SYSTEM FROM WHITE BELT TO THIRD DEGREE BLACK BELT, OR SANDAN LEVEL.

REASON BEING BECAUSE TO TEACH THE MARTIAL ARTS YOU NEED TO HOLD THIS RANK OF SANDAN WHICH IS REFERED TO AS SENSEI OR TEACHER.

THIS DVD IS CALLED "" *THE ART OF DEFENSE* "". IN THIS DVD I PERFORMED ALL MY MATERIAL IN A SEMINAR FORMAT.

I USED MY TWO PRIVATE STUDENTS ... KAITI AND BRIAN, AND MY GOOD FRIEND SENSEI MIKE AS MY UKES.

UKES IN THE MARTIAL ARTS ARE WHAT WE REFER TO AS ATTACKERS.

THIS PROJECT CAME OUT FANTASTIC AS WELL.

EACH FILM THAT I HAVE MADE I LIKE TO SHOW A DIFFERENT PROSPECTIVE, OF MY MARTIAL ARTS KNOWLEDGE.

I DO NOT SHOW ANYTHING REPEATED FROM A PREVIOUS DVD. THIS MAKES THE COLLECTION UNIQUE.

ALL MY DVDS COME WITH AN OPENING AND CLOSING SPEECH. THEY ALSO HAVE SPECIAL THOUGHTS THAT I WISH TO PROJECT THAT SCROLL EITHER IN THE START OR FINISH.

ALSO THERE IS A FULL SOUNDTRACK ON EACH. I DO THIS BECAUSE I WANT TO ENTERTAIN THE VIEWER WITH SIGHT AND SOUND.

THIS IS A HUGH PART OF CATCHING THE EYE OF ALL POTENTIAL VIEWERS. NOT JUST THE MARTIAL ART PRACTITIONERS.

ONE POINT OF INTEREST IN DOING THIS IS THE FOLLOWING ... ALL THE MUSIC THAT I PICK FOR MY DEMOS IS PUT IN AFTER ALL THE FILMING IS COMPLETED.

IT IS AMAZING HOW WELL IT FITS INTO ALL THE MOVEMENT. I WAS ACTUALLY ONCE ASKED HOW THIS IS?

WELL WHEN I START WORKING ON MY PROJECTS I START LISTENING TO ALL TYPES OF MUSIC THAT I HAVE INTEREST IN.

THEN ONCE I DECIDE ON A TRACK PARIED WITH A KATA I PRACTICE THAT KATA THINKING OF THE MUSIC IN MY HEAD.

THIS GOES ON FOR MONTHS. HOWEVER I NEVER ACTUALLY PRACTICE WITH THE MUSIC PLAYING.

I KNOW THIS SOUNDS CRAZY, BUT I THINK IT HAS A LOT TO DO WITH ALL MY YEARS PLAYING AND STUDING MUSIC.

NEVER THE LESS … EVERYTHING FITS TOGETHER AND COMPLEMENTS ONE ANOTHER PERFECTLY.

SO IF YOU ENJOY READING MY BOOKS MAKE SURE YOU CHECKOUT MY DVD COLLECTON AS WELL.

AS FOR MY NEXT DVD PROJECT I AM NOT SURE WHEN I WILL ACTUALLY FILM IT?

BUT I DO KNOW IT IS GOING TO BE CALLED "" *WEAPONS VS. WEAPONS* "".

THERE WILL BE TWO DVDS ON THIS SUBJECT. THE FIRST WILL BE ALL WOODEN WEAPONS.

THE SECOND WILL BE ALL BLADED WEAPONS. THE KEY FACTOR BETWEEN THE TWO WILL BE THE USE OF THE STAFF.

WHAT DEDICATION INVOLVES :

DEDICATION:

" TOTAL DEVOTION TO SOMETHING WITHOUT SELFISH AGENDA "

IS ONE OF THOSE WORDS THAT MOST PEOPLE CLAIM, BUT IN FACT HAVE NO RECOLLECTION AS TO THE TRUE MEANING OF ITS ORGIN.

WITH THIS BEING SAID … LET ME JUST GIVE YOU A FEW IDEAS OF HOW DEDICATION RELATES TO MY LIFE.

WHEN STARTING A PROJECT AS THIS BOOK IT TAKES COUNTLESS HOURS TO STRUCTURE, PLAN, AND PREPARE INFORMATION.

ALSO YOU NEED TO KEEP IN MIND THE FOLLOWING AS WELL:

I HAVE A FULL TIME JOB, A FAMILY, A HOME TO MAINTAIN, STUDENTS TO INSTRUCT, AND MY PERSONAL TRAINING TO ACCOUNT FOR.

THEN AFTER ALL OF THAT I AM AN AUTHOR AS WELL AS A PROFESSIONAL MARTIAL ARTISTS.

DURING A WORK WEEK … I AVERAGE IN THE LEAST FOURTY THREE HOUR ALONG WITH FIFTEEN MILES OF WALKING EACH DAY FOR FIVE DAYS.

THEN WHEN I GO HOME I HAVE SEVERAL CHORES TO ACCOMPLISH THERE BOTH INSIDE AND OUT.

NEXT I HAVE MY PERSONAL TRAINING FOR WHICH I SPEND AN AVERAGE OF SIXTEEN HOURS PER WEEK.

LASTLY I THEN HAVE THE TIME THAT I SPEND TEACHING MY PRIVATE STUDENTS.

SO AFTER ALL THE ABOVE I NEXT GOTO MY WIFE AND SON, AND GIVE BOTH OF THEM HUGS AND KISSES.

THEN BEFORE I START MY WORK IN WRITING I ASK THEM IF THERE IS ANYTHING THEY NEED, OR THAT I MAY DO FOR THEM.

IF THEY REPLY YES THEN I GET THEIR REQUEST FINISHED FIRST. NOW IS THE TIME I BEGIN MY PROJECTS!

NOW ANOTHER BIG PART OF DEDICATION IS FOLLOWING THREW WITH YOUR WORK TO THE END OF ITS COMPLETION.

SO WHEN IT COMES TO DONATING MY TIME, FINANCES, AND MY RESOURCES TO A CHARITY IT ISN'T JUST A ONCE OF YEAR SORT OF THING.

IN THIS RESPECT I PHRASE THESE TYPE OF PEOPLE: *"" LOOKING FOR A DEDUCTION ""*

MY PERSONAL BELIEF AND I HOLD STRONG TO THIS IS:

 "" IF YOU ARE TRULY PASSIONATE ABOUT A CHARITY … IT ISN'T JUST A ONCE A YEAR TIME OF THING.

IT IS AN EVERYDAY OCCURENCE OF EVENTS WHICH MAKES THE LIFE OF THOSE IN NEED A BETTER ONE!   KYOSHI {QS} FARADAY … ""

THIS IS WHY ALL THE BOOKS THAT I PUT OUT ABOUT MY LIFE …

I DECIDE ON A CHARITY THAT I FIND MEANING TO IN MY LIFE, AND DONATE A CERTAIN PERCENTAGE OF SALES TO THAT CHARITY FOR LIFE!

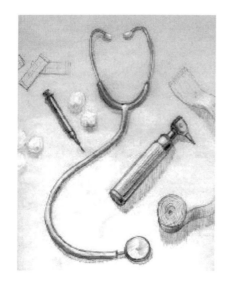

!! PROUD SUPPORTERS OF THE RELAY FOR LIFE !!

"" TAMMY & I; ON OUR WAY TO THE LOCAL RELAY FOR LIFE   ""

"" SEPTEMBER 10TH 2010 ROCKETLAND AUBURN MA 01501 "'

AS FOR ALL THE OTHER BOOKS AND DVDS THAT I PUT OUT … THOSE ARE ABOUT MY SYSTEM THAT I TEACH IN THE STUDY OF MARTIAL ARTS.

TAIKYOKUKEN KEN SHO RYU

THE MONEY THAT IS EARNED FROM THESE IS USED TO PROVIDE EXTRA FUNDS FOR MY FAMILY AND I.

MOST OF THE TIME THIS IS WHAT IS USED FOR ALL OF OUR TRAVELING THAT WE DO.

IN THE NEAR FUTURE :

THE FUTURE IS CONSTANTLY CHANGING … WHAT IT ALL COMES DOWN TO IS:

DETERMINATION & TIME

I LOVE TO MAKE PLANS. HOWEVER; I HAVE COME TO UNDERSTAND THAT PLANS ARE ALL WELL AND FINE …

SOMETIMES NO MATTER HOW HARD YOU TRY TO MAKE THEM WORK IT JUST DOESN'T HAPPEN THE WAY YOU PICTURED!

BUT DO NOT BECOME DISCOURAGED OVER THIS. KEEP ON WORKING HARD, AND MAKE YOUR DREAMS COME TRUE!

FOR ME SOMETIME IN THE NEAR FUTURE I WOULD VERY MUCH LIKE TO BREAK INTO THE FILM INDUSTRY.

I AM NOT LOOKING FOR INSTANT FAME OR FORTUNE. BUT I AM WILLING TO WORK HARD AND TAKE DIRECTION LEADING INTO MY DREAM.

BUT KEEPING IT REAL I WOULD LIKE TO START SMALL BY PERHAPS COLLABORATING ON A NEW PROJECT WITH OTHER GREAT MARTIAL ARTISTS OF MY TIME.

SUCH MARTIAL ARTISTS LIKE:

MY MENTOR GRANDMASTER RON VAN CLIEF.

MASTER CYNTHIA ROTHROCK, MASTER MARK DACASCOS, AND ANOTHER GOOD FRIEND OF MINE GRANDMASTER ANTHONY G. ELAM.

IF THIS IS IN MY PATH NEXT I WILL EMBRACE THE OPPORTUNITY.

IN FACT ANY PROJECT THAT I MAYBE ABLE TO WORK IN WITH SUCH GREATS WOULD BE AWESOME.

IF IT WAS MEANT TO BE … OR IF IT ISN'T … SO BE IT. AT LEAST I CAN SAY I TRIED!

HONESTLY I AM AT THAT POINT IN MY LIFE WHERE I AM STARTING SERIOUSLY TO RE - THINK MY LIFE.

CALL IT THE MIDLIFE CRISIS STAGE I GUESS? AS FOR THE PAST IT IS THE PAST.

AS FOR NOW WE LEARN FROM OUR MISTAKES FROM THE PAST! NOW FOR THE FUTURE WE LOOK TO IMPROVE UPON THOSE MISTAKES!

ALL THESE YEARS EVERYTHING THAT I HAVE DONE IN THE FIELD OF MARTIAL ARTS … I HAVE DONE FOR FREE.

SUCH AS MY LAST BOOK **LIMELIGHT TO THE DEVIL'S PARADISE**.

I GAVE AWAY ALL THE MONEY FROM THE SALE OF THIS BOOK, TO THE BREAST CANCER SOCIETY FOR THE RELAY FOR LIFE, AND THE DANA FARBER CANCER INSTITUTE IN BOSTON MA.

AS OF TODAY 01 - 01 - 2011 THIS BOOK HAS GROSSED $ 4,068.00. MINIS THE COST OF PRODUCTION AND SHIPPING OF $ 1,700.65 …

THEN PROMOTIONAL COSTS { % OF SALES IN BOOK STORE OF SIGNING TO OWNER & ADVERTISING MARKET } $ 971.35 …

MY TOTAL PROFIT AND DONATION OF THE DIFFERENCES FROM EXPENSES $ 1,396.00! GIVING DIRECTLY TO THE FINE CHARITY.

EACH AND EVERY YEAR FOR LIFE 15% OF THE TOTAL SALES OF THIS BOOK BASED FROM SEPTEMBER TO SEPTEMBER WILL BE DONATED TO THIS CHARITY.

I CALL THIS A COMPLETE SUCCESS!   THIS BOOK BY TH WAY WAS AVAILABLE FOR SALE SINCE AUGUST 17TH 2010.

YOU CAN FIND IT AVAILABLE FOR SALE ALONG WITH ALL MY OTHER PRODUCTS MENTIONED AT:

WWW.LULU.COM

&

WWW.AMAZON.COM

&

WWW.THRUTHEYEARS.COM

THINKING OVER THIS NOW I WOULD LIKE TO IMPROVE THE LIFE OF MY FAMILY TOO!

WHAT BETTER WAY TO DO SO THAN BY DOING SOMETHING THAT NOT ONLY BENEFITS OTHERS, BUT ALSO IS SOMETHING THAT I LOVE TO DO.

SO FOR THE TIME BEING I PLAN TO RELEASE SEVERAL BOOKS AND DVDS OF MY OWN STARTING IN 2011 - 2012.

AT THIS TIME THE EVE OF THE NEW YEAR TO BE 2011 I HAVE FINISHED TWO NEW DVDS.
ONE IS CALLED: *A TRIBUTE TO THE ORIENT*, AND THE OTHER IS ENTITLED: *THE ART OF DEFENSE*.

IN BOTH OF THESE I SHOW CASE THE TECHNIQUES WITHIN MY SYSTEM OF TAIKYOKUKEN KEN SHO RYU.

BESIDES THOSE DVDS, AND THIS BOOK … I AM ALSO WORKING ON TWO OTHER BOOKS.

ONE IS GOING TO BE CALLED: *THE FIVE ANIMALS OF TAIKYOKUKEN KEN SHO RYU*, AND THE OTHER WILL BE: *THE PHILOSOPHY'S OF TAIKYOKUKEN KEN SHO RYU.*

THEN IF TIME ALLOWS MY IDEA FOR MY FOURTH DVD FROM MY SYSTEM WILL BE: *WEAPONS VS. WEAPONS.*

THESE ARE THE THOUGHTS THAT I HAVE FOR NOW, AS TO THE NEAR FUTURE …

LIVING THE MARTIAL WAY IS WHAT I DO! IT ISN'T A PHRASE JUST TO TALK ABOUT.

IT IS THE WAY OF LIFE THAT I HAVE BECOME ACCUSTOMED TO, AND LIVE EACH DAY BY!

QUICK FUN FACT'S SHEET :

BORN: *MICHAEL PAUL STELMACH MAY 12TH 1970*

MOTHER RE - MARRIED: *MICHAEL PAUL WILLARD*

GRANDPARENTS ADOPTED ME: *AGE SIX*

TOOK GRANDPARENTS NAME: *OFFICIALLY CHANGED 1995 WORCESTER COURT SYSTEM TO ... MICHAEL PAUL FARADAY*

HAIR COLOR: *BROWN*

EYE COLOR: *BLUE*

HEIGHT: *5 ' 7*

WEIGHT: *128 LBS*

CURRENTLY RESIDING: *AUBURN MA 01501*

RETIREMENT LIVING GOAL: *SCOTTSDALE ARIZONA*

RELIGION: *BORN PROTESTANT ... STUDY & BELIEVE IN ZEN!*

POLITICAL VIEW: *DEMOCRAT*

NICKNAME: *QUICKSILVER*

TATTOO'S: *HAVE THREE CURRENTLY.*

1ST IS A DRAGON HOLDING A YING - YANG. THIS REPRESENTS ALL MY YEARS STUDING THE ART OF KENPO.

2ND IS A BONE TIGER UNDER A TORREY GATE. THIS REPRESENTS ALL MY YERS OF STUDING THE ART OF SHOTOKAN.

3RD IS SAMURI JACK. THIS REPRESENTS ALL THE YEARS OF DRIFTING AROUND THE WORLD WHILE LEARNING LIFE'S LESSONS!

FAVORITE COLOR: *RED*

FAVORITE DRINK: *MONSTER ENERGY BLUE CAN*

FAVORITE ADULT DRINK: *JAMESON IRISH WHISKY*

ALL TIME FAVORITE HOLIDAY MOVIE: *IT'S A WONDERFUL LIFE!*

ALL TIME FAVORITE MARTIAL ARTS MOVIE: *ONLY THE STRONG!*

FAVORITE ACTIVITY: *BOGGIE BOARDING*

FAVORITE MUSIC STYLE: *ALTERNATIVE { ANGRY WOMEN }*

ALL TIME VOTE FOR BEST BAND EVER: *THE BEATLES! HANDS DOWN.*

FAVORITE FOODS: *CHINESE, ITALIAN, & MEXICAN*

BEST CONCERT'S I HAVE ATTENDED: *STEVIE NICKS, GLORIA ESTAFON, & ALANIS MORISSETTE*

LIKES: *SPENDING TIME WITH FAMILY & TRAVELING ALL OVER THIS CRAZY WORLD!*

DIS - LIKES: *WINTER, LAZY PEOPLE, & THE TELEPHONE!*

"" NEW YEARS EVE 2011 YUMMIES CHINESE "'

THE UNITED POSTAL SERVICE :

IF THE AMERICAN PUBLIC ONLY KNEW WHAT ACTUALLY HAPPENS ON A DAILY BASIS BOTH INSIDE AND OUT WORKING FOR THIS FEDERAL AGENCY!

YOU WOULD NEVER BELIEVE ME IF I TOLD YOU! BEST CASE SITUATE IS …

YOU WOULD THINK THAT I WAS MAKING UP FAIRY TALES! HOWEVER; YOU CAN NOT MAKE THIS STUFF UP!

IT IS ALL TRUE … IT IS BETTER THAN WORKING FOR THE PEACE CORPS. THIS IS THE TOUGHEST JOB YOU WILL EVER LOVE.

THE EVENTS THAT HAPPEN NOT ONLY IN THE BUILDING, BUT OUT IN THE STREETS AS WELL!

THIS IS WHERE I DEVELOPED TWO OF MY TOP TEN FAVORITE PERSONAL QUOTES:

1ST ONE IS : *" FUCK THE MAN "* THE 2ND IS : *" STUPIDITY IS AN EPIDEMIC, AND IT IS RUNNING RAMPID AROUND HERE! "*

NOW … PLEASE DO NOT GET ME WRONG ON THE CONCEPT. THE POSTAL SERVICE HAS PROVIDED FOR MY WAY OF LIVING, AND MY FAMILIES WAY OF LIFE!

HOWEVER; … HERE IS THE TRUTH OF FACT! IF I WASN'T MARRIED, AND DIDN'T HAVE A CHILD …

I WOULD HAVE LEFT THIS COMPANY A LONG TIME AGO! BUT THERE IS NO WHERE ELSE THAT I CAN MAKE THIS TYPE OF PAY.

NEVER MIND ALL THE BENEFITS TOO. SO YOU LEARN HOW TO COPE WITH ALL THE NONE - SENSE.

BELIEVE ME WHEN I TELL YOU THIS … *" THE STRESS FACTOR WORKING HERE IS WAY OUT OF CONTROL! IN THIS INDUSTRY. "*

THERE IS REALLY NO NEED FOR THIS, BUT THE PEOPLE IN MANAGEMENT THAT HAVE NEVER LEFT THE COMFRT AND SAFETY OF THEIR OFFICE CHAIRS …

NEVER MIND ACTUALLY TRYING TO CARRY AND DELIVER THE MAIL! MAKE IT THIS WAY.

FOR WHICH I STRONGLY BELIEVE IS OUT OF SPITE! THE CARRIERS ARE THE BACKBONE OF THIS COMPANY.

THERE ARE CONTRADICTIONS UPON CONTRADICTIONS! … … … … … …

THE RULES AND THE REGULATIONS FOR ONE SET OF EMPLOYEES ARE DIFFERENT FROM ANOTHER GROUP OF THE SAME EMPLOYEES.

BUT WE ALL WORK FOR THE SAME COMPANY? WHY IS THIS? WELL AFTER TWENTYTWO YEARS NOW I HAVEN'T A CLUE YET WHY!

WHEN I ATTENDED COLLEGE … I HAD ONE PROFESSOR WHO STATED :

"" *A HAPPY WORK FORCE IS A PRODUCTIVE WORK FORCE!* ""

BUT THE REFLECTION OF THIS WISDOM AND TERMINOLOGY DOESEN'T CARRY WITHIN THE UNITED STATES POSTAL SERVICE!

INSTEAD WE HEAR SUCH THOUGHTS AS: "" *YOU USED TO BE FASTER! YOU ARE A POOR WORKER! WHATS WRONG WITH YOU! CAN'T YOU WORK ANY FASTER? YOU ARE A BUM! YOUR JUST LAZY!* ""

I COULD GO ON FOR DAYS WITH THE REMARKS, BUT NONE OF THESE ARE A POSITIVE REINFORCEMENT.

HOW ABOUT … "" *NICE JOB TODAY! THANK YOU FOR ALL YOUR HARD WORK!* OR *HOW ABOUT GOODMORNING?*

OR *IT IS NICE TO HAVE YOU FOR AN EMPLOYEE! THANK YOU.* ""

ALTHOUGH WITH ALL THESE PROBLEMS WITHIN THE SERVICE I WAS RECONIZED TWICE.

IN BOTH CASES THEY WERE FOR OUTSTANDING ACHIEVEMENT. BY GONG ABOVE AND BEYOND THE DUTIES OF A LETTER CARRIER.

THE AWARDS WERE LABELED: DIVERSITY ACHIEVEMENT. THEY WERE IN THE FORM OF PLAQUES,   AND THEY ALSO CAME WITH A NICE CASH AWARD TOO!

THE FIRST ONE I RECEIVED WAS FOR $ 100. 00, AND TE SECOND WAS FOR $ 200.00. THIS WAS A NICE TOUCH IN THE LEAST.

THANK YOU. AS FAR AS I KNOW … I HAVE BEEN THE ONLY CARRIER TO EVER RECEIVE THESE AWARDS DURING MY EMPLOYMENT HERE.

BUT BEFORE AND AFTER I RECEIVED THESE AWARDS I ALSO RECEIVED THE WORDS OF GREAT WISDOM MENTIONED ABOVE!

THE PROBLEM HERE IS THIS ... I HAVE NEVER CHANGED. THE POST OFFICE IS CONSTANTLY CHANGING.

NOW WHEN THEY DECIDE TO MAKE THESE CHANGES WE ARE EXPECTED TO MAKE THEM WORK!

EVEN IF THESE CHANGES ARE IMPOSSIBLE TO MAKE WORK IN THE FIRST PLACE.

NINTY PERCENT OF THE TIME THESE SO CALLED IMPROVEMENTS BACK FIRE!

BUT STILL IT IS BECAUSE WE DO NOT WORK HARD ENOUGH. BULL SHIT!

BUT ONE ASPECT IS CONSTANT, AND THAT IS THAT MANAGEMENT NEVER CHANGES!

BECAUSE I DO WORK FOR A FEDERAL BRANCH OF THE UNITED STATES GOVERNMENT ...

I HAVE DECIDED TO TELL A COLLECTION OF SHORT STORIES, BUT OMIT THE NAMES.

SO I MAY PROTECT THE INNOCENT AND SHIELD THE IDOTS!

TO TALK ABOUT MY MANY ENCOUNTERS OVER THE YEARS OF WALKING WHAT I CALL THE CONCERETE JUNGLE WOULD BECOME A NOVEL!

BEING PRESSED FOR TIME AND ISSUE OF SPACE IN THIS BOOK IS THE REASONING BEHIND MY DECISION FOR THIS SECTION.

THE STORY COLLECTION :

IN THE BUILDING ...

IT IS SAD TO SEE A FELLOW WORKER HAVE TO TAKE THEIR NAME BADGE OFF TO SEE HOW TO SPELL THEIR NAME CORRECTLY!

THEN HAVE THIS SAME PERSON COME UP TO YOU, AND TELL YOU THAT YOUR STUPID!

IT IS SAD WHEN YOU WALK INTO THE REST ROOM, AND THE CLEANINESS IS SO POOR THAT YOU WAIT UNTIL YOU CAN FIND A PLACE ON THE ROAD TO USE!

IT IS SAD THAT YOU CAN NOT HAVE A SOUND CONVERSATION WITH ANOTHER PERSON!

IF YOU SPOKE TO THEM IN PROPER ENGLISH … THEY ARE UN - ABLE TO UNDERSTAND YOU.

BUT IF YOU SPEAK IN STRONG PROFANITY TO THEM … THEY UNDERSTAND YOU PERFECTLY CLEAR.

SO IT IS SAD THAT YOU HAVE TO BECOME PROFICIENT IN PROFANITY TO HAVE A INTELLIGENT CONVERSATION WITH AN EDUCATED PERSON!

THIS HOWEVER ALSO IS TRUE OUT ON THE STREETS TOO!!!

BUT BY FAR THE BEST I HAVE EVER HEARD, AND TRUST ME THAT I HAVE HEARD QUITE A BIT …

WAS WHEN A CARRIER CALLED IN SICK, BECAUSE THE DAY BEFORE DURING A WIND STORM THAT AN ACORN HAD FALLEN FROM A TREE.

HITTING THEM IN THE HEAD! THEY SAID THEY WANTED MANAGEMENT TO BE AWARE OF THE ISSUE IN CASE A TRIP TO THE HOSPITAL WS REQUIRED.

BUT FOR THE TIME BEING THEY ONLY SUFFERED FROM A SEVERE HEADACHE!

I KNOW THIS ALL REALLY SOUNDS OFF THE WALL! BUT IT IS ALL TRUE! I CAN'T BELIEVE IT EITHER.

LIKE I SAID BEFORE … YOU JUST CAN'T MAKE THIS STUFF UP.

THE TRUTH DOES HURT, BUT THIS STUFF IS REALLY HAPPENING! VERY SAD.

OUT IN THE STREET …

HERE ARE SOME OF THE BEST LINES THAT I HAVE EVER HEARD WHILE DELIVERING MY ROUTE …

"" HEY MAILMAN … I KNOW YOU NOT TO BRIGHT BEING A PAPERBOY, BUT COULD YOU TELL ME WHAT TIME IT IS? ""

FIRST OF ALL I DO NOT WEAR A WATCH. SECOND DO SEE THE IRONY HERE?

"" WHY IS MY MAIL NOT BEING DELIVERED? ""

IF YOU LIVE IN A MULTI - APARTMENT BUILDING OR SUCH ... IF YOU DO NOT PUT YOUR NAME ON OR INTO A BOX ... HO DO I KNOW WHERE YOU LIVE OR WHO YOU ARE?

IF YOU DO NOT KNOW WHERE YOU LIVE THEN EITHER DO I! I HAVE LOST ALL MY PSYCHIC ABILITIES!

"" HOW COME EVERYTIME IT RAINS ... MY MAIL IS WET!? ""

SORRY TO TELL YOU, BUT THE MAIL IS AS DRY AS I AM! THERE IS NO CHOICE ABOUT IT, AND I AM DOWN RIGHT SOAKED!

"" HEY BABY HOW WOULD YOU LIKE TO DELIVER ME A PACKAGE? ''"

THE DAILY OFFERS OF PROPENSITY ARE NUMEROUS!

SOME PEOPLE ACTUALLY BELIEVE THAT THE STREET THEY LIVE ON IS THE ONLY STREET THAT I DELIVER TO ALL DAY.

I HATE TO BREAK IT TO YOU ... HOWEVER; I COVER A WALKING RADIS OF APPROX: FIFTEEN MILES PER DAY, AND DELIVER TO APPROX: 650 CUSTOMERS EACH DAY.

ALL THIS IN AN EIGHT HOUR PERIOD OF TIME, FOR WHICH IT TAKES ME ABOUT ONE HOUR AND FOURTYFIVE MINUTES TO ORGANIZE.

ANOTHER CONCEPT OF BELIEFE TO THE CUSTOMERS IS THAT WE PRINT THEIR BILLS IN THE BACK OF OUR TRUCK.

LISTEN ... WHEN WE RECEIVE YOUR MAIL ... THEN YOU GET IT THAT SAME DAY.

NOTHING IS HELD BACK! I HOPE YOU UNDERSTAND THIS? ...

LIKE I EXPLAINED BEFORE ... THIS STUFF IS NO LIE! IT IS UNBELIEVABLE WHAT PEOPLE REALLY THINK!

OH YES THIS TOO ... I CAN'T EVEN GIVE YOU A NUMBER FOR ALL THE TIMES A WOMAN HAS COME TO THE DOOR NAKED TO GET THE MAIL!

YES IT IS TRUE. WOMEN DO CRAZY ACTS! JUST TO TRY TO GET YOU TO ENTERTAIN THEM.

PLEASE REMEMBER … THESE ARE ONLY A SMALL FRACTION OF THE MANY EXPERIENCES THAT I ENDURE ON A NORMAL DAY.

COMPASSION AND THE POST OFFICE :

THE CAR …

THESE NEXT FOUR STORIES INVOLVE THINGS THAT HAVE HAPPENED TO ME, AND HAVE OCCURRED DURING MY DUTIES.

ONE DAY WHILE PERFORMING MY DUTIES A LETTER CARRIER … I WAS STRUCK BY A MOVING VEHICLE!

WHAT HAD HAPPENED WAS AN ELDERLY WOMAN DECIDED TO PEG HER GAS PEDAL WHILE BACKING OUT OF HER DRIVEWAY.

THE ONLY PROBLEM WITH THIS WAS … SHE DIDN'T LOOK BEFORE BACKING FOR ONE, AND FOR TWO SHE NAILED ME!

I WAS BLINDED BY THE EVENT DUE TO THE PROPERTY SITS UP ON A HUGH HILL, AND THE PATH LEADING TO THE FRONT OF THE DRIVEWAY HAS A HUGH STONE WALL ADJACENT TO IT.

SO UNTIL YOU COME TO THE END OF THIS PROPERTY … YOU CAN NOT SEE ANYTHING!

COMING OR GOING! SO WHEN I DID SEE THE CAR COMING FOR ME I KNEW ENOUGH TO TURN TO MY SIDE AND PROTECT MY FRONT FROM THE IMPACT.

IN DOING THIS MY ARM, SHOULDER, AND LEG TOOK THE BLUNT FORCE OF THE IMPACT, RATHER THAN MY CHEST, RIBS, AND FACE!

STILL TO THIS DAY YOU CAN SEE THE IMPRINT OF MY FIST IN THE TRUNK OF HER CAR.

I NEVER TOOK HER TO COURT OR ASKED FOR ANYTHING. SHE WAS OLD AND I KNEW IT WAS AN ACCIDENT.

PLUS SHE APPOLOGIZED RIGHT AWAY! THEN I WENT TO THE HOSPITAL.

I WAS THERE FOR PRETTY MUCH THE REST OF THE DAY. THEY HAD THOUGHT THAT MY HAND WAS FRACTURED.

BUT AFTER THE SWELLING WENT DOWN THEY DISCOVERED IT WASN'T.

I HAD SUFFERED ONLY SEVERE SWELLING AND BONE BRUISING. REALLY BADLY!

NOW THE NEXT DAY WHEN I AWOKE FOR WORK I WAS IN SO MUCH PAIN!

I CALLED IN SICK TO WORK. THEY ASKED ME WHY? … I TOLD THEM HOW ABOUT BECAUSE I WAS HIT BY A CAR YESTERDAY ON THE ROUTE!

THEY THEN TOLD ME … "" *WE DO NOT BELIEVE YOU! IF YOU DO NOT SHOW FOR WORK TODAY … YOU ARE GOING TO HAVE TO GET A NOTE! OR WE WILL NOT PAY YOU FOR THE DAY.* ""

YES BELIEVE IT. THE BEST PART IS THEY WERE AT THE HOSPITAL WITH ME AFTER THE ACCIDENT.

THE THREAT …

UPON DELIVERING THE MAIL ONE DAY … A MAN HAD YELLED OUT TO ME FROM ACROSS THE STREET.

HE SCREAMED AT ME, BECAUSE HE DIDN'T RECEIVE A PAPER. I THEN EXPLAINED TO HIM THAT I WAS SORRY ABOUT THIS.

BUT THERE WASN'T ANY PAPER WITH HIS ADDRESS ON IT. HE THEN TOLD ME …

"" *IF I CAN NOT HAVE A PAPER THEN HOW WOULD YOU LIKE IT IF I GOT MY GUN, AND SHOT YOU?* ""

SO I BEGAN TO SLOWLY RETURN TO MY TRUCK. THEN I NOTICED THE MAN FOLLOWING ME AROUND IN A CAR!

SO AT THIS POINT I TOOK IT AS IF HE WAS SERIOUS! I THEN DROVE TO THE NEAREST BUSINESS T CALL FOR HELP.

PROTOCAL FOR THE GOVERNMENT IS TO CALL THE OFFICE FIRST. THEN THEY TAKE THETTER FROM THERE.

WHEN MY SUPERVISOR ANSWERED THE PHONE … I EXPLAINED WHAT WAS GOING ON!

THEN THERE WAS SILENCE!   …   …   …   …   THEN I WAS ASKED THE FOLLOWING QUESTION …

"" *HOW FAST CAN YOU RUN?* "" I WAS FLOORED! I COULDN'T ACTUALLY BELIEVE THIS WAS HAPPENING TO ME!

SO THEN I ANSWERED … "" *I CAN NOT RUN FASTER THAN A CAR, OR A BULLET!* ""

THEN THEY HUNG UP ON ME! SO I CALLED THE POLICE MYSELF. END OF STORY.

THE POLICE CAME AND TOOK CARE OF THE REST FROM THIS POINT ON.

THE DOG …

THIS ONE IS ONE OF THE MORE RECENT EVENT'S THAT HAPPENED. THIS EVENT TOOK PLACE ON NOVEMBER 10TH 2006.

WHILE I WAS WALKING UP ONE SIDE OF A STREET … ON THE OTHER SIDE THERE WAS A MAN RAKING UP HIS LAWN.

I SAID HELLO TO HIM, AND HE JUST IGNORED ME. SO I THOUGHT OK. WHAT EVER!

ABOUT TEN MINUTES LATER … I WAS AT THE HOUSE BEFORE HIS. NOW BEING ON HIS SIDE OF THE STREET.

AS I LEFT THAT YARD, AND PROCCEDED TO THIS MANS HOME A ROTTY HAD JUMPED OVER THE STONEWALL OUT OF NOWHERE!

IT WAS THE MANS DOG. IT LATCHED ONTO MY FOREARM. THE PAIN WAS INTENSE!

I YELLED TO THE MAN ASKING HIM FOR HELP IN REMOVING HIS DG FROM MY BODY!

HE THEN PICKED UP HIS RAKE, AND PLACED IT UPSIDE DOWN. NEXT HE LEANED ON IT TO REST, AND JUST WATCHED!

I WILL NEVER FORGET THIS DAY FOR AS LONG AS I LIVE. TO HIM IT WAS A SHOW.

THERE WAS BLOOD EVERYWHERE! THE ONLY THING I KNEW FOR SURE WAS THIS:

ONE I CAN NOT LET THIS GOTO THE GROUND OR I AM DONE. SECOND I NEED TO REMOVE THIS BEAST FROM MY ARM! QUICK!!!

THE ONLY WAY I WAS ABLE TO DO THIS WAS BY HITTING THIS MONSTER DOG IN THE THROAT WITH A THRUST PUNCH!

NEXT THE DOG STARTED TO CHOKE AND WIMPER … THEN IT LET GO, AND FELL TO THE GROUND FREEING UP MY ARM.

MEAN WHILE THE POLICE WERE CALLED, BY A CONCERNED ON LOOKER WHO HAD WITNESSED THE WHOLE ORDEAL.

WHEN THE MAN WAS APPROACHED BY THE POLICE, AND THE POSTAL OFFICIALS …

 HE SAID : *"" I DIDN'T SEE ANYTHING! YOUR CARRIER ISN'T HURT. ""*

I REMEMBER MY BOSS SCREAMING AT THIS GUY: *"" DO YOU SEE ALL THE BLOOD ALL OVER THE SIDEWALK?! … OR THAT IS RUNNING DOWN MY CARRIERS ARM? ""*

THEN THE MAN REPLIED : *"" OH … MY DOG WAS ONLY PLAYING WITH HIM. ""*
SO I THEN SAID : *"" SEE YOU IN COURT BUDDY! ""*

I NOW HAVE EIGHT SCARS ON MY RIGHT ARM. OVER TIME THEY HAVE BEEN GETTING SMALLER, BUT THE MEMORY WILL LAST FOREVER!

AFTER BEING RELEASED FROM THE HOSPITAL IT WAS DISCOVERED THAT I WAS ALLERGIC TO THE ANTIBODY THAT WAS PRESCRIBED TO ME.

SO BECAUSE OF THE ALLERGIC SIDE REACTIONS I HAD TO TAKE TIME OFF FROM WORK.

GUESS WHAT … ? THE POST OFFICE ONCE AGAIN TOLD ME THAT I NEEDED A DOCTORS NOTE!

CAN YOU BELIEVE IT? WELL ITS TRUE! SO DO YOU REALLY WONDER WHY ALL MAIL PERSONNEL ARE CRAZY?

I THINK THE ACTIONS OF MANAGEMENT ARE THE PROOF OF THE MANY PROBLEMS OF OUR COMPANY!

I TRUST I HAVE PROVIDED JUST ENOUGH TO GIVE YOU AN IDEA OF WHAT IT IS WE GO THREW ON A DAILY BASIS IN THE POSTAL SERVICE.

HERE IS ONE EXTRA STORY FOR YOU … FROM MY MAIL ROUTE OUT IN WEBSTER MA 01570.

ON A SUMMER MORNING WHILE WALKING MY ROUTE I CAME TO A HOUSE THAT WAS A TWO FAMILY CONDO TYPE.

IT IS ON A CORNER LOT ADJACENT TO TWO MAJOR STREETS. ON ONE SIDE THERE IS A HEDGE THAT RUNS THE LENGTH OF THE PROPERTY.

NOW THE MAN WHO LIVES ON THE SECOND FLOOR OF THIS HOUSE IS THE PROPERTY OWNER.

AS I CAME TO THE EDGE OF THE HEDGE I HEARD WHAT SOUNDED LIKE A VACUUM CLEANER?

AS I TOOK THE CORNER THERE WAS THE PROPERTY OWNER GOING TO TOWN VACUUMING UP THE TOWN SIDEWALK!

I TRIED TO KEEP A STRAIGHT FACE AND NOT PAY ATTENTION TO THIS BIZARRE SIGHT.

I DO NOT KNOW ABOUT YOU … BUT I FIND THIS TO BE WAY OUT THERE!

ANYWAYS I HAD TO GO UP TO HIS BOX AND DELIVER HIS MAIL. THEN HE SAW ME AND SHUT THE VACUUM OFF.

THEN HE LOOKED AT ME AND SAID : "" *HI HOW IS YOUR DAY?* ""

I REPLIED : "" *OK HOWS YOURS?* "" HE SAID : "" *GREAT!* "" THEN HE STARTED BACK DOING HIS SIDEWALK CLEANING!

WHEN I FINISHED PUTTING THE MAIL FOR THE HOUSE INTO THE BOXES I SAW YET ANOTHER STRANGE SIGHT …

THE MAN NOW HAD TAKEN THE ATTACHMENT PIECE OFF, AND NOW WAS VACUUMING THE LINES IN THE CEMENT SIDEWALK THAT ARE SPACED OUT EVERY FOUR FEET.

SORRY BUT NEVER HAVE I EVER SEEN SUCH A SIGHT! BETTER THAN THIS WHEN I GOT TO THE NEXT HOUSE THAT OWNER WAS OUT TOO.

SO I ASKED HIM … "" *WHATS WRONG WITH YOUR NEIGHBOR?* "" HE SAID : "" *NOTHING WHY?* "'

"" DON'T YOU FIND WHAT HE IS DOING TO BE JUST A LITTLE WEIRD OR CRAZY? "'

HE SAID : *"" NO. ""* OK NOW THIS REALLY IS STRANGE. IS IT JUST ME? WHAT DO YOU THINK?

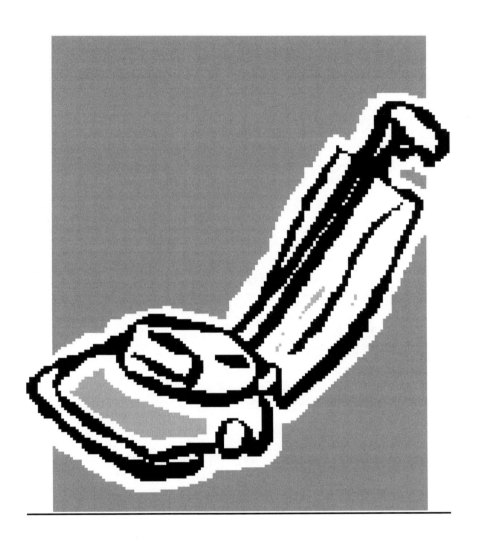

"" YES I AM SERIOUS! I REALLY WITNESSED THIS ACT. ""

THE UNDERLINING MESSAGE, THE FORMULA, & CLOSING STATEMENT:

THE MESSAGE WITHIN

IN EVERYTHING THAT I DECIDE TO DO THERE IS A PURPOSE. THERE IS MEANING FOR WHICH YOU CAN SEE, AND ALSO THAT YOU CAN NOT!

TO HELP GUIDE YOU THROUGH WHAT IT IS I WOULD LIKE YOU TO REALIZE I LIKE TO PROVIDE CLUES OF THOUGHT …

THIS PROCESS OF THOUGHT WILL LEAD YOU TO THE ASWERS OF TRUTH BEHIND THE LESSONS OF LIFE THAT I HAVE EXPERIENCED!

THE TITLE OF THIS BOOK CAME TO ME WHILE I WAS ON BREAK SITTING IN THE PARKING LOT OF A BUSINESS ON MY MAIL ROUTE.

THAT LOCATION IS 138 LAKE ST { TALS PLACE } WEBSTER MA 01570.

IT ISN'T JUST A HEADING THAT I PICKED OUT FROM THE BLUE. IT IS THE STORY OF MY JOURNEY OF TRAVEL THROUGH MY TRAINING IN THE MARTIAL ARTS.

IT DEPICTS MY LIFE IN WHOLE AND HOW THE FIVE RULES ARE PART OF MY NORMAL DAILY ROUTINE!

EACH AND EVERY DAY OF MY LIFE. ALSO EACH AND EVERY TOPIC THAT I SPEAK ABOUT AND DESCRIBE IN DETAIL REFERS TO THE TITLE OF THIS BOOK.

THE FIVE RULES … THEY ARE NOT JUST A SET OF RULES TO FOLLOW. THAY ARE THE CODE OF CONDUCT FOR WHICH I LIFE MY ENTIRE LIFE!

I HOPE EVERYONE WHO HAS TOOK THE TIME TO READ THIS HAS ENJOYED IT.

I ALSO HOPE THAT ONCE AGAIN JUST LIKE FROM MY OTHER BOOK " LIMELIGHT TO THE DEVIL'S PARADISE " YOU HAVE LEARNED SOMETHING.

SOMETHING THAT WILL HELP AID YOU IN THE DECISIONS OF CHOICE THAT LEADS TO YOUR PATH IN YOUR DESTINY.

THE FORMULA

{ STRESS X PROJECT / TIME = T. B. B. OVER LIFE. }

* T. .B. B. = TRUE BLACK BELTS { OVER COME AND ADAPT TO LIFES MANY COMPLEXITIES! }

CLOSING STATEMENT

"" IF WE ALL WORK TOGETHER, IN THE TRUE SPIRIT OF MARTIAL ARTS TRADITION ...

TOGETHER WE WILL CREATE AN AWESOME SPECTALE OF SPORT AS WELL AS TRAINING ...

FOR ALL MARTIAL ARTISTS TO ASPIRE TO! THE CLASS OF LIFE YOU RESIDE IN HAS NO BEARING! ...

WE ARE ALL EQUAL UNDER THE SAME SKY AND SHOULD BE HELPING ONE ANOTHER ...

SO LET US RAISE OUR BARS, AND SET NEW STANDARDS FOR WHICH WE CAN ALL BE PROUD TO BE A PART OF!

BY: KYOSHI PROFESSOR " QUICKSILVER " MICHAEL P. FARADAY

" LIFE ... LIBERTY ... JUSTICE ... "

CREDITS :

KYOSHI {QS} FARADAY
PROFESSOR IN THE ART OF
TAIKYOKUKEN KEN SHO RYU
HEAD INSTRUCTOR OF
U.S.A. INTERNATIONAL MARTIAL ARTS

KYOSHI:

A KYOSHI IS A PHILOSOPHER WHO IS ABLE TO RELATE ALL ASPECTS OF THE MARTIAL ARTS FROM HIS TRAININGS IN LIVING THE MARTIAL WAY …

BOTH PHYSICALLY AS WELL AS MENTALLY.

IN HIS BELIEFS ~ TRADITIONS ~ AND SPIRIT.

I HOLD THE RANK OF KYOSHI 7TH DAN PROFESSOR;

" IN THE ART OF TAIKYOKUKEN KEN SHO RYU "

HEAD INSTRUCTOR & OWNER : U.S.A. INTERNATIONAL MARTIAL ARTS.

MY NICKNAME IN THE ARTS IS: QUICKSILVER.

CREDITS OF TRAINING:

BEGAN MY TRAINING AT THE YOUNG AGE OF THRITEEN.

{ FITNESS & BOXING ~ WITH THE MAN REFERED TO AS UNCLE … }

{ PI LUM KUNG - FU ~ SIFU RUBAN RODRIGUES }

{ GO JU RYU ~ YONDAN 4TH DEGREE CARL PAGALIONE }

{ THE ART OF KENPO ~ SENSEI JOHN GIAQUIANTO }

{ KEN RYU KENPO ~ SHIHAN MASTER 7TH DAN ALAN D' ALLESSANDRO }

{ AMERICAN KENPO ~ GODAN 5TH DAN SHIHAN MASTER CHARLES TARR }

{ TRADITIONAL SHOTOKAN ~ SHIHAN MASTER 7TH DAN WAYNE MELLO }

{ RVCS : RON VAN CLIEF SYSTEM OF MARTIAL ARTS }
~ UNDER GRANDMASTER RON VAN CLIEF ~

{ CHINESE GOJU ~ SHIDOSHI GRANDMASTER RON VAN CLIEF }

SPECIAL TRAINING :

MASTER ~ DON " THE DRAGON " WILSON

MASTER ~ JEFF " THE PERFECT WEAPON " SPEAKMAN

GRANDMASTER ~ OSO TAYARI CASEL

GRANDMASTER ~ GEORGE ALEXANDER

SHIHAN MASTER 8TH DAN ~ CHRISTINE BANNON RODRIGUEZ

MASTER ~ BILL " SUPERFOOT " WALLACE

GRANDMASTER ~ BRAM FRANK

GRANDMASTER ~ MARK SHUEY " THE CANE MASTER "

MASTER ~ CYNTHIA " THE LADY DRAGON " ROTHROCK

EXPERIENCE :

1995 ~ 2000

STATE CHAMPION ~ MA / RI / CT / ME / VT / NH

MASSACHUSETS STATE CHAMPION THREE TIMES RUNNING.

THREE TIME NATIONAL CHAMPION UNITED STATES.

FOUR TIME INTERNATIONAL TOP TEN MARTIL ARTISTS.

1999 ~ 2005

MEMBER OF THE UNITED STATES MARTIAL ARTS TEAM : TEAM AMERICA.

{ COMPETITOR 2000 - 2005 / COACHING STAFF 2003 - 2005 }

2000 ~ 2005

SIX TIME WORLD CHAMPION ALL CONSECUTIVELY!

{ AUSTRILIA / 2X MAINLAND UNITED STATES / IRELAND

HONO LULU HAWAII / MEXICO }

2001

CHUCK NORRIS KICK DRUGS OUT OF AMERICA PROGRAM

2005

OFFICAL LICENSED CERTIFIED CENTER JUDGE AND REFREE:

{ KRANE RATINGS INTERNATIONAL & WORLD ORGANIZATION OF MARTIAL ARTS ATHLETES }

SEMINARS :

2004 - 2010

* I HAVE TAUGHT SEVERAL SEMINARS THROUGHOUT THE YEARS. HOWEVER; THE BEST ONE I EVER PROVIDED WAS AT:

THE WORLD HEAD OF FAMILY SOKESHIP, IN UNIVERSAL STUDIOS FLORIDA, IN THE GRANDBALL ROOM AT THE ROYAL PACIFICA HOTEL.

FOR WHICH I HAD THE UNIQUE PLEASURE TO DEMO MY MATERIAL TO SUCH GANDMASTERS AS:

GRANDMASTER SOKE FRANK SANCHEZ ~ GRANDMASTER BRAM FRANK ~ GRANDMASTER MARK SHUEY ~ GRANDMASTER GARY DILL ~ GRANDMASTER GLENN WILSON

JUST TO NAME A FEW OF THE MANY LEGENDS OF OUR TIME THAT WERE IN THE AUDIENCE.

INDUCTION'S : AWARD'S : MEMBERSHIP'S :

INDUCTION'S & AWARD'S :

NOVEMBER 27TH 2009

UNIVERSITY OF MARTIAL ARTS SCIENCE HALL OF FAME AWARD

{ ST THOMAS }

DECEMBER 1ST 2009

OFFICALLY PROMOTED TO THE RANK & TITLE OF:

KYOSHI SHIHAN 7TH DAN PROFESSOR:

IN THE STUDY OF KE SHO RYU KENPO

BY: **GRANDMASTER RON " THE BLACK DRAGON " VAN CLIEF**

JANUARY 21TH 2010

ACTION MARTIAL ARTS MAGAZINE HALL OF FAME & SPIRIT AWARDS:

{ EXCELLENCE IN THE TEACHING OF MARTIAL ARTS / TROPICANA ATLANTIC CITY NEW JERSEY }

MAY 29TH 2010

WORLD HEAD OF FAMILY SOKESHIP :

&

INTERNATIONAL MARTIAL ARTS ACHIEVEMENT AWARDS HALL OF FAME :

{ MASTER INSTRUCTOR OF THE YEAR / UNIVERSAL STUDIOS FLORIDA }

JANUARY 22ND 2011

ACTION MARTIAL ARTS MAGAZINE HALL OF FAME & SPIRIT AWARDS :

{ UNITED STATES AMBASSADOR OF GOODWILL FOR EXEMPLARY CONTRIBUTIONS TO THE MARTIAL ARTS / TROPICANA ATLANTIC CITY NEW JERSEY }

MEMBERSHIP'S :

MARCH 3RD 2010

*LIFETIME MEMBERSHIP AWARDED INTO { **K.I.O.** }*

KOGAKUSHIN INTERNATIONAL ORGANISATION

MARCH 15TH 2010

ACCEPTED INTO THE WORLD HEAD OF FAMILY SOKESHIP COUNCIL

{ REFERRED BY: G.M. RON VAN CLIEF & ACCEPTED BY: G.M. SOKE FRANK SANCHEZ }

APRIL 20TH 2010

RECOGNIZED INTO THE GOLD SHIELD PROJECT

{ PROGRAM BY: ACTION MARTIAL ARTS MAGAZINE & GRANDMASTR SIFU ALAN GOLDBERG; FOR CERTIFIED WORLDWIDE INSTRUCTORS. }

SEPTEMBER 14TH 2010

INDUCTED INTO THE AMERICAN TEMPLE TRAINING UNION { A.T.T.U. }

{ HONORARY SHA RYU / STYLE OF: SHA SOO DOO JITSU RYU }

BY: GRANDMASTER ANTHONY ELAM

YOU CAN FIND MORE INFORMATION ABOUT THIS ORGANIZATION AND ME AT:

WWW.SHAPOERYU.COM

AUTHOR :

THE FIVE RULES, A PATH TO BECOMING A MASTER

{ PRIVATE JOURNAL UN - PUBLISHED }

LIMELIGHT TO THE DEVIL'S PARADISE

THE FIVE RULES, A PATH TO BECOMING A MASTER

BOOK SIGNINGS :

KENSHO RYU KENPO KARATE DOJO

BOOKLOVERS GOURMET

* IN THE WORKS CURRENTLY : BARNES & NOBLE

AVAILABLE SOON ...

THE FIVE ANIMALS OF TAIKYOKUKEN KEN SHO RYU / 2011

THE PHILOSOPHY OF KYOSHI FARADAY / 2011

IN THE NEAR FUTURE ...

LIVING THE DREAM

FEATURED CREDITS / BOOK'S & FILM'S :

BOOK :

2004

SELF - DEFENSE; FOR MEN, WOMEN AND CHILDREN

BY: ALAN D ' ALLESSANDRO

2010

INSTANT DEFENSE

BY: RON " THE BLACK DRAGON " VAN CLIEF

* WAITING FOR RELEASE *

MAGAZINE:

2010

ACTION MARTIAL ARTS MAGAZINE : ISSUE # 76

INSIDE KUNG - FU MAGAZINE : W.H.F.S.C. REVIEW ... SUMMER ISSUE

FILM :

2000

WORLD MARTIAL ARTS GAMES SYDNEY AUSTRILIA

{ OLYMPIC STADIUM / HOMEBUSH BAY PRODUCTIONS APRIL 1ST & 2ND }

2010

SELECTED TO BE IN THE FILMING OF : THE P.B.S. DOCUMENTARY.

RON VAN CLIEF THE BLACK DRAGON EXPERIENCE

{ ON THE ISLAND OF ST. THOMAS. SADLY UNABLE TO ATTEND DUE TO PREVIOUS COMMITMENT. }

DVD'S :

2009

NOVEMBER : U.S.A. INTERNATIONAL MARTIAL ARTS PRODUCTIONS VOL I.

{ A LOOK INTO BUNKI }

2010

OCTOBER : U.S.A. INTERNATIONAL MARTIAL ARTS PRODUCTIONS VOL II.

{ A TRIBUTE TO THE ORIENT }

NOVEMBER : U.S.A. INTERNATIONAL MARTIAL ARTS PRODUCTIONS VOL III.
{ THE ART OF DEFENSE }

"If we all work together in the true spirit of martial arts tradition, together we will create an awesome spectacle of sport, as well as training for all martial artists to aspire to! Let us raise our bars and set new standards for which we can all be proud to be a part of!" - Michael P. Faraday

Thank You To:
My Uncle for his donation in the production of this film.

Sensei John Giaquianto & Master Chuck Tarr for being a part of this DVD.

This has been a Thru The Years Production
ThruTheYears.com

This is dedicated to my beloved wife Tammy and my son Mason

U.S.A. International Martial Arts
Michael P. Faraday
faradaypower@msn.com

U.S.A. International Martial Arts—Michael P. Faraday

U.S.A. International Martial Arts
Michael P. Faraday

"Becoming a master is a lifetime of achievements! Your mind and your body are now fused together and act as one." - Michael P. Faraday

VOL I.

" " FILMED IN NOVEMBER 2009 IN SHREWSBURY MA.

THIS DVD WAS THE 1ST DVD I EVER SHOT. IT CONTAINS THREE DIFFERENT VERSIONS OF TWO KATAS.
ONE EMPTY HANDED TRADITIONAL KATA & ONE EXTENSION OF ARM WEAPONS KATA OF MY OWN MATERIAL.

1ST IS DOWN TRADITIONALLY. 2ND IS PERFORMED AS A BUNKI. 3RD IS SHOWN IN SLOW MOTION. " "

VOL II.

"" FILMED IN OCTOBER 2010 IN SHREWSBURY MA.

THIS DVD DEMONSTRATES ALL MY REQUIRMENTS FROM SHODAN 1ST DEGREE BLACKBELT TO KYOSHI 7TH DEGREE BLACKBELT.

THERE ARE FOURTEEN KATAS DIVIDED INTO ONE EMPTY HANDED KATA & ONE EXTENSION OF ARM WEAPON KATA.

TWO TOTAL KATAS FOR EACH LEVEL. ALSO EACH LEVEL CONTAINS A DIFFERENT WEAPON OF INTEREST. ""

The Art Of Defense - U.S.A. International Martial Arts~Kyoshi Quicksilver Faraday

THE FOLLOWING PROGRAM HAS OVER 185 TECHNIQUES TAUGHT IN A SEMINAR FORMAT. FILMED ON NOV. 14TH 2010.

SPECIAL THANK YOU TO SENSEI MIKE MILLETT, KAITIE FLYNN & BRIAN WILLARD FOR BEING MY UKE'S.

YOURS IN THE ARTS ~ QUICKSILVER

This has been a Thru The Years Production
ThruTheYears.com

U.S.A. International Martial Arts
Kyoshi QS Faraday
faradaypower@msn.com

DVD VIDEO

The Art Of Defense
A Look Into The Techniques Of
Taikyokuken Ken Sho Ryu

Kyoshi Michael Faraday

U.S.A. International Martial Arts ®

VOL III.

"" FILMED IN NOVEMBER 2010 IN SHREWSBURY MA.

THIS DVD CONTAINS ALL TECHNIQUES FROM MY SYSTEM OF TAIKYOKUKEN KEN SHO RYU FROM 10TH KYU WHITEBELT TO SHODAN 1ST DEGREE BLACKBELT.

FROM BASIC, TO INTERM, TO ADVANCED : TECHNIQUES & FIGHTING. ""

ACKNOWLEDGEMENTS :

ABOVE ALL OTHERS   ...   I WOULD LIKE TO THANK MY FAMILY. ESPECIALLY MY WIFE TAMMY, AND MY SON MASON.

BECAUSE THE TWO OF THEM HAVE TO ENDURE ME DAY IN AND DAY OUT!

TO BE PERFECTLY HONEST IT ISN'T EASY TO UNDERSTAND ME OR MY THOUGHTS ON A GOOD DAY.

HOWEVER; THEY SEEM TO DO A GREAT JOB KEEPING UP WITH ALL MY ACTIVITIES.

I COULDN'T DO IT WITHOUT YOU GUYS. MY LIFE IS COMPLETE BECAUSE OF YOU.

NEXT I WOULD LIKE TO ACKNOWLEDGE THE TEACHINGS OF MY MENTOR AND SENSEI.

GRANDMASTER RON VAN CLIEF, OR AS I ADDRESS HIM SHIDOSHI. THESE PAST THREE CALENDAR YEARS HAVE BEEN AMAZING!

THANK YOU FOR EVERYTHING THAT YOU PROVIDE TO ME IN ALL ASPECTS OF MY MARTIAL ARTS TRAINING.

I ALSO NEED TO SAY THANK YOU TO:

GRANDMASTER SOKE FRANK SANCHEZ / W.H.F.S.C.

GRANDMASTER SIFU ALAN GOLDBERG / ACTION MARTIAL ARTS

GRANDMASTER ANTHONY ELAM / AMERICAN TEMPLE TRAINING UNION

MASTER CYNTHIA ROTHROCK

AaRON RICHMAN / PRESIDENT OF THE MAA FIGHT COUNCIL

SANDAN MICHAEL MILLETT

LIZ POPLAWSKI / OWNER & MY PRODUCER AT THRU THE YEARS PRODUCTIONS.

LULU.COM & AMAZON.COM FOR CARRYING MY PRODUCTS.

DEBRA HORAN / OWNER BOOKLOVERS BOOK STORE

CHRIS CHARRON / SOUNDS EASY DJ SERVICES { FIXING MY COMPUTER & RETRIEVING THESE LOST FILES FOR THIS BOOK! }

LASTLY ... MS. KAITI FLYNN & BRIAN WILLARD / MY PRIVATE STUDENTS

ALL THE MATERIAL IN THIS BOOK IS TRUE AND HAS BEEN SOLELY WRITTEN BY ME MICHAEL P. FARADAY. A.K.A. KYOSHI QUICKSILVER FARADAY.

ALSO ALL PICTURES WITHIN THIS BOOK ARE FROM MY PRIVATE COLLECTION.

MOST OF THESE PICTURES WERE TAKEN BY MY WIFE TAMMY JEAN FARADAY.

FINAL EDITING AND ALL LAYOUTS WERE ALSO PERFORMED BY MYSELF.

I WOULD LIKE TO TAKE THIS TIME TO THANK EVERYONE WHO HAS SUPPORTED ME IN ALL MY ENDEAVORS.

THIS HAS BEEN A DIVISION OF U.S.A. INTERNATIONAL MARTIAL ARTS PRODUCTIONS AND COPYRIGHTS.

FOLLOW YOUR HEART ... TO ALL YOUR DREAMS!

WISHING YOU ALL THE VERY BEST:

KYOSHI " QUICKSILVER " FARADAY

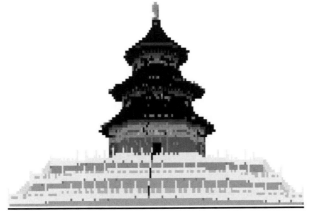

BY: MICHAEL P. FARADAY

2009

"" THIS WAS THE YEAR THAT THE FIRST EDITION OF THIS BOOK; " THE FIVE RULES ..... A PATH TO BECOMING A MASTER " WAS NOTATED.

PICTURED IS THE FRONT COVER ART WORK AND DESIGN FROM MY PRIVATE JOURNAL THAT WAS SPECIFICALLY WRITTEN FOR G.M. VAN CLIEF TOWARDS MY PROJECT TO ACHIEVE MY 7TH DAN.

SINCE THEN WHILE TAKING THE PRIVATE EDITION AND RE - WRITING ITS MATERIAL INTO THIS VERSION ... IT HAS WHAT ACTUALLY HAS BECOME A WHOLE NEW BOOK!

SO FOR ALL PERSONAL REFRENCES THIS IS NOW MY THIRD BOOK, FOR WHICH TWO HAVE BEEN PUBLISHED BY: LULU.COM 12 ~ 22 ~ 10. ""

" " THIS PAGE WAS TAKEN STRAIGHT OUT OF ONE OF OUR FAMILY SCRAPBOOKS THAT TAMMY AND I MADE.

THESE PICTURES DEPICT A REFLECTION OF TIME SPENT ON TEAM AMERICA.

TOP LEFT TO BOTTOM RIGHT:

SYDNEY AUSTRILIA 2000 ~ HONOLULU HAWAII 2002 ~ KILLARNEY IRELAND 2001 ~ MEXICO 2003. " "